Fundamentals of Investment

An Irish Perspective

Brian O'Loughlin
and Frank O'Brien

GILL & MACMILLAN

Gill & Macmillan
Hume Avenue
Park West
Dublin 12
with associated companies throughout the world
www.gillmacmillan.ie

978 0 7171 3983 5

Index compiled by Cover to Cover
Print origination in Ireland by
Carrigboy Typesetting Services, Co. Cork

*The paper used in this book is made from the wood pulp of managed forests.
For every tree felled, at least one is planted, thereby renewing natural resources.*

A catalogue record is available for this book from the British Library.

Fundamentals of Investment

An Irish Perspective

To Belinda and Geraldine for their encouragement and support

Support Material for
Fundamentals of Investment, An Irish Perspective
by Brian O'Loughlin & Frank O'Brien

Dynamic and easy to use, online support material for this book:

Provides lecturers with:
- PowerPoint slides
- Web links to financial sites and data
- Self-assessment problems
- Multiple choice questions.

To access lecturer support material on our secure site:
1) Go to *www.gillmacmillan.ie/lecturers*
2) Logon using your username and password. If you don't have a password, register online and we will email your password to you.

Provides students with:
- Web links to financial sites and data
- Self-assessment problems
- Multiple choice questions.

To access student support material
1) Go to *www.gillmacmillan.ie/student*
2) Click on the link for Student Support material

Contents

Chapter one

Introduction

Saving and investing have always been everyday issues that impact on the lives of everyone, and a critical feature of developed economies is a strong and vibrant financial services industry. Throughout the 1980s and 1990s the Irish financial sector has grown and evolved into an advanced and innovative industry. The success of the Irish Financial Services Centre (IFSC) has added a strong international dimension to an already diverse and sophisticated industry. The numbers employed in the sector have grown in tandem and the variety of jobs has widened considerably.

This book is primarily aimed at those working (or planning to work) in the financial sector, particularly those employed in functions where investment services and products are important. Such services and products are ubiquitous across the industry as the demand for savings, investment and protection products has risen with the growth in the Irish population.

The Irish financial services industry has responded well, by and large, to the needs of the growing economy. In tandem with this the legal and regulatory structure has moved forward and the establishment of the Irish Financial Services Regulatory Authority (IFSRA) was an important milestone. The Financial Regulator was formally established on 1 May 2003 as the single regulator for virtually all financial services in Ireland, with the passing of the Central Bank and Financial Services Authority of Ireland Act, 2003. The scale of the industry can be appreciated from the following information gathered from the Central Bank, the Central Statistics Office and the Financial Regulator:

- The total assets of credit institutions stood at €722,545m at end-2004.
- Employment in the banking and insurance sectors alone stood at 52,600.
- The net asset value of collective investment schemes was €434,784m at end-2004.
- The market capitalisation of the Irish Stock Exchange stood at €209,616m at end-2004.

Source: Annual Report of the *Financial Regulator*, May '03/Dec. '04.

The international financial sector is now a significant contributor to the Irish economy, with employment in the three core sectors of banking, funds and insurance being in the region of 17,600 at end-2004. In addition, employment in ancillary services such as legal, accounting, etc. would be significant. Despite the low rate of corporation tax that applies in Ireland the total yield of corporation tax from international financial sector companies was €663m in 2004, which represented 12.4% of total corporation tax collected in the State.

Staff education and training are critical to the continued development of the Irish financial services industry. In most sectors of the industry employees must now attain relevant professional qualifications, as well as industry qualifications from industry bodies such as the Institute of Bankers, the Life Industry Association, the Insurance Institute and others. This textbook has been written with the needs of this group to the fore, although it will also be of benefit to third-level students who are studying investments for the first time. For the latter group this book provides an Irish-based perspective that usefully supplements the many excellent international introductory textbooks.

ORGANISATION OF THE BOOK

The book introduces the basic building blocks of investment and reviews the operations of the industry from a variety of perspectives. These include the retail investor, the pension fund investor and also the perspective of the professional fund manager. The approach adopted is to introduce investment concepts and issues in a discursive manner. As far as practicable, examples and illustrations are presented in an Irish setting.

CHAPTER SUMMARIES

Chapter 2 focuses on the mainstream investment assets – fixed interest, equities, property and cash. The key characteristics of each asset are outlined and basic valuation concepts such as dividend yield, price earnings ratio (PER) and gross redemption yield are introduced. How securities markets are organised and the methods by which securities are issued and sold to investors are set out. The distinction between primary markets and secondary markets is explained and the mechanism by which an initial public offering is brought to the market is described. This chapter concludes with an outline of how securities are issued and traded on the Irish Stock Exchange.

Chapter 3 builds on the introduction to bonds in Chapter 2 and provides a fuller analysis of bonds, including the valuation of bonds and the calculation of the flat yield and the gross redemption yield (GRY) or yield to maturity (YTM). This chapter will help the reader to develop an understanding of how to value a bond by applying the time value of money concept. The nature of the inverse relationship between changes in interest rates and bond prices is examined and the important concept of duration is explained. The term structure of interest rates and its various applications are discussed.

In Chapter 2 we discuss the basic characteristics of equity securities and how they are issued and traded on stock exchanges. In Chapter 4 we examine ways in which we can analyse and assess the investment merits of a company's shares. The questions that investors are interested in seeking answers to include:

- What is the fair price for a share and how can we calculate it?
- What are the key financial ratios relevant to an analysis of the investment prospects of a company?
- What yardsticks should be employed to compare one share with another?
- Are there ways to establish the investment value of an equity market?
- How can equity markets in different countries be compared with one another?

Chapter 4 shows how discounted cash-flow techniques can be used to estimate the fair price of a share. The chapter then goes on to describe the most commonly used relative valuation techniques such as the price earnings ratio and the dividend yield.

Chapter 5 discusses the alternative of indirect investing, used by many investors. With indirect investing the investor pools his assets with those of others to create a single pool of money that is then managed by professional investment managers in accordance with a well-defined investment strategy. A key point about indirect investing is that the investor is not directly responsible for the asset, although he is exposed to the same market risk as if he did hold the asset directly, and he also reaps whatever investment return those assets generate (less management fees and expenses). In Ireland the unit-linked funds offered by life assurance companies form the backbone of the industry. Latterly, the emergence of mutual funds – called open-ended investment companies or OEICs – has occurred as a result of EU Investment Services Directives. Once an OEIC is regulated in one EU country it can be sold throughout the EU. The basics of how these collective investment schemes (CIS) are priced are discussed. The role of investment advice and ensuring that individual investors are sold investment funds appropriate to their particular circumstances is a key issue that is addressed in this chapter.

Chapter 6 introduces the key concept of risk and starts by distinguishing among the investor, the gambler and the speculator. It examines the relationship between risk and return and sets out the different sources of investment return. What risk means to different investors is explored and the subjective nature of risk is examined. The quantitative concept of risk as defined and measured by Markowitz is examined. The implications of the Markowitz approach are extended to the implications for portfolio construction.

Chapter 7 develops further the important concept of Markowitz diversification. This chapter shows how a concept such as the correlation coefficient can be used to construct portfolios. The concept of the efficient frontier is discussed and the impact on the efficient frontier of introducing a risk-free asset is explored. The separation theorem is also discussed.

Markowitz portfolio theory is normative, in the sense that it describes how investors should go about the task of selecting portfolios of risky securities. Capital market theory tries to explain how security prices would behave under idealised conditions. The most widely known model is the capital asset pricing model (CAPM). The CAPM is attractive as an equilibrium model because it can be applied to the job of portfolio construction relatively easily. It does have a number of weaknesses and alternative theories have been developed, the most important of which is arbitrage pricing theory (APT), although here we limit ourselves to the CAPM.

Chapter 8 is entitled The Real Economy and the Markets and here the central importance of growth and inflation is identified in determining asset prices and in driving both the real economy and the financial markets. The relevance of the economic cycle in influencing the asset allocation decision is discussed. Periods of speculative excess are examined to isolate their common denominators and to identify the insight that there is a difference between the market price of a security and its intrinsic value.

Chapter 9 introduces pension schemes and the legal and regulatory framework within which they operate. The role and responsibilities of pension fund trustees are outlined, particularly with regard to the fund's investments. The particular risks attaching to pension fund investment are described and investment objectives outlined. The central role of the trustees in determining investment strategy is discussed.

Chapter 10 examines the fund management industry, its scope, recent development, role and organisational structure. The key elements of investment management firms are introduced – philosophy, process, people and performance – and investment styles and skill sets are explored. The industry's investment decision-making processes and risk-control frameworks are outlined.

Chapter 11 deals with the measurement of investment returns. The calculation methodologies most commonly used are described and their suitability for comparing returns across managers is discussed. Risk-adjusted return methodologies are also covered. The attribution of performance over the various sources of return is briefly outlined. The Chartered Financial Analyst (CFA) Institute's Global Investment Performance Standards for the calculation and presentation of investment returns are described. The chapter concludes by discussing Investment Style Analysis and Manager Selection.

Chapter 12 analyses derivative contracts, which now form an intrinsic part of the global financial fabric. Derivatives first emerged in a significant way in agricultural commodities markets in Chicago in the mid-nineteenth century. Although financial derivatives made their appearance quite early in the history of stock markets, they have really come to prominence only since the early 1980s. Today, financial derivatives play a central role in all developed financial markets. This chapter focuses on describing basic futures and options contracts and analysing how they can be used either to manage risk, or to speculate on the price movements of underlying securities.

Chapter 13, Investment Arithmetic, is a catch-all chapter that sets out to bring together the key quantitative yardsticks and financial ratios that are commonly used by investment practitioners. A brief description is provided for each concept, together with illustrative examples where appropriate. Readers will find it useful to refer to this chapter when they wish to clarify the meaning of financial and valuation ratios that crop up regularly in any discussion of investments.

Finally, in Chapter 14 we present an analysis of long-term historical investment returns. A model for evaluating prospective investment returns is developed and shows that prospective returns are likely to be lower than those achieved in the 1980s and 1990s. The implications of this for pension funds, in particular, are explored.

GUIDE TO USING THE BOOK

Readers who are using this book as part of their preparation for the investment modules of the various financial industry qualifications can be selective in their chapter selection. The book is organised to facilitate those students who are working full time in the industry, and the following reading plan will comprehensively cover what is required for many investment modules:

Chapter 1   Introduction
Chapter 2   Securities Markets
Chapter 5   The Retail Investor's Choices
Chapter 6   Investment, Investors and Risk
Chapter 8   The Real Economy and the Markets

Learning objectives are outlined at the beginning of each chapter. At the end of each chapter there is a summary and selected chapters finish with multiple-choice and/or self-assessment questions.

Chapter two

Securities Markets and the Investment Assets

In this chapter the focus is on the mainstream investment assets – fixed interest, equities, property and cash. The key characteristics of each asset are outlined and basic valuation concepts such as dividend yield, price earnings ratio (PER) and gross redemption yield are introduced. How securities markets are organised and the methods by which securities are issued and sold to investors are set out. The distinction between primary markets and secondary markets is explained and the mechanism by which an initial public offering is brought to the market is described. This chapter concludes with an outline of how securities are issued and traded on the Irish Stock Exchange.

Learning Objectives

After completing this chapter you should:
- Have an understanding of the mainstream investment assets and the key characteristics of each security type
- Be able to distinguish between the Primary and Secondary markets for securities and be aware of the key players involved in the markets
- Be knowledgeable about the structure of the Irish Stock Exchange and how the market is organised.

SECURITY TYPES

In this section the focus is on the mainstream investment assets – bonds, both fixed-interest securities and index-linked securities, equities, property and cash. The term 'bonds' is often used to refer to fixed-interest securities only, even though fixed-interest securities are just one type of bond. The characteristics of other types of bond are also described in this chapter.

However, we will follow the market convention and the discussion on bonds refers to fixed-interest securities, unless specifically stated otherwise.

Bonds (Fixed-Interest Securities)

Fixed-interest securities or bonds are loans raised by borrowers from investors at fixed rates of interest for fixed periods of time. The borrower may be a government, a government agency, a state or a corporation. The lender or investor may be an insurance company, a bank, a pension fund or a private individual.

Typically the borrower, or issuer of the bond, undertakes to pay the investors a fixed rate of interest each year for the fixed period (or fixed term) and to repay principal, i.e. the capital amount originally borrowed, when the loan becomes due (or matures) at the end of the period. Essentially bonds are loans with pre-specified terms and conditions; they have been used by borrowers and lenders for centuries and provide returns in the form of income and repayment at maturity. The early bonds were issued by governments, often for the purposes of funding wars or colonial escapades. The UK was a leader in this regard and by the nineteenth century there was an active market in British government securities.

Bonds issued by the UK Government are often referred to as Gilt Edged Securities or Gilts. The term 'gilt edged' has its origins in the gilt embossing on the certificates, which denoted ownership of the bonds. In time, however, it came to signify the high levels of quality and security attaching to bonds issued by the UK Government. Historically, the Irish bond market was closely linked to the British market, and in fact historically the Irish Stock Exchange was a constituent part of the London Stock Exchange. The Irish Stock Exchange is now an independent exchange that is governed by the Stock Exchange Act, 1995. The fact that the Irish £ exchange rate was fixed at parity to sterling up to 1979 cemented this link even further. Now, as a founding participant in the euro, the Irish Government bond market effectively forms part of the Eurozone bond market.

Bonds are divisible and are typically denominated in nominal units of €100 for bonds issued by Eurozone borrowers. The fixed rate of interest refers to the rate payable annually per €100 nominal and normally on maturity bonds are repayable at par, i.e. at €100 per €100 nominal.

Listings of bonds appear frequently in the financial press and in lists prepared by investment houses and stockbrokers. A bond is identified by its fixed rate of interest (or coupon), its issuer and its redemption date. For example, an Irish Government bond (or stock) is described below:

Government Stock

4.5% Treasury 18.4.2020

The coupon on this bond is 4.5% and this means that the issuer, the Irish government, will make an annual interest payment of €4.50 to the holder of each €100 nominal of the bond up to and including the maturity date. On the maturity date (18.4.2020) the issuer will pay the holder €100 per €100 nominal of the bond. It is useful to visualise these payments in the form of a 'Timeline' as illustrated in Figure 2.1.

Figure 2.1 Timeline – 4.5% Treasury 2020

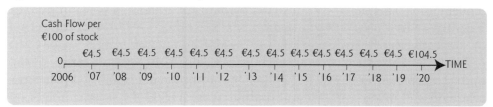

If we imagine that today is 18.04.2006, we can see that the cash flows that will be generated by this bond can be set out with certainty. Starting in April 2007 an interest payment of €4.50 will be made annually per €100 of stock. At the maturity or redemption date a final interest payment of €4.50 is made, plus €100 (the nominal value of the bond).

Bonds issued by governments are usually quoted on a stock exchange and therefore trade freely on the open market. Bond prices are quoted per €100 nominal. Between the issue of a bond and its final repayment (or redemption) its market price will fluctuate around €100 depending on the investment environment, most particularly interest-rate levels, and the interaction of buyers and sellers. Therefore, it is more often the case that investors purchase bonds at a price that is different from its nominal or par value. Referring to our timeline, the par value of €100 establishes only the cash amount that will be repaid to the investor on the maturity date. Assume that for the bond identified in the previous paragraph we find that today this bond is priced at €111 per €100 nominal. It will therefore appear as follows in listings of bonds:

Government Stock   *Price*

4.50% Treasury 18.4.2020   111.00

From this information the returns available to an investor who is willing to hold the stock to redemption may be calculated. The investor receives two returns.

Annual Yield or Running Yield.

This is the annual cash payment (investment income) of €4.50 for each €100 nominal of stock purchased. As the investor paid €111 for each

€100, he receives a cash income yield each year between now and 2020 of:

$$\frac{4.50 \times 100}{111} = 4.05\%$$

In addition, the investor must take into account the movement from the purchase price of €111 to the €100 at which the bond will finally be redeemed on 18.4.2020. Because the price of the bond is trading above the par value, this is a negative amount of €100 – €111 = –€11 over the period of some fourteen years.

Again it is useful to visualise what is going to happen in terms of the timeline depicted in **Figure 2.2.** The line AB shows that the bond price will gradually fall towards €100 and on the maturity date the price of the bond will be exactly €100.

Figure 2.2 Projected Capital loss when Bond is purchased above par value

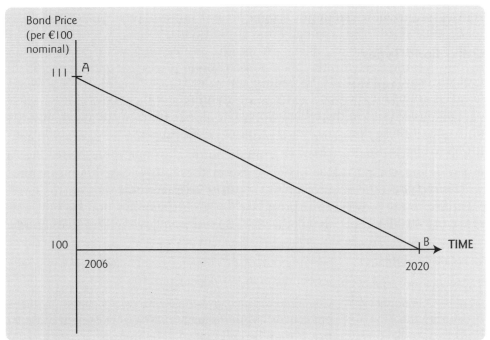

Gross Redemption Yield (GRY) or Yield to Maturity (YTM)

The Annual Yield discussed above does not take this amount into account. A second yield calculation – the Gross Redemption Yield (GRY) or Yield to

Maturity (YTM) – takes into account both the annual income and the loss (or gain, if the bond price is below par) from the current price of €111 to the value on redemption of €100. In the case of the bond discussed above, because the current price of €111 is above (at a premium to) €100, the GRY will be lower than the Annual Yield.

Conversely, a bond which is priced below (at a discount to) its par value will have a GRY that is above its Annual Yield.

Incorporating this information on returns into our bond listing extends its identification as follows:

Government Stock	Price	Annual Yield	Gross Redemption Yield
4.50% Treasury 18.4.2020	111.00	4.05%	3.52%

Strictly speaking, the GRY is the interest rate at which the bond's price equals the discounted present value of all future payments (in our example €4.50 each year until 2016 and €100 on 18.4.2020).

Investment decisions in the fixed-interest sector – which stocks to buy or sell – are normally made on the basis of Gross Redemption Yield. The GRY is discussed in more detail in Chapter 3.

Other Bond Types

Not all bonds issued are fixed-interest securities, although fixed-interest bonds account for the lion's share of outstanding bonds in issue. Other types of bond are set out in the table below. This is not an exhaustive list, and the only one of these that we discuss in more detail is index-linked or inflation-protected bonds.

Bond Type	Key Characteristic
Floating Rate Bonds	Coupon payment is variable and usually set with reference to money-market interest rates.
Zero-Coupon Bonds	Such bonds have no coupon (pay no interest), but trade at a deep discount to par value of €100.
Convertible Bonds	Coupon payments are normally fixed for a period of time, but on redemption the holder will have the right to convert into some other security.
Index-Linked Bonds	Coupon payments and the final redemption payment are linked to the inflation rate. Each year the coupon paid increases by the relevant rate of inflation and the redemption value also increases in line with the rate of inflation.

Index-Linked Securities

Fixed-interest securities, described above, are constrained by their terms of issue. Annual interest payments and eventual repayment of capital on the redemption date are fixed and will not change, regardless of changes in the inflationary background. Inflation erodes the purchasing power of the annual interest payments and the final capital repayment, as investors in fixed interest discovered to their heavy cost in the high-inflation period of the 1970s and early 1980s.

In response to the need of investors for a degree of protection against inflation, and to facilitate continued funding of government borrowing, the UK authorities in 1981 issued index-linked securities. Over subsequent years a relatively small number of governments have followed suit – the US, Australia, Canada, France and Sweden – though in all cases index-linked securities play a relatively minor role in government funding compared to conventional fixed-interest securities. In Ireland the Housing Finance Agency, a government-guaranteed body, issued index-linked securities in very small volumes in the 1980s. There are no longer any outstanding issues of these securities listed on the Irish stock exchange. Because of the open-ended nature of the promise to compensate investors for inflation, index-linked securities are almost entirely the preserve of government or government-backed issuers.

Index-linked securities protect the investor against the impact of inflation by linking both interest payments and the eventual payment on redemption to an index of retail or consumer prices.

Therefore, when an investor buys an index-linked stock he receives a return that will rise with inflation, but that will be constant in real terms, i.e., in terms of purchasing power.

The conventions for denominating and describing fixed-interest securities apply also to index-linked securities:

Index-Linked Bonds	Price	Real Yield
UK 2.5% Index-Linked 2024	226.35	1.5%
US 3.625% Index-Linked 2028	127.88	2.1%

A UK investor, therefore, buying the UK Government 2.5% Index-Linked 2024 receives over the remaining life of the stock a real yield of 1.5%, i.e. in excess of inflation. If UK inflation in the period to 2024 is 3% p.a., his return in nominal (cash) terms will be 4.5% per annum; if inflation rises to 5% his return will be 6.5% p.a. nominal. The UK Government has undertaken to compensate the investor for whatever level of inflation occurs in the period to 2024. Real rates of return available on index-linked securities are important in their own right for bond selection within the index-linked sector, but also as a government-guaranteed benchmark for evaluating returns on the other investment assets.

Calculating The Real Rate of Interest

The real rate of interest (or return) is given by the expression:

$R_r = (1 + R_n)/(1 + i) - 1$

where: R_r = real rate of interest
R_n = nominal rate of interest
i = inflation rate.

Therefore, if inflation is 3% and the gross redemption yield on long-term, fixed-interest bonds is 5%, the real rate of interest is:

$R_r = (1 + .05)/(1 + .03) - 1 = .0194$, i.e. 1.94% p.a.

Note that simply subtracting the rate of inflation from the nominal yield gives a close approximation.

Equities

An equity investment is an investment in the ordinary shares (or share capital) of a limited company. The equity investor is a part-owner of the company and this part-ownership is represented by a share certificate which sets out the number of shares owned. The proportion of the company owned by the investor is determined by the relationship between the number of shares owned, as defined by the share certificate, and the total number of shares in existence (in issue). This is illustrated in the table below:

Company	Total No of Shares in Issue	No of Shares Owned by Investor A	% of Company Owned by A
Company X	1,000	10	1%
Company Y	1,000	1,000	100%
Company Z	1,000,000	50,000	5%

Where the investor invests in the securities discussed earlier, fixed-interest and index-linked, he has a contractual relationship with the issuer to receive the interest payments and final redemption payment as set out in the terms of issue. He is entitled only to these returns; there is no entitlement to any further participation.

The position of the equity investor is dramatically different. His share certificate identifies his co-ownership of the company: of its lands, buildings, plant and machinery; its stocks, work in progress and finished goods; its products, market shares and brand names; its client lists and customer goodwill; the strategic expertise of its management team and the operational skills of its workforce.

Within the legal framework of the company these assets and attributes combine to generate a stream of profits into the future. The equity investor, as co-owner, participates pro rata to his shareholding in this stream of future profits or earnings.

On the one hand, where the company is successful and enjoys powerful growth in profits, the equity investor may enjoy very large returns. After the company has paid its workforce, its various suppliers, its bank for any interest charges arising and its taxes, all the remaining surplus, no matter how large, belongs (is attributable) to the ordinary shareholders.

On the other hand, if the company is unsuccessful and plunges into bankruptcy, all those with a legitimate claim on its assets must be satisfied before any repayment is due to shareholders. Typically, when a company fails there is little or nothing left for shareholders. Shareholders, of course, enjoy the benefit of limited liability; they have the rather small comfort of knowing that they cannot lose more than 100% of their investment!

The equity investor typically may expect to receive two types of return from an investment in a company:

i)   an income return, based on the annual dividend (or distribution to shareholders) paid out of profits paid each year
ii)   a capital return, based on the increase in the share price as it rises to reflect a rising stream of profits into the future.

The income return – the dividend – is relatively stable and typically will rise, reflecting higher dividends as profits increase. However, in periods of difficult trading dividend payments may be reduced (or cut) or suspended altogether.

The capital return is uncertain and volatile, especially in the short term. It is subject to fluctuations in the company's own profitability and to external fluctuations in interest rates and in the stock market. In the long run the generality of share prices may be expected to rise, since they reflect higher profits as the economy grows. At any particular point in time, however, the share price in the stock market is determined by the interaction of buyers and sellers, i.e., it is subject to the laws of supply and demand.

Calculating Earnings Per Share (EPS) and Dividends Per Share (DPS)

Shareholders and investment analysts normally assess the investment merits of a company with reference to a variety of valuation metrics that are usually calculated on a per-share basis. The two most commonly used ratios are earnings per share (EPS) and dividends per share (DPS). The numerical example here illustrates how these important ratios are calculated:

ABC plc

Excerpts from ABC's Profit & Loss Account (€ millions)
Profit After Tax   €120 m
Dividends Paid   €40 m
Retained Earnings   €80 m

Current Share Information:
Number of Shares in Issue 1,000 million
Share Price   €2 per share
Market Capitalisation = shares in issue x share price

$$1{,}000 \text{ million} \times €2 = €2{,}000 \text{ m}$$

Earnings Per Share = Profit After Tax/No. of shares in issue

$$€120m / 1{,}000 \text{ m} = 12.0 \text{ cent}$$

Dividends Per Share = Dividends Paid/No. of shares in issue

$$€40 \text{ m} / 1{,}000 \text{ m} = 4.0 \text{ cent}$$

The income return – which is based on a tangible, cash dividend – is measurable and is normally expressed as a dividend yield, calculated as follows:

$$\frac{\text{Dividend per share (cents)} \times 100}{\text{Share price (cents)}}$$

Therefore, for ABC plc with its share price standing at 200c, and assuming it has just paid an annual dividend of 4c per share:

$$\text{Dividend Yield} \quad \frac{4c \times 100}{200c} = 2\%$$

Normally the shareholders will expect the dividend to rise over time as, hopefully, the profits of the company increase. The capital return is uncertain and therefore cannot be quantified in advance.

The Price Earnings Ratio (PER)

The most commonly used convention for measuring and comparing company valuations is the Price Earnings Ratio or PER.

A company may be expected to generate a stream of profits into the future. The shareholder is a part-owner of that stream of profits.

Earnings per share is a measure of the amount of profit after tax earned in a financial year, which is attributable to each share issued by the company.

The PER is a profit-based measure of the company's perceived worth, relating share price to earnings per share.

With ABC plc's share price at 200c and earnings per share (EPS) of 12c in its most recent financial year:

$$\text{Price Earnings Ratio:}$$
$$\frac{200c}{12c}$$
$$= 16.7 \text{ times}$$

The higher the PER, the greater the expectation for future growth in earnings.

See Chapter 4 for a full analysis of the yardsticks employed to value equities.

Property

A property investment is an investment in bricks and mortar. Property investment may embrace both residential and commercial properties. In Ireland, on the one hand the private investor is heavily involved in the residential property market (houses, apartments, holiday homes). On the other hand, institutional involvement by pension funds and life companies in residential property is relatively low, both in Ireland and the UK. This is in contrast to the US and Continental Europe, where institutional investors are significant players in the residential property market. Commercial property investments typically include offices, retail shops and industrial buildings (factories, warehouses). Developing opportunities include factory outlets (out-of-town retail shopping malls) and leisure centres. Property, especially commercial property, is a 'big ticket' activity. Involvement in the direct property market, i.e., where the investor owns the building, requires large resources – potentially very large. For this reason the market in commercial property is dominated by institutional investors and very high net worth individuals and families.

A variety of investment vehicles have been developed to enable smaller investors to indirectly access commercial property investment, including quoted property companies, e.g., Land Securities in the UK; property unit trusts, e.g., IPUT in Ireland; and property unit-linked funds promoted by the life assurance industry.

Like equities, property returns are not guaranteed. The returns enjoyed by the property investor depend on the success of the building in attracting tenants who, over time, will be willing to pay rising rents. Location is the critical factor in determining the long-term success of a property investment.

A particularly attractive feature of the Irish and UK office-property markets from an investment perspective is the convention of the long leases incorporating upwards-only rent reviews, normally after 5–7 years. This provides high visibility of rental returns.

A key investment attraction of property is that it offers the prospects for a relatively high income that grows over time.

This income return is measured by the Rental Yield as follows:

$$\frac{\text{Current Rent Receivable}}{\text{Property Value}} \times 100\%$$

Assume that Investor A, owner of an office building valued at €10m, let the building three years ago at a rental of €0.5m per annum.

Rental Yield:
$$\frac{€0.5\ m}{€10.0\ m} \times 100 = 5\%$$

A second yield calculation, with applications in property valuation and in comparing different properties, is the **Equivalent Yield**. The Equivalent Yield allows for an uplift in the existing rent to current rental values.

Assume in the example above that the building could currently be let at €0.75m per annum, compared to the €0.5m agreed three years ago.

Equivalent Yield:
$$\frac{€0.75\ m}{€10.0\ m} \times 100 = 7.5\%$$

Investors in property may also benefit from capital appreciation, as capital values rise to reflect rising rents. Just like equities, such capital appreciation is uncertain and will depend on how well a particular property performs in terms of rental income growth. Capital appreciation will also be a function of overall trends in the economy; in particular, movements in interest rates and bond yields exert a large influence.

Cash or Bank Deposits

Cash is normally regarded as a short-term investment and not usually as a suitable investment vehicle for long-term investors. In fact, cash plays three roles within investors' strategies.

i)   It may be held to meet short-term obligations or liabilities, e.g. to meet payments to current pensioners.

ii)   It may be a temporary home for funds as the investor awaits more attractive opportunities than those currently available.

iii)   It may be an investment vehicle in its own right and held for longer periods if the investment environment is adverse. Holding cash will cushion the investor from the impact of falling values in the other investment assets and, importantly, will provide the wherewithal to buy the other assets when they have fallen into low ground. In other words, cash can play an important role as a diversifier of investment risk.

Cash returns, i.e., interest on deposits – no matter how low – always look attractive if the other assets are generating negative returns.

A critical consideration for the investor is to determine the appropriate term (or duration) of the deposit. Cash may be placed on deposit from periods ranging from one day (or overnight) out to one year, or even longer in the case of more sophisticated money-market instruments. Key considerations in determining the deposit term include:

• the investor's view of the outlook for interest rates;
• the investor's requirement to access the deposit to take advantage of market opportunities as they emerge;
• the availability of other sources of finance, including cash flows.

Perhaps even more critical is the creditworthiness of the deposit-taking institution. The marginal improvement in deposit rates that might be achievable by moving a deposit from a strong bank to a weaker bank will rarely compensate the investor for the loss of the deposit if the weaker bank should fail.

Uniquely among the investment assets, cash generates only one stream of return. The nominal value of the deposit is always fixed in absolute terms. An investor who puts €100 on deposit will always receive €100 on maturity of the deposit. Capital value is fixed; there is no capital return, positive or negative.

The investor receives an income return only. The interest rate will be fixed for the duration of the deposit, and if the deposit is renewed or rolled over the interest rate for the succeeding period will be set at the levels then prevailing.

Cash therefore provides certainty of income return only for relatively short periods. Because of fluctuations in interest rates there is no certainty of long-term income return, either in absolute (nominal) or real (after inflation) terms.

Investment Assets and Alternative Investments

Our discussion has concentrated on the traditional investment assets of bonds, equities, property and cash. The vast bulk of funds invested resides within these asset categories either directly, or indirectly through financial products. There is much debate about so-called alternative investment categories such as commodities and hedge funds. It is arguable whether these are alternative asset classes, or are merely different forms of trading strategies. In this introductory chapter we confine ourselves to the traditional asset classes, and the table below sets out the key characteristics of each major asset class.

Asset	Type of Return	Advantages	Disadvantages
Cash	Interest income only	Capital is secure	Rate of return lower than other assets
Bonds (Fixed Interest)	Income return is known in advance; prospect of capital appreciation if bond is traded	Bonds issued by developed-world governments considered to be risk free (credit risk); cash flows are definite	Returns are not protected against inflation; long-term returns are likely to be lower than property or equities
Bonds (Index-linked)	Income return starts low but rises in line with inflation; principal amount at maturity rises in line with cumulative inflation over the life of the bond	Provides automatic protection against inflation by raising the coupon payments and the principal sum to be paid at maturity in line with the relevant inflation index	Likely to under-perform in a low-inflation environment
Property	Income in the form of rents which can be expected to grow over time; prospects for capital appreciation	Total returns will reflect the performance of the relevant local economy	Transaction costs are very high and property investments can be very illiquid
Equities	Income in the form of dividends which can be expected to grow over time; prospects for capital appreciation	Total returns will reflect the performance of individual companies	Asset class that experiences the highest volatility of returns

HOW SECURITIES ARE ISSUED

Companies issue and sell securities to investors in order to finance their operations, as well as to expand their businesses. Usually companies issue equity and long-term corporate bonds to fund their long-term capital needs. Governments issue bonds to fund borrowing needs that may include a deficit on day-to-day spending and spending on capital projects such as building a new roads infrastructure.

A market where a company or a government issues new securities for cash is referred to as a primary market. New sales of Irish government bonds, sales of new shares by, for example, Ryanair all occur on the **primary markets**. Where the issuer is selling securities for the first time, the issue is referred to as an initial public offering (IPO). One of the most high-profile and controversial IPOs on the Irish market was the sale of Eircom shares by the Irish government in 1999. At the time equity markets had been rising for several years and telecom stocks had become the darlings of the market. The owner of Telecom Éireann (name later changed to Eircom) was the Irish government, which saw the flotation of Eircom as the first step in a process of bringing share ownership to a wide range of ordinary individuals. The government embarked on a major publicity campaign to market the shares to the ordinary public, most of whom had never invested directly in the stock market before. The process of setting the sale price and deciding on the marketing campaign was highly complicated.

Exhibit 2.1 EIRCOM CASE STUDY
Finance Friday, 16 July, 1999

'Plotting Success in State's Largest Flotation'

Finance Editor Cliff Taylor details the behind-the-scenes negotiations which led to the Telecom Éireann flotation.

After a year working on the project to sell Telecom Éireann, the final meeting was tense. At what price would the Telecom shares be floated?

Gathered in Government Buildings Tuesday of last week were the Cabinet members charged with making the decision and their civil servants. The Minister for Public Enterprise, Ms O'Rourke, was arguing for a price of under £3 (€3.81) to allow a significant gain for the public who had invested. On the other side, the Minister for Finance, Mr McCreevy, countered that the strong demand for the shares justified a high price.

The ministers had heard different recommendations from the two corporate finance advisers to the Government at the beginning of the meeting. Mr Colm Doherty of AIB

➡

Corporate Finance had pushed for a price of £2.95, while Mr Russell Chambers of Merrill Lynch had said that, such was the demand, the shares should be priced as high as £3.37. Now the ministers had to decide.

In the end, it was up to the Taoiseach, Mr Ahern, to broker a compromise. Nobody could agree on a round number as the debate went back and forward between £3 and £3.10. So a price of £3.07 was struck, closer to the position advocated by AIB than by Merrill Lynch. At least it was a round number in euros – €3.90.

The deal was done and it was decided the shares would be floated at a price which valued Telecom above most other European telecommunications firms and more highly than the company's management had itself wanted. After an anxious 24 hours, the shares floated at a hefty premium and have held most of the gains since then. While the decision to go for a stock market offering was taken in March 1998, the real work started almost exactly a year ago, with the appointment of AIB Corporate Finance and Merrill Lynch as joint Government advisers. AIB played the lead role in the hugely successful Irish side of the campaign and was seen as more than holding its own against the international heavyweights from Merrill Lynch.

One steering group – including the key players from the Government, the company and the advisers – was established to oversee the whole process and four working groups looked after the various elements of the flotation. Much of the initial work was done quietly. The company and its advisers worked on a detailed review of its operations. Every aspect of the company's business was mapped out and a painfully slow process of drawing up the prospectus and confirming and reconfirming every figure was gone through.

Telecom's chief executive, Mr Alfie Kane, the company's project co-ordinator, Mr Donagh McGovern, Mr John O'Donnell of AIB Corporate Finance, Mr Sean Carney of Merrill Lynch and Mr Nigel Higgins of ABN-Amro Corporate Finance, which was advising the company, were all centrally involved in the complex financial work which went into the prospectus.

In tandem with this, the group working on the politically sensitive aspect of the flotation – the offer to the public – got to work. It had been given a clear mandate from the Government to maximise public involvement. Work on how to do this began in earnest towards the end of last year. This group included Mr Roy Barrett, head of AIB's stockbroker, Goodbodys – subsequently appointed as Telecom's own brokers – and Mr Gerry O'Sullivan, head of corporate affairs at Telecom, along with representatives of the PR and advertising advisers and the Department of Public Enterprise.

Extensive research was commissioned, including both quantitative surveys and focus groups around the State. The results indicated that people were very interested in buying the shares, but, equally, they knew little or nothing about investing in the market. The trick was to devise a campaign which got the basic information across, without patronising people.

Companies from Dublin and London – Drury Communications and Dewe Rogersen – got the £1 million (€1.27 million) PR contract, while Ian Young's Irish International

➡

advertising agency was put in charge of managing the advertising campaign, which was to cost some £2 million. It was they who suggested the re-mix – by Donal Lunny – of the catchy Dulam an tune, which was central to the TV campaign. Meanwhile, at Minister O'Rourke's suggestion, every household in the State was sent details of the flotation – with this approach chosen in favour of using Telecom's own customer register.

To deal with the public interest, a share office was established, staffed by 200 people, to deal with queries and help the public at every stage of the process. Alongside this central office, a "local face" was put on the campaign through the branches of AIB – Goodbodys' parent – where the huge task was undertaken to train 3,000 staff on the registration and application process. The other key decision on the retail offer was what incentive to offer the public to invest. Again the research findings were called into play. They showed that many people saw themselves as holding the share in the long term. For this reason it was decided to opt to give a bonus share at the end of the first year – one free share for every 25 held – rather than give a discount on the issue price.

In the course of the negotiations, a number of crunch issues emerged before the final debate on the price. One was the lengthy negotiations with Telecom's strategic alliance partners, KPN of the Netherlands and Telia of Sweden. The first problem here emerged when a merger was announced between Telia and the Norwegian state company, Telenor. As Telenor was a shareholder in Esat Digifone – the competitor of Telecom's Eircell – it was immediately clear that either it or Telia would have to sell its Irish holdings If the merger goes ahead, Telia will be the seller. There were lengthy discussions on the formula by which its shares would be sold, which would not allow KPN to take a stake of more than 29.9 per cent for 18 months at least.

There were also heated discussions – with KPN in particular – at the time the price range for the share sale was announced. KPN, it has emerged, feared the range was on the high side and indicated clearly that this was an issue for it. After lengthy toing and froing, a clause was written in to the prospectus which tied the price which KPN must pay the Government to increase its stake to the float price, or an average of the trading price on the market, whichever turned out to be the lower, protecting the Dutch company if the share price did fall.

And then, of course, came the shenanigans in the Telecom boardroom. Acting on the advice of AIB and Merrill Lynch, Ms O'Rourke had restructured the board, persuading most of the existing members to leave and appointing new members with either telecoms or public company experience. Among the new appointees were Mr Pat Molloy, former chief executive of Bank of Ireland, and Mr Jim Flavin of DCC. Another was incoming chairman and US telecoms heavyweight, Mr Brian Thompson, who was touted as the key man who would sell the flotation in the US.

But just two months later, Mr Thompson rang the Government to inform it he had been offered a new position as chairman and chief executive of international telecoms group, Global TeleSystems (GTS). He did not indicate that he saw a problem with this and may not have even realised that GTS had a small operation in Ireland.

➡

Telecom's advisers, however, discovered this and, after a series of transatlantic telephone calls, Mr Thompson issued a statement that "regretfully but appropriately" he was resigning his position. The PR message was sent out that the float was not affected and Ms O'Rourke, forced to move quickly, decided to appoint Mr Ray MacSharry as chairman.

Accountant Mr Ron Bolger, who had stepped aside as chairman for Mr Thompson to be appointed but had remained on the board, resigned the day after, angry that he had been passed over a second time. He had been heavily involved in the company business for a number of years and Mr MacSharry had quickly to take up the baton with the flotation fast approaching. But such was the momentum behind the flotation that – barring a market collapse – there was never any prospect of it not going ahead.

It was becoming increasingly clear that the retail marketing campaign was working well, assisted by the advertising campaign and the link through the AIB network. All kinds of records were set. Almost 1.2 million people registered for shares and just under half of these, 574,000, went ahead to purchase, a much higher conversion from registration to application than seen in any other comparable major flotation. Some 20 per cent of the adult population will own shares. The next highest in major telecom flotations was Telstra in Australia, where 14 per cent of the population bought shares, while the typical figure for European telecom initial public offerings is 3 to 5 per cent of the public. The Government aim of encouraging private share ownership was clearly met, with at least 60 per cent of Telecom's shareholders believed to be first-time purchasers of stock. With retail interest so strong, the Telecom sector in favour and "Ireland" a good story to sell, the institutional investment interest was always going to be strong. Around 112 meetings were held with major institutions in the runup to the float and 107 of these institutions applied for shares, along with many more who were not met individually.

In total, more than 600 institutions received an allocation. Broken down, 33 per cent of the institutional shares went to Ireland; 24 per cent to Britain; 21 per cent to Europe; 20 per cent to the US; and the remainder to the rest of the world. It is this strong interest from major institutions, most of whom got fewer shares than they wanted, which has supported the shares in early trading, a trend private investors hope will continue in the weeks ahead.

© **The Irish Times**

The key players in the sale of new securities, either an IPO or the sale of new securities by an already-listed company, are:

i)   THE ISSUER
ii)   THE ORIGINATING INVESTMENT BANK
iii)   THE UNDERWRITING SYNDICATE – usually the originating investment banker will put together a syndicate of banks that will agree to underwrite the issue. This ensures that if investors back off

from purchasing the new securities at the last minute, the syndicate will buy the securities from the issuer at a pre-agreed issue price

iv)   THE SELLING GROUP OF INVESTMENT BANKERS AND STOCK-BROKERS – this will usually comprise the underwriting syndicate (or the stockbroking arms of the syndicate members), possibly plus selected domestic and overseas brokerage houses

v)   INVESTORS – these will include pension funds, insurance funds and unit trusts, as well as private investors.

After the IPO

Once securities are listed on a stock exchange, further issues can be made through a variety of routes. Any new securities issued will be exactly the same as the existing securities in terms of par value, rights to dividends, voting rights, etc. Companies whose shares are listed on an exchange can issue and sell new shares to existing and new shareholders through either a **Placing** or a **Rights Issue**.

In a Placing, new shares are issued by a company and sold to investors, who may already be existing shareholders but would normally include new investors. The sale of the shares will normally be organised by an investment bank (or a syndicate of banks for a large issue) appointed by the company. Usually the price of new shares will be pitched at a level that is close to the most recently traded price of the existing shares.

In a Rights Issue, new shares are offered only to existing shareholders. Usually the price of the new shares will be pitched at a significant discount to the most recently traded price of the existing shares. Companies will usually take the rights-issue route when the amount of new capital being raised is large relative to its current market capitalisation. Rights issues are normally underwritten (for an underwriting fee) by the company's stockbroker or investment bank. From the company's perspective this guarantees that it will raise the targeted new capital.

From the perspective of the current shareholders in a company, a rights issue is attractive in that they have the option to retain their existing percentage stake in the company. An example illustrating the mechanics of a rights issue shows why this is so.

Rights Issue

A company has 1m shares in issue with a current market price of 40c. It has just announced a rights issue of 1 new share for every 3 shares held at a price of 30c per new share. The rights offer will be open for 21 days and during that period shareholders will be able to trade the nil-paid rights as well as the existing shares. Prior to the announcement of the rights issue a shareholder with 3 shares had an investment valued at:

$$3 \times 40c \text{ (original market value)} = €1.20$$

If this shareholder takes up his rights on the closing date of the offer, he will then have the following:

$$
\begin{array}{lr}
\text{3 shares @ 40c} & = €1.20 \\
\underline{\text{1 new share (cost 30c)}} & = \underline{€0.30} \\
\text{4 shares valued at} & €1.50 \\
\end{array}
$$

Therefore: each share is valued at €1.50/4 = €0.375

Each share now has a theoretical value of 37.5c and this is known as the theoretical x-rights price.

During the offer period a shareholder can trade in the rights or what is known as the nil-paid shares, which will have a theoretical value of:

$$
\begin{array}{ccc}
\text{Ex-Rights price} - \text{Subscription price} & = & \text{Nil-Paid price} \\
37.5c \quad\quad - \quad\quad 30c & & = 7.5c \\
\end{array}
$$

A shareholder who does not wish to take up his rights can sell the nil-paid shares in the market. In this way shareholders who choose not to take up the rights offer are not disadvantaged compared with those shareholders who subscribe for the new shares.

A shareholder who decides to subscribe for the new shares will of course increase his monetary stake in the company. However, his percentage stake will remain exactly the same pre and post the rights issue. This is because the mechanism of a rights issue ensures that a subscribing shareholder with (say) 1% of the company will take up 1% of the new issue. Shareholders who do not subscribe will see their percentage stake in the company decline, i.e., they will suffer some dilution. This does not involve any loss in value, since the shareholder has not invested any further funds in the company. Furthermore, the nil-paid shares can be sold in the market so that non-subscribing shareholders do not suffer any loss if the new shares are priced at a discount to the 'old' shares. In some cases non-subscribing shareholders may use the proceeds of the sale of their nil-paid rights to subscribe for a fraction of their rights entitlement.

From the perspective of shareholders, and particularly small shareholders, the rights-issue mechanism of selling additional shares is attractive and equitable. There are, however, some drawbacks from the company's per-spective, namely:

- There is usually a significant time-gap between the announcement of a rights issue and the subscription date. Shareholders must be provided with full and detailed information regarding the issue to ensure that they are fully informed about the prospects for the business. All relevant available information concerning the business must be made available to share-holders so that they can make an informed investment decision. During the offer period the market in the company's shares will be subject to normal market volatility. Clearly, adverse market developments outside of anyone's control could severely jeopardise the eventual success of the issue. Because of this risk most companies will pay investment banks an under-writing fee to underwrite the issue if shareholders shun the issue for whatever reason. This clearly adds to the cost of selling new shares.
- Because of the onerous rules regarding a rights issue and the time involved, companies generally use this capital-raising mechanism sparingly. Therefore, rights issues will normally be resorted to only for major corporate events, such as a take-over, a major expansion or a major capital reconstruction.

While a rights issue has some disadvantages in terms of cost and management time, it is the favoured mechanism for raising substantial additional capital in Europe. Where the number of new shares being sold is less than 10% of the outstanding issued share capital a company has the option of using a Placing to sell the new shares. Stock exchanges usually have rules regarding such placings to ensure that existing shareholders are equitably treated. In Ireland the price of the new shares must be at a discount of no more than 5% to the most recently traded price and the amount of shares issued cannot exceed 10% of the issued share capital. Placings have the advantage of much more rapid execution than a rights issue and the associated transactions costs are significantly lower.

From the perspective of company treasurers the availability of the rights-issue alternative is a critical benefit of having a stock market listing. In a scenario where a company is going through a very difficult time, most sources of long-term finance tend to dry up. Banks are reluctant to extend finance to weak companies and bond investors are likely to shun issues of corporate bonds from distressed companies. Also, in times of overall market weakness even strong companies can find it difficult to raise finance at an acceptable cost. In such circumstances a company that requires long-term finance has the option of bringing a rights issue to the market. The price at which the shares are pitched may be low, implying a high cost of equity to the company. However, if the company requires extra finance for survival then this is the price that it must pay. The key point is that for quoted companies access to the capital market virtually never dries up. An example is Waterford Wedgwood, a company that has been struggling through very difficult business conditions for several years. Nevertheless, in December 2003, it raised €38.5m in a 3-for-1 rights issue to acquire Royal Doulton and to strengthen its balance sheet.

Exhibit 2.2 WATERFORD WEDGWOOD CASE STUDY

Waterford Wedgwood Completes Rights Issue

Una McCaffrey

Waterford Wedgwood has completed the €38.5 million rights issue it launched before Christmas as part of a major refinancing programme. The firm said yesterday 88.07 per cent of the new shares on offer had been taken up, with the remainder placed by Davy Stockbrokers at 21 cents per share.

The rights issue, which was fully underwritten by Davy, was priced at 18 cents per unit and was made on a three-for-11 basis. All of the company's main shareholders took up their entitlement, with the O'Reilly and Goulandris families, who between them own a quarter of Waterford Wedgwood, spending some €10 million in the process. The offering was also taken up in full by Waterford's remaining directors, a number of whom raised their holdings in the company as the issue neared its Christmas Eve closing date. The issue was, however, partly shunned by Waterford's 25,000 smaller, individual investors, of whom just 9,000 chose to take up their entitlement.

The reluctance of smaller shareholders to become involved accounted for a portion of the 11.93 per cent "rump" left over after the issue had closed. The rump also included the entitlements of overseas investors, who were excluded from the issue from the start. This block was placed with unnamed institutions at 21 cents per unit, thus bringing the total raised to €39.2 million before expenses. The fully-paid units traded positively in Dublin yesterday, climbing two cents to 23 cents.

© **The Irish Times**

STOCK EXCHANGES

A stock exchange will normally prescribe criteria for listing in terms of the history of the company, its profits and capital, the integrity of management, and other factors relevant to potential investors in the business. The Irish Stock Exchange was originally part of the London Stock Exchange, but it is now an independent exchange that is governed by the Stock Exchange Act, 1995. The Act provides a legislative framework for the regulation of stock exchanges and their member firms (stockbrokers). The legislation was enacted in order to implement the provisions of the EU Investment Services

Directive (ISD), which requires member states to implement the provisions of that directive in national law. The Act nominates the Irish Financial Services Regulatory Authority (IFSRA) as the supervisory authority for stock exchange member firms. In accordance with the ISD, stockbrokers authorised by IFSRA are entitled to provide stockbroking services to clients in other EEA member states.

Listing of Securities

The Irish Stock Exchange (ISE) is the designated competent authority for the listing of securities in Ireland. Any company that wishes to be admitted to the Official List is expected to comply with the basic conditions set out in the 'Listing Rules'. Some of the key provisions are set out below:

- The company must be validly organised under the laws of its country and must be operating in conformity with its articles of association.
- The securities must be freely transferable and at least 25% of any class of shares must be in the hands of the public.
- Under the Companies Act, all fundraising exercises require a full prospectus to be prepared.
- The ISE has laid down minimum advertising requirements concerning a prospectus. For example, in an 'Offer for Sale', where new shares are being sold, a mini-prospectus or 'offer notice' must appear in at least one newspaper.
- Issues of equity securities must be offered to existing shareholders in proportion to their shareholdings, i.e., by way of a rights issue. This protection is meant to avoid the shareholders' interests being diluted. The law is prepared to remove this protection if shareholders themselves vote on it and they can entitle their directors to issue shares on a non-pre-emptive basis at any time within the following five years. Most Irish-quoted companies have sought the approval of shareholders to issue shares on a non-pre-emptive basis up to 10% of the already-issued share capital.

Definitions: 'Offer notices' and 'mini-prospectuses' are documents containing specific details drawn from the listing particulars or prospectus, including application forms. Information will also be provided of the addresses and times at which copies of the full prospectus are available to the public.

Formal notices are advertisements giving outline details of the issue and the addresses and times at which copies of the listing particulars are available to the public.

Continuing Obligations of Listed Companies

All applicants to the Official List automatically agree to comply with the conditions set out in the 'Continuing Obligations'. Some of the key requirements are set out below:

- A company must notify the ISE of any price-sensitive information.
- Directors' dealings must be announced and restricted to specified time periods.
- Explanatory circulars must be sent to shareholders regarding major acquisitions or disposals of assets.
- The company must have permission from shareholders to repurchase its own shares.
- A company must issue a half-yearly report within four months of the period end and a preliminary statement of annual results within four months of its year-end. Annual accounts must be produced within six months of the company's financial year-end.

The objective of these various listing requirements and continuing obligations is to ensure that a fair and orderly market is maintained in the company's listed securities at all times.

Dealing on the Irish Stock Exchange

The ISE operates a different dealing system for Irish government bonds and for equity and other quoted securities.

Irish Government Bonds

The Irish government bond market revolves around the primary dealers who are recognised by the National Treasury Management Agency (NTMA) and who apply for registration by the ISE as a primary dealer for Irish government bonds. The primary dealers are responsible for quoting continuous two-way prices in Irish government bonds. Primary dealers therefore commit their own capital as they act as principals when dealing in Irish bonds. As a recognised primary dealer a firm takes on certain obligations, which include quoting firm, two-way prices in those bonds specifically notified by NTMA, subject to minimum sizes and maximum bid–offer spreads. The existence of a continuous market in Irish government bonds enables stockbrokers to efficiently execute client orders in government bonds.

Primary dealers are granted certain privileges in return for making bid and offer prices. These include:

- exclusive access to funding by NTMA through auctions of bonds;
- access to NTMA for the purposes of borrowing and lending stock.

Irish Equity Market

Unlike the Irish government bond market, there are no primary dealers in Irish equities. Rather, the market in listed company shares is 'created' by the buy and sell orders that are generated by investors in Irish shares. The equity market may be characterised as an 'order-driven market'. In June 2000 the ISE moved to an electronic order-driven system called ISE Xetra. This system is the product of a strategic alliance between the ISE and the Deutsche Börse in Germany. The Xetra trading system is accessible by all member firms of the ISE through an IT package that provides their dealing rooms with direct access to the central trading system. Investors still give their buy and sell orders to stockbrokers, who then enter orders into the electronic system. Deals then occur when the system matches buy and sell orders. The key advantage of this system is that it is cost-effective, as the cost of supporting primary dealers or market makers is avoided. A disadvantage is that there may be periods when it is difficult to trade in some shares, when there may be a very small number of active orders in the system.

SUMMARY

- Investment alternatives available to investors include fixed-interest securities (bonds), index-linked securities, equities, property, and cash or bank deposits.
- Equities and bonds are generally highly marketable and are easily traded on recognised stock exchanges.
- Deposits are non-negotiable, but are usually accessible at short notice and therefore are highly liquid.
- Property investments are marketable, but because of the large value per unit and high transactions costs property is a highly illiquid investment.
- Equity and property investments provide investors with returns that are closely linked to the performance of the overall economy and are therefore referred to as real assets. Cash and fixed-interest securities provide no such link to economic growth and may be referred to as nominal assets.
- The key risk facing investors in long-term, fixed-interest securities is that of unanticipated inflation. In contrast, index-linked securities promise returns that rise in line with inflation and therefore offer investors a risk-free real return.

➡

- A market where a company or government issues new securities for the first time is referred to as a primary market and such issues are referred to as initial public offerings (IPOs).
- Once issued on a stock market, securities can be bought and sold by investors on a daily basis on what is known as the secondary market.
- Once listed on a stock exchange, companies can issue further tranches of securities through either a rights issue or through a placing of new shares with investors.
- The Irish Stock Exchange is the designated competent authority for the listing of securities in Ireland.
- The Irish Stock Exchange operates different dealing systems for Irish government bonds, and for equity and other quoted securities.
- The Irish government bond market revolves around the primary dealers who are recognised by the National Treasury Management Agency (NTMA) and who apply for registration by the ISE as a primary dealer for Irish government bonds.
- The market in listed company shares is 'created' by the buy and sell orders that are generated by investors in Irish shares. The equity market may be characterised as an 'order-driven market'. In June 2000 the ISE moved to an electronic order-driven system called ISE Xetra.

QUESTIONS

1. **Holding all other factors constant, which of the following is/are TRUE?**

   A. A bond sold at discount will experience a rise in price over time to reach par value.

   B. A bond sold at premium will experience a rise in price over time to reach par value.

   C. A bond sold at premium will experience a decline in price over time to reach par value.

   1. B & C only
   2. All of the above
   3. A & C only
   4. A only

2. **Why do investors invest in fixed-income securities?**

   A. A steady stream of income offered over the life of the bond's obligations.

   ➡

   B. A return of principal when the bond matures.

   C. It is possible to earn capital gains when interest-rate movements are correctly predicted.

      1. None of the above

      2. A & B only

      3. All of the above

      4. B & C only

3. Regarding bonds, which of the following statement(s) is/are FALSE?

   A. The vast majority of fixed-income securities have a specified repayment schedule and must mature at some future date.

   B. Since stocks regularly pay dividends, stocks are fixed-income securities.

   C. At the time the bond is issued, the coupon payments for a typical bond are specified and remain fixed for the life of the bond.

   D. A buyer will get the principal back when a bond matures, assuming there is no default by the issuer.

4. Regarding the holder of an ordinary share, which of the following is/are FALSE?

   A. Is guaranteed a specified dividend return.

   B. Is senior to bondholders in terms of payment.

   C. As the owner, can best be described as the residual claimant.

   D. Has unlimited liability and is responsible for any loss created by the firm.

      1. A, B & C only

      2. A, B & D only

      3. None of the above

      4. D only

Questions 5 and 6 are based on the summary information below for ABC plc.

	€ Million
Sales	200
Operating Profit	30
Profit after Tax	20
Dividend	10
Retained Profits	10

ABC has 200 million shares in issue and the current market price is 100c.

➡

5. What are ABC's Earnings Per Share (EPS), and its dividend yield?

   A. 1c; 2.5%
   B. 100c; 5.0%
   C. 10c; 5.0%
   D. 10c; 10%

6. What is ABC's Price Earnings Ratio (PER)?

   A. 20
   B. 6.7
   C. 10
   D. 13.3

7. Which of the following statements is FALSE?

   A. Investment returns from property investment depend on the success of the building in attracting tenants who over time will be willing to pay rising rents.
   B. Property unit-linked funds promoted by the life assurance industry enable small investors to invest in the commercial property market.
   C. Unlike equities, property returns are guaranteed and therefore property is a lower-risk investment than government bonds.
   D. Commercial property investments typically include offices, retail shops and industrial premises such as factories and warehouses.

Exercise

Exhibit 2.3 concerns the Eircom IPO on the Irish Stock Exchange. After reading this identify all the relevant players and which category they fall into, i.e., who was the Originating Investment Bank, who was the seller of the shares, who are the stockbrokers engaged to sell the issue, etc.? Construct a flow chart plotting the movement of shares from the owner to the final group of investors, and plot the flow of cash from the final investors to the owner (the Irish government in this case).

Exhibit 2.3

Stockbroking firms invited to take part in Telecom share offer

By BRENDAN MCGRATH, Markets Editor

All of the Irish stock-broking firms have been invited to become involved in the offering of an estimated £1 billion (€1.26 billion) of Telecom Éireann shares to the public, even though the Irish retail offering is being directly handled by AIB Capital Markets and its stock-broking subsidiary, Goodbody.

This move to bring in the other brokers as agents is seen as an attempt by the Government to ensure that the maximum possible interest in Telecom shares is generated among private investors.

The marketing campaign for the retail offering of Telecom shares will begin on April 22nd with a mail-shot to every household in the State, followed by an intensive advertising campaign involving print, radio, television and outdoor media.

The Government has also finalised the syndication and underwriting of the global institutional offering of shares. AIB Capital Markets and Merrill Lynch are the global co-ordinators and lead managers, and four co-lead managers have now been appointed: ABN Amro, Dresdner Kleinwort Benson, Morgan Stanley and SG/Paribas.

Half the 35 per cent of Telecom shares being sold by the Government will be directed towards the retail offering, and the general public will be invited to pre-register for an allocation of shares. While this pre-registration does not involve an obligation to buy, those who do pre-register will receive priority when it comes to the final allocation of Telecom shares.

Similarly, the stock-broking firms have been invited to pre-register their own private clients and will receive a commission on any shares that their clients take up in the retail offering. One condition attached to the involvement of the brokers is that they must have dealt at least once in the past year for each private client they pre-register for a priority allocation.

For the global institutional offering, the four co-lead managers were chosen from almost 30 applicants and a final shortlist of 12. It is understood that the four were chosen for a combination of criteria, including geographical spread, expertise in telecoms research, distribution network and their ability to work as a group.

Lead manager Merrill Lynch and co-lead manager Morgan Stanley will be responsible for the marketing of Telecom shares to American investors, Dresdner Kleinwort Benson will be responsible for the UK and Germany, SG/Paribas will deal with France and ABN Amro will look after Dutch investors as well as being involved with lead manager AIB Capital Markets in the marketing to Irish institutions.

Initially, the global offering will involve a series of road-shows in various locations worldwide. These will be followed by one-to-one presentations to the bigger institutional investors. Exactly how many shares will be allocated to the various regions in the global offering has not yet been decided.

Chapter three

Investing in Bonds

This chapter extends the analysis of bonds begun in chapter 2. Issues such as the valuation of bonds and the calculation of the flat yield and the gross redemption yield (GRY) or yield to maturity (YTM) are examined in detail. The term structure of interest rates is discussed, as well as the important concept of duration.

Learning Objectives

After completing this chapter you should:
- **Be familiar with the various bond yield measures, most importantly the gross redemption yield**
- **Have an understanding of how to value a bond applying the time value of money concept**
- **Understand the nature of the inverse relationship between changes in interest rates and bond prices**
- **Be familiar with the term structure of interest rates**
- **Be able to use a bond's duration to estimate the impact of a change in yield on the price of a bond.**

Bonds (or fixed-income securities) usually provide a return in the form of regular interest payments and the repayment of their capital value on their maturity or redemption dates. Bonds are generally a more reliable source of ongoing income than many other asset classes, as they provide a predefined income stream and the repayment of principal at maturity. This sets them apart from equity securities, where the future dividend income stream is uncertain and where there is no maturity date. Likewise the certain future investment-income stream associated with bonds contrasts with the uncertain future rental-income stream associated with property. Not surprisingly, equities and property tend to be more volatile investment categories than bonds. Essentially bonds are loans with pre-specified terms and conditions; they have been used by borrowers and lenders for centuries and provide returns in the form of income and repayment at maturity. The early bonds were issued by governments, often for the purposes of funding wars or colonial escapades. The UK was a leader in this regard and by the nineteenth century there was an active market in British government securities. Title to these early bonds was by way of a certificate which was embossed with gilt edging. As a result British government securities came to be referred to as 'gilt-edged' securities and to this day are still referred to as such.

WHY BOND MARKETS HAVE DEVELOPED

The development of bond markets reflects the benefits that such investment securities offer to both the issuers (borrowers) and investors (lenders). In Ireland the vast majority of bonds are those issued by the Irish government and this is a pattern that is common in most economies. Corporations also issue bonds and corporate bonds are identical to government bonds except for one important difference. The default risk of bonds issued by governments in the developed world is infinitesimal and these securities are viewed by investors as being risk-free. Bonds issued by corporations are subject to default risk, the extent of which is determined by the financial strength of the respective company and an assessment of its future prospects. Investors (lenders) will require compensation for this credit risk in the form of a higher interest rate. Our discussion on bonds that follows relates to government bonds and examples are confined to the Irish government bond market. However, the characteristics of bonds are generic and apply equally to bonds issued by a wide variety of issuers.

ATTRACTIONS TO ISSUERS AND INVESTORS

Cost and flexibility are the key attractions to the issuers of bonds. By funding their borrowing requirements in this way governments have created the conditions for the development of large and liquid bond markets, thus creating a very cost-effective way for governments to fund their borrowing requirements on an ongoing basis. The ability to issue bonds with varying maturity dates ensures that interest payments and eventual repayment of bonds can be timed to coincide with any specific set of cash-flow needs. For investors, bonds offer a steady and secure future income stream with extremely low default risk in the case of most government bonds. For corporate bonds the work of credit rating agencies such as Moody's and Standard & Poors ensures that an efficient market exists that enables company credit risk to be priced. Because the characteristics of bonds are very different from other assets such as equities and property they are the key to enabling investors to diversify risk.

CHARACTERISTICS OF BONDS

Bonds are essentially loans that are negotiable, i.e., they can be bought and sold after they are issued, and therefore a bond has a set of terms and conditions that protects the purchaser or investor by obliging the borrower to repay specified amounts at certain intervals. Although the prospectus of any new bond issue is a long legal document, there are three key components that establish the essentials of the contractual relationship between the borrower and the lender. These are:

- par value
- coupon
- term to maturity.

Par Value: The par value is sometimes referred to as the face value, nominal value or redemption value of a bond. Irish government bonds typically have a par value of €100. One unit of a bond therefore has a nominal value of €100. The price at which a bond is issued may be higher or lower than this par value, and the market prices of bonds already in issue will usually diverge from the par value. As well as being a nominal unit of value, the par value has real economic significance, as this is the amount of money that the issuer will repay to the holder on the maturity date of the bond.

Coupon: The coupon is the interest rate set as part of a bond's terms and conditions. This interest rate is calculated on the *par value* of a bond and not the issue price of the bond. Therefore, the amount of interest paid by a bond issuer is calculated by multiplying the coupon interest rate by the par value of the bond. Irish government bonds usually pay this interest once a year.

> A holder of €10,000 nominal of the 4% Treasury 2010 holds 10,000/100 = 100 units of this bond. Each unit will pay annual interest of €100 * .04 = €4. With 100 units this investor will receive annual interest on his holding of 100 * €4 = €400.

Time to Maturity: This is the length of time between the date the money is invested and the date it is subsequently repaid by the borrower. The maturity date or redemption date is the day the issuer repays the bond's par value.

For an investor the par value, coupon interest rate and the redemption date provide sufficient information to establish the investment parameters of a bond. A schedule of cash flows that are determined by the terms of the bond can easily be established, and this schedule provides the basis on which bonds can be valued and priced.

PRICING AND VALUING BONDS

An investor who wishes to put funds on deposit will generally look at interest rates offered on deposits in the marketplace and will place his funds with the institution that offers the highest interest rate for the particular period chosen. The deposit product that offers the highest rate of interest clearly is the one that offers the best 'value' to the prospective investor. Assessing the investment worth of bonds has similarities with the above but, given the characteristics of bonds, the process is much more complicated. A good starting point is to define the various interest rates or yields that apply to a fixed-interest bond; there are three of these.

i)   **Coupon Rate:** This is the annual interest paid divided by the par value of the bond, expressed as a percentage.

ii)   **Flat or Running Yield:** This is the actual annual coupon payable divided by the current market value of the bond, which usually differs from the par value, again expressed as a percentage.

iii)   **Gross Redemption Yield:** This takes into account all the future coupon payments due on the bond, together with the redemption value (which is the bond's par value), and relates these future payments to the current price of the bond in the market. The Gross Redemption Yield (GRY) is expressed as a percentage per annum and is the most useful measure of the worth or value of the bond. It is sometimes referred to as the Yield to Maturity (YTM).

Exhibit 3.1 contains the list of Irish Government bonds that appears daily in the *Irish Times*. The information published for each bond includes:

• coupon
• redemption date
• market price
• yield (which is the GRY).

Exhibit 3.1 List of Irish Government Bonds

Government Stocks

	Euro price	Yield
3.5% Try 18/10/05	101.46	1.618
12½ Cap 15/12/05.........	100.81	2.352
8 Try 18/08/06	104.08	2.466
9 Cap 01/09/06	105.02	2.597
4.25 Try 18/OCT/07.........	102.78	2.728
8¼ Cap 30/07/08...........	113.86	2.899
6 Try 18/08/08	108.00	2.907
3.25% Try 18/Apr/09.......	100.88	2.963
4.00% Try 18/04/10........	103.25	3.196
8½ Cap 01/10/10...........	123.77	3.223
8¾ Cap 30/09/12...........	133.11	3.352
5% Try 18/04/13	110.65	3.348
8¼ Try 18/08/15.............	138.92	3.476
4.60 Try 18/04/16..........	109.10	3.535
4.50 Try 18/Apr/20..........	108.65	3.710

(Courtesy NCB Stockbrokers)

The Flat Yield or Running Yield can be easily calculated for each bond; let's take the 5% Treasury 18/04/13 as an example. This bond matures on 18 April 2013, which is a crucial piece of information for the calculation of the GRY. However, the redemption date has no relevance to the calculation of the flat yield. For the above bond the flat yield is calculated using the formula:

$$\frac{\text{Coupon}}{\text{Price}} \times 100 = \frac{5}{110.65} \times 100 = 4.52\%$$

Because the bond is trading above par, the flat yield is lower than the coupon – 4.52% versus 5%. An investor who invests €1,000 in this bond will receive €45.20 interest for each year that he holds the bond. This can be compared with deposit interest of €20 that would be received on a €1,000 deposit if the deposit interest rate were 2% per annum for the same period. While the flat yield is useful, it presents only part of the return picture of a fixed-interest bond. Figure 3.1 illustrates that the value of the bond will move from €110.65 to €100 if it is held to maturity.

Figure 3.1 5% Treasury 2013, Price Movement if Held to Maturity

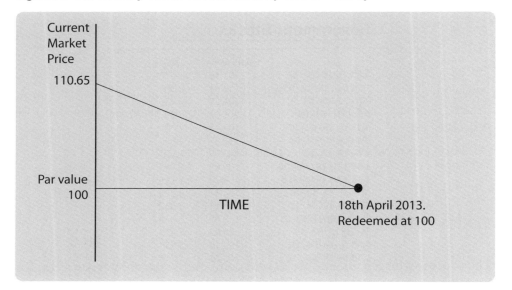

On the maturity date the bond will be redeemed at its par value of €100, so that a capital loss of €10.65 will be sustained if the bond is held until it matures. Clearly in order to accurately assess the investment value of the bond, this future capital loss must be taken into account.

Gross Redemption Yield (GRY)

The GRY is calculated in a way that takes into account all the future cash flows that are associated with a particular bond. There are two very important assumptions made in the calculation of GRY. These are:

i)   The bond is held until its maturity date.
ii)   All coupons are reinvested immediately when received and achieve a GRY that is identical to today's GRY.

To understand the GRY concept, we need to digress into a discussion of the time value of money. It is intuitively clear that future or deferred income is not as valuable as immediate income. This manifests itself in the financial markets as a rate of interest on low-risk assets such as cash, and an expected rate of return on risky assets such as equities. In other words, savers or investors need a reward if they are going to save for tomorrow rather than spend today. Example 3.1 illustrates how the value of a deposit grows over time to a much larger future value.

Example 3.1. The Future Value (FV) of a deposit

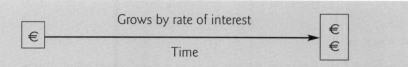

Grows by rate of interest

Time

€1,000 is deposited at a fixed annual rate of interest of 5% with interest credited once a year. Deposit to last for a term of 10 years. Value of deposit after one year is calculated as:

€1,000 * (1 + r), where r = rate of interest expressed as a decimal
€1,000 * (1 + 0.05) = €1,050
Value of deposit after 10 years is calculated as:
€1,000 * (1 + r)^n, where n = term of deposit in years
€1,000 * (1 + 0.05)^{10} = €1,629.

The process whereby money grows at a compound rate of interest to reach a future value as we move forward in time can be reversed if we examine what happens as we move back in time. Example 3.2 illustrates how a sum of money to be received in the future can be translated into the equivalent value in today's money.

Example 3.2. The Present Value (PV) of a sum to be received in the Future

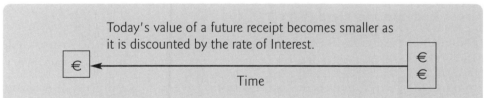

Today's value of a future receipt becomes smaller as it is discounted by the rate of Interest.

Time

A payment of €1,000 is to be received in exactly one year. The rate of interest or discount rate is 5%. The payment in today's money (the present value) may be calculated using the formula: €1,000/(1 + r), where r = the rate of interest or the expected rate of return, commonly referred to as the discount rate. Therefore, the PV of this expected receipt is €1,000/1.05 = €952.

If this payment were to be received in 10 years' time the PV may be calculated using the formula: €1,000/(1 + r)^n, where n = the number of years to wait before payment is received. Now the PV of this expected receipt becomes €1,000/(1.05)^{10} = €614.

This example illustrates that the PV of a future payment is calculated by dividing the expected payment by one plus the rate of interest to the power of the number of years to wait for the payment. Clearly, the higher the rate of interest (discount rate) the lower will be the present value, and the longer the time period the lower will be the present value.

Example 3.3 sets out the future cash flows associated with the 3.25% Treasury 2009, taken from the list of Irish government bonds.

Example 3.3 Calculating the Present Value of a Government Bond, 3.25% Treasury 2009

Interest		€3.25	€3.25	€3.25	
Redemption Amount				€100	

	19 April 2006	2007	2008	18 April 2009	Time

To calculate the present value we need to decide on a rate of discount; in this case r = 3%

Cash flows	Year	Cash Flow	Present Value Calculation	PV of end Payment
	2007	3,25	$\frac{3.25}{1.03}$ =	3.16
	2008	3.25	$\frac{3.25}{(1.03)^2}$ =	3.06
	2009	103.25	$\frac{103.25}{(1.03)^3}$ =	94.49
				100.71

Imagine the government is selling this bond for the first time and is seeking bids from investors. You are considering investing in this bond, but you have to decide on a price. What you need to do is to work out what the future pay-outs of the bond are worth in today's money. You therefore need to work out the present value of the interest payments and the final redemption amount. We can apply the technique illustrated in Example 3.2 to calculate the present value of each cash flow associated with this bond. To do this we need a discount rate. In this example, the discount rate should be the rate of return that we require if we are to be enticed to invest in this bond. Let's assume that we would be happy with a return of 3% per annum. This then becomes the discount rate that can be plugged in to our present-value calculations, as illustrated in Example 3.3.

We have now calculated the present value of the cash flows that will be generated by this bond at €100.71. We can interpret this as meaning that if we pay this price for the bond, it will deliver to us a return of 3% per annum. If the government prices the bonds at 100.71, then an investment in this bond will yield an annual return of 3%. If the bond is priced lower than that, then it will deliver a return greater than 3% p.a. A price higher than 100.71 implies a return of less than 3% p.a. (in which case we would not invest in the bond).

Where the price of the bond is known, we can apply the same formula to establish the rate of return that this price implies. Example 3.4 illustrates this and it can be seen that when the price of the bond is known there is only one unknown to solve in the equation, namely the discount rate, r.

Example 3.4. Calculating the Gross Redemption Yield (GRY)

3.25% Treasury 2009

$$\text{Price} = \frac{\text{Coupon 1}}{1 + r} + \frac{\text{Coupon 2}}{(1 + r)^2} + \frac{(\text{Coupon 3} + \text{Par value})}{(1 + r)^3}$$

r = the discount rate, which is also the GRY of the bond.

If this is April 2006, and given the current price of the bond as 102.85, the GRY is calculated by inserting the known information into this equation:

$$102.85 = 3.25/(1 + r) + 3.25/(1 + r)^2 + 103.25/(1 + r)^3$$

This discount rate is in fact the gross redemption yield of the bond. It is quite a difficult equation to solve, but we can rely on financial calculators to do the job for us, or we will often be simply given information on both the price and GRY of the bond. In the example the GRY as published is 2.5%, which is the discount rate that brings the sum of the present values of the cash flows associated with the bond to the current price of €102.85.

Inverse Relationship between the Price and GRY of a Bond

Closer inspection of Examples 3.3 and 3.4 illustrates the relationship between changes in the discount rate (r) and the price of the bond. A rise in the interest rate or discount rate (r) will reduce the present value of each future cash flow. Since the price or value of the bond is equal to the sum of these present values, it is clear that any rise in interest rates will lead to a FALL in the price of a bond. Example 3.5 illustrates what happens to the price of the 3.25% Treasury 2009 when there is a rise in the GRY from 3% to 4%.

Example 3.5 The Impact of a higher GRY on the Value of a Bond

$r = 3\%$ and $r = 4\%$

Cash flows	Year	Cash Flow €	Present Value $r = 3\%$	$r = 4\%$
	2007	3.25	$\dfrac{3.25}{1.03} = 3.16$	$\dfrac{3.25}{1.04} = 3.13$
	2008	3.25	$\dfrac{3.25}{(1.03)^2} = 3.06$	$\dfrac{3.25}{(1.04)^2} = 3.01$
	2009	103.25	$\dfrac{103.25}{(1.03)^3} = 94.49$	$\dfrac{103.25}{(1.04)^3} = 91.79$

Sum of present Value of Cash Flows =
Price of Bond =   **100.71**   **97.93**

The present value of each expected cash flow falls and hence the price of the bond (which equals the sum of the PVs) falls to €97.93, compared with the price of €100.71 when r was 3%. Once a bond is issued, its price will constantly fluctuate in response to changes in long-term interest rates. A rise in interest rates reduces the price of a bond and a fall in interest rates increases the price of a bond. This is a precise mathematical relationship.

MANAGING A BOND PORTFOLIO

The inverse relationship between market yields and bond prices is the basis for understanding, valuing and managing bonds. A bond fund manager who correctly anticipates changes in market yields can exploit this relationship. In recent years bond yields have declined quite sharply, leading to an uplift in the value of fixed-interest bonds. The magnitude of change in the capital value of a particular bond in response to a change in market yields will depend on variables that are unique to each bond, i.e., the coupon and the time to maturity.

The Impact of Maturity

An important concept is that for a given change in market yields, changes in bond prices are directly related to time to maturity. From Example 3.5 we can see that the rise in GRY from 3% to 4% led to a fall in the price of the 3.25% Treasury from 100.71 to 97.93, a decline of –2.8%. Given another bond with exactly the same coupon but with 4 years to maturity, we can calculate its value in the same way. With a discount rate of 3% the value of this bond is 100.92, which falls to 97.29 when the discount rate rises to 4%. This is a fall of −3.6% and in general it is the case that longer-dated bonds are more sensitive to interest-rate changes than are shorter-dated bonds.

Figure 3.2 Bond Prices, Time to Maturity and Interest-Rate Changes

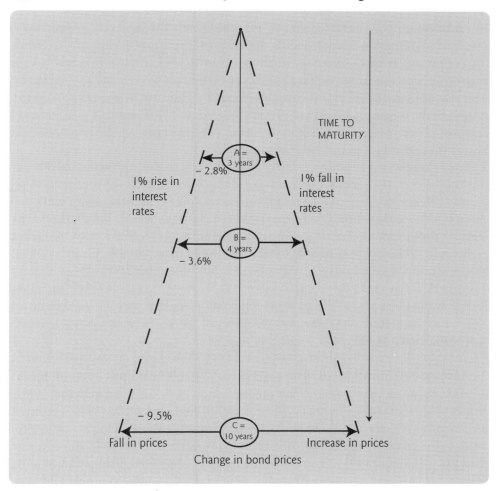

Figure 3.2 illustrates this relationship as a series of pendulums. Bond A is quite short and a rise in interest rates causes this pendulum to swing to the left, indicating a fall in price. For longer-dated bonds the pendulum becomes longer, and hence swings over a wider arc for the same change in market yields. Bond B is a 4-year bond which falls in price by −3.6% for the same 1% rise in yield. Bond C is a 10-year bond which falls in price by −9.5%. The greater sensitivity of longer-dated bonds is due to the longer wait for the

receipt of the later coupons and particularly the longer wait for the final redemption amount, so consequently the discounting mechanism is working over a much longer period of time. The principle illustrated here is a stark one: other things being equal, bond price volatility is a function of maturity and therefore long-term bonds fluctuate more than do short-term bonds.

The Effects of Coupon

In addition to the maturity effect, the change in the price of a bond as a result of a change in market yields depends on the coupon rate of the bond. Referring again to Figure 3.2, if the coupon is very high it will result in a higher proportion of expected cash flows being received in the earlier years. The pendulum becomes weighted towards its fulcrum and hence its arc is dampened. So a second principle is that bond price volatility and bond coupon rates are inversely related. Other things being equal, high-coupon bonds fluctuate less than low-coupon bonds.

The relationship between bond yields and bond price movements was set out by Burton Malkiel in 1962, when he set out a number of theorems such as the effect of time and coupon on bond price volatility that we have discussed here. For bond fund managers and investors Malkiel's theorems lead to the important conclusion that a decline in interest rates or market yields will cause a rise in bond prices, and the highest volatility will occur in longer-maturity bonds and low-coupon bonds. Therefore:

i)   A bond buyer, in order to receive the maximum price impact of an expected fall in interest rates, should purchase low-coupon, long-maturity bonds.
ii) If an increase in interest rates is expected, an investor already holding bonds should switch into shorter-maturity bonds with high coupons.

While these theorems are sufficient to enable investors to structure their bond portfolios, they are not sufficiently precise in today's sophisticated financial world. Investors managing bond portfolios need measures that take into account all the bonds' cash flows, and that also take into account any changes that occur in volatility as the overall level of market yields changes. Such measures are available and are called 'duration' and 'convexity'; they are explained later in this chapter.

The Term Structure of Interest Rates

So far our discussion has centred on the characteristics of a typical fixed-interest bond issued by the government of a developed economy. The fact that most governments have several bonds in issue, with different maturity dates, gives investors the ability to create bond portfolios that can closely match their respective investment objectives. Taking bonds issued by the Irish government as an example, we can see that we have a set of bonds that are homogeneous in a number of important respects:

- They all have the same issuer, and therefore the risk of default is exactly the same for each bond. In the case of Irish bonds this risk is so small that these bonds have no practical risk of default.
- All these bonds are subject to the same tax, legal and regulatory regimes.

This homogeneity allows us to analyse the investment characteristics of a bond market as a whole, in addition to the characteristics of each individual bond. This provides a wealth of extra information regarding the current structure of interest rates. The relationship between time to maturity and yields for a particular category of bonds at a particular point in time is referred to as the **term structure of interest rates**. The term structure of interest rates is usually plotted as a **yield curve** and can be quite easily done by plotting pairs of yield and time to maturity on a scattergram. In Figure 3.3 yield curves for the Irish, UK and US government bond markets are plotted.

Figure 3.3 Yield Curves – Ireland, UK, US

Implications of theories of the term structure of interest rates	Impact on the slope of the yield curve
Expectations regarding future short-term interest rates • expectations for a rise • expectations for a fall	• Upward slope • Downward slope (inverted)
Capital Risk	Upward slope
Income Risk	Downward slope (inverted)
Excess demand for long-dated bonds (15 years +)	Inverted from 15 years out
Excess supply of medium-term bonds (5–15 years)	Yield curve with a humped shape

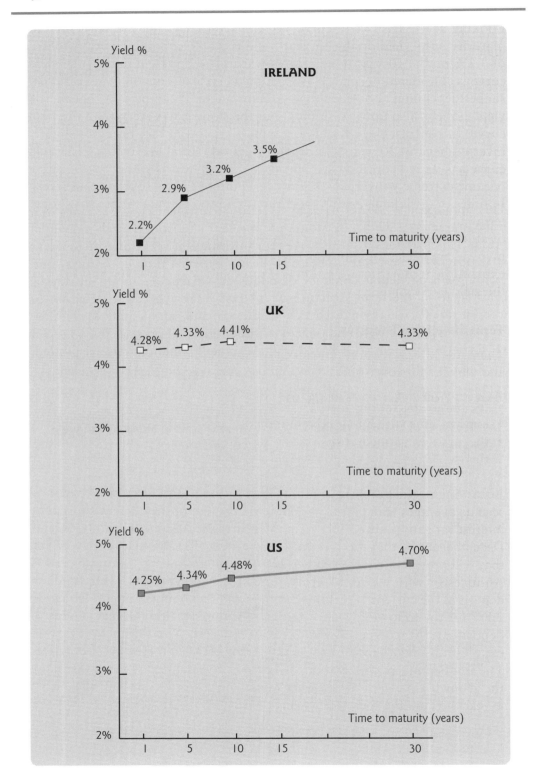

Looking at the Irish yield curve, we can see that yields rise with time to maturity – the yield on the 15-year bond is 3.5%, compared with the yield of 3.2% on the 10-year bond. The upward slope apparent in the Irish yield curve is considered normal. However, the curve can take on many different shapes depending upon economic circumstances. It can be seen that the US yield curve is also upward sloping, but the slope is less steep than the Irish curve. In contrast the UK curve is quite flat, and in fact becomes slightly inverted beyond 20 years. At different periods the shape of the Irish yield curve has varied enormously. During the currency crisis in 1992 the curve became extremely inverted, as short-term interest rates rose to crisis levels. In times of crisis such as this short rates tend to rise much more than long-term rates, and an inverted yield curve is often considered to be the precursor of an economic recession. However, most observations about yield curves involve tendencies and not exact relationships. Theories have developed to explain the term structure of interest rates and why the shape and slope of the yield curve change over time.

Term Structure Theories

There are several theories advanced to explain the shape of the yield curve and why it shifts over time. They can be categorised into the following:

- the pure expectations theory
- expectations with a risk premium theory
- the market segmentation theory (a variation is the preferred habitat theory).

According to the **pure expectations theory**, long-term interest rates can be seen as averages (calculated as geometric means) of the current short-term interest rate and future short-term interest rates. Assume that today is end-December 2006, that the current 1-year rate is 3%, and that the 1-year rate that will prevail at end-December 2007 for the following 12 months is 4%. An investor who wishes to invest funds for two years can place funds on deposit at the current 1-year interest rate, and then reinvest at end-December 2007 for the following year. Alternatively, the investor can place funds on deposit at the current 2-year rate of interest. According to the pure expectations theory investors are indifferent between these two alternatives. The implication of this is that the current 2-year interest rate must equal the geometric mean of these 1-year rates. The geometric mean of the current 1-year rate and the forward 1-year rate is:

$$\sqrt{(1.03 \times 1.04)} - 1 = .035 \text{ or } 3.5\%$$

If the pure expectations theory is an accurate explanation of the level of long-term interest rates, then the yield curve can be used to infer market expectations of future interest rates. In the example above, if we know the 1-year rate of 3% and the 2-year rate of 3.5%, we can deduce the 1-year forward rate as:

$$\sqrt{1.03 \times (1 + f)} = 1.035, \text{ where f = 1-year forward rate}$$
$$[1.03 \times (1 + f)] = (1.035)^2 = 1.07$$
$$1 + f = (1.07)/(1.03) = 1.04$$

Therefore   f = .04 or 4%.

While this equation has been limited to just two years, it does apply more generally, so that forward rates of interest can be calculated for virtually any chosen period of time. Several governments now issue bonds with a maturity of 50 years, so that we have yield curves in some markets that stretch out to 50 years. There is one important caveat regarding the pure expectations theory, which is that it assumes that investors are risk-neutral. A risk-neutral investor is defined as one who is not concerned about the possibility that interest-rate expectations will not prove to be correct, so long as potential favourable deviations from expectations are as likely as unfavourable ones. However, it is generally assumed that investors are risk-averse. Risk-averse investors are prepared to forgo some investment return in order to achieve greater certainty in regard to the value of investments and the income from them.

The likely existence of risk aversion leads into the '**Expectations with a Risk Premium Theory**'. This could mean that the yield curve should normally slope upwards, because longer-dated maturities have higher volatility than shorter-dated ones. Risk-averse investors will demand a risk premium for the longer-dated bonds, thereby pushing up their yields relative to shorter-dated bonds. This theory provides a logical explanation as to why a yield curve normally slopes upwards. The tendency towards an upward slope could be further reinforced by borrowers' preference to borrow for long periods in order to reduce uncertainty. Such borrowers would presumably be prepared to pay a premium for longer-dated issues. However, the other side of this coin is that some investors may prefer long-dated bonds because they provide greater certainty of income flows compared with other assets. For example, bank deposits over the long term provide a very uncertain stream of future income. Therefore, such investors may be prepared to pay a premium (accept a lower yield) for longer-dated bonds, which would tend to flatten the shape of the yield curve.

The third theory of the term structure of interest rates is the **market segmentation approach** and a variation called the '**preferred habitat hypothesis**'. The essential idea here is that demand and supply conditions may vary across the maturity spectrum, and it is excess demand or supply that determines yields for different maturities. Therefore, short-term yields are determined by the interaction of supply and demand for short-term funds. Long-term yields are determined by the interaction of a different set of borrowers and lenders. Under this hypothesis the yield curve could have almost any shape, depending on the number of different maturity segments.

Concluding Comments on Yield Curve Theories

This discussion highlights the fact that there is no single, elegant explanation for the behaviour of the term structure of interest rates. Indeed, the 'theories' discussed here are really a series of explanations for the observation that yield curves change shape on an ongoing basis. Each 'theory' has its merits, but none is capable of providing a comprehensive explanation of the yield curve. These theories can provide a checklist for the important task of analysis of the term structure of interest rates.

The Measurement of Bond Price Volatility

Earlier in this chapter we identified maturity and coupon as being the determinants of the sensitivity of a bond's price to changes in the overall level of interest rates. A single statistic that captures the impact of both coupon and maturity would be very useful when it comes to managing bond portfolios. Fortunately there is such a concept, called 'duration', which was conceived over 50 years ago by Frederick Macauley.

Duration Defined: Duration can be thought of as the average number of years it takes for an investor to get his money back. More formally, it measures the weighted average maturity of a bond's cash flows on a present-value basis. Duration is expressed in years and **Example 3.6** illustrates how it is calculated.

Example 3.6 Calculating Duration

$3\frac{1}{4}$ % Treasury 2009	$r = 3\%$, Price $= 100.71$		
Period (t)	**Cash Flow**	**Present Value Cash Flow (PVCF)**	**t $\times$ PVCF**
1	3.25	3.16	3.16
2	3.25	3.06	6.12
3	103.25	94.49	283.47
Total		100.71	292.75

Macauley Duration $= 292.75/100.71 = 2.9$ Years ➡

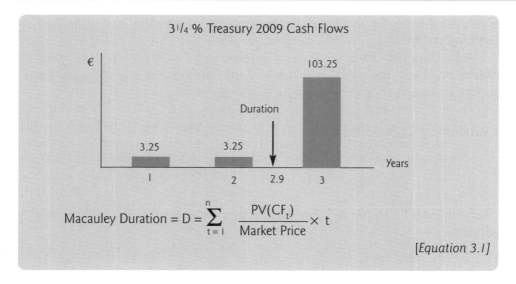

$$\text{Macauley Duration} = D = \sum_{t=1}^{n} \frac{PV(CF_t)}{\text{Market Price}} \times t$$

[Equation 3.1]

This example illustrates that the present value of each cash flow is weighted by the time (in years) to wait for the receipt, and these weights are totalled and divided by the price of the bond to give the Macauley Duration of the bond in years.

Understanding Duration

An examination of the Macauley Duration equation shows that the calculation of duration depends on three factors:

i)   The maturity of the bond: duration lengthens with time to maturity, holding the GRY and coupon payments constant.

ii)   The coupon payments: higher coupons lead to a faster recovery of money invested, so that higher coupons result in shorter duration compared with lower-coupon bonds. Therefore, coupon is inversely related to duration.

iii) The gross redemption yield, GRY, is inversely related to duration (holding coupon and maturity constant).

Uses of Duration

The two most important uses of duration are: first, it gives us the *effective life* of a bond; and second, it is a measure of bond price sensitivity to interest-rate movements. Regarding the former, duration allows us to compare bonds with different maturities and coupons on a consistent basis. Furthermore, the duration of a bond portfolio can also be calculated, so that different portfolios can be compared with one another and bond portfolios can be compared with the duration of the respective liabilities that they may be seeking to match.

Regarding the latter, bond price changes are directly related to duration. More precisely, the percentage change in a bond's price, given a change in interest rates, is proportional to its duration, so that duration can be used to measure interest-rate exposure. A modification needs to be made to duration in order to apply it for this purpose, whereby Macauley Duration is divided by one plus the GRY (1 + GRY) to give what is termed Modified Duration:

$$\text{Modified Duration} = D^* = D/(1 + GRY)$$

Referring to Example 3.6, we can calculate the modified duration of this bond as:

$$MD = 2.9/(1 + .03) = 2.82$$

How do we interpret this number for modified duration? Unlike duration it is not a period of years; rather, it is a number that when multiplied by a change in the yield of a bond gives us the percentage change in the price of the bond. Referring again to Example 3.6, we can calculate the change in the price of this bond for any given change in yields (or interest rates) by applying the equation:

$$\Delta P/P = -D^* \, \Delta r$$

where: ΔP = change in price
          P = price of bond
          $-D^*$ = modified duration with a negative sign
          Δr = instantaneous change in yield in decimal form.

[Equation 3.2]

If there was an instantaneous rise in yields of one percentage point, then the price of the 3.25% Treasury 2009 would change as follows:

$$\text{Change in price} = -2.82 \times .01 = -.0282 \text{ or } -2.82\%$$

Therefore, a one-percentage-point rise in yields would lead to a fall in the price of this bond of (100.7 × .0282) = €2.84 per €100 nominal. On this basis it would seem that we can interpret the modified duration number as being the percentage change in the price of a bond for a one percentage point change in yield. Unfortunately, Equation 3.2 is only an approximation. For very small changes in yield (up to about 20 basis points) it gives a result that is very close to being correct. For changes in yield of one or two percentage points there will be quite a large discrepancy compared with the true actual change in the price of a bond. However, we can interpret a bond's modified duration as giving us the percentage change in the price of a bond for a one percentage point change in yield, as long as we remember that this is an approximation.

While the modified duration number may be sufficient in many situations, the effective management of bond portfolios requires a more precise calculation.

The reason why modified duration is an approximation is that it produces symmetric percentage price change estimates. In the example above, applying the equation to a percentage point fall in yield would produce the same absolute bond price change (+2.82%). In other words, it operates as if the price–yield relationship were linear, whereas this relationship is not in fact linear, but is curvilinear.

Convexity

We refer to this curved nature of the price–yield relationship as the bond's convexity. More formally, convexity is the term used to refer to the degree to which duration changes as the GRY changes. Figure 3.4 illustrates why an adjustment to the modified duration calculation needs to be made for the convexity of a bond.

Figure 3.4 Using Modified Duration 3.25% Treasury 2009

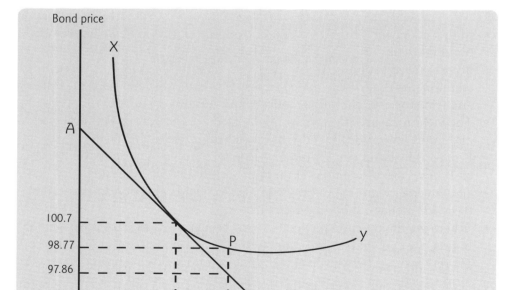

The MD calculation results in a fall in the price of the 3.25% Treasury 2009 to 97.86 from 100.7 for a rise in GRY to 4% from 3%. The MD relationship is represented by the line AB, whereas the true relationship at the 3% GRY is more properly represented by the curve XY. This curve indicates that the price fall should be read from point P (indicating a fall in price to 98.77). In general, modified duration overestimates price falls (rising yields) and underestimates price rises (falling yields). For very small changes in yield the discrepancy is immaterial, but for larger changes in yield it becomes significant.

Convexity varies for different bonds and, just like duration, it is a function of coupon, maturity and yield. Convexity:

- is positively related to maturity, therefore it is larger for long-dated bonds;
- is negatively related to coupon; it is larger for low-coupon bonds;
- is negatively related to yield; it is larger when yields are low.

Convexity calculations can be made, similar to those for modified duration, to give a percentage change in the price of a bond due to a change in yield. This can be added to the approximate price change calculated using duration. The result will still be an approximation, but it will be a big improvement on the calculation based solely on duration.

SUMMARY

- Both lenders and borrowers benefit from the existence of well-developed bond markets.
- Bonds are essentially loans that are negotiable and the three key components that define the contractual relationship between the issuer and investor are: par value, coupon and term to maturity.
- The yield measures that investors look to are the Flat or Running yield and, more importantly, the gross redemption yield (GRY).
- Bonds are valued using present-value techniques, whereby the bonds' cash flows are discounted at an appropriate rate of interest.
- The inverse relationship between market yields and bond prices is the basis for managing bond portfolios.
- Where we have a homogeneous set of bonds, such as Irish government bonds, we can analyse the characteristics of a bond market as a whole; the relationship between time to maturity and yields is referred to as the term structure of interest rates and is normally depicted as a yield curve.
- Duration can be thought of as the average number of years that it takes for an investor to get his money back.

> • Modified Duration can be used to calculate the sensitivity of bond prices to changes in interest rates for small changes in rates.
> • For large changes in yield, the convexity of a bond needs to be used to adjust the duration calculation.

QUESTIONS

1. **A two-year government bond (3% Exchequer 2005) has a fixed coupon of €3 per €100 nominal of the bond. Your broker has quoted you a purchase price of €98 per €100 nominal but you don't trust him. The two-year rate of interest offered by your bank is 4% p.a. Is your broker offering you a better deal than that offered by the bank?**

   A. Yes
   B. No

2. **10% is equivalent to _____ basis points.**

   A. 10
   B. 100
   C. 1,000
   D. 10,000

3. **Irish 10-year Government Bonds typically yield more than 6-month Irish Exchequer Bills primarily because of the:**

   A. Default risk differential
   B. Expected inflation premium differential
   C. Liquidity differential
   D. Maturity differential.

4. **Holding all other factors constant:**

   A. A bond sold at a discount will experience a rise in price over time to reach par value.
   B. A bond sold at a premium will experience a rise in price over time to reach par value.
   C. A bond sold at a premium will experience a decline in price over time to reach par value.
   D. Both A and C are true statements.

   ➡

5. Why do investors invest in fixed-income securities?

A. A steady stream of income offered over the life of the bond's obligations.

B. A return of principal when the bond matures.

C. It is possible to earn capital gains when interest-rate movements are correctly predicted.

D. All of the above.

6. Which of the following statement(s) is/are TRUE?

A. Investors should shorten the maturity of the portfolio when interest rates are expected to fall.

B. Investors should lengthen the maturity of their portfolio when interest rates are expected to rise.

C. Investors will have a preference for low-coupon bonds over high-coupon bonds when interest rates are expected to rise.

    1. C only
    2. None of the above
    3. All of the above
    4. A & B only

7. If interest rates are expected to fall, which of the following bond strategies yields the largest capital gains?

A. Buy short-term and high-coupon bonds.

B. Sell long-term and low-coupon bonds.

C. Buy long-term and low-coupon bonds.

D. Sell short-term and high-coupon bonds.

8. 'Duration' is:

A. Always equal to the maturity of the bond

B. Equal to double the maturity of the bond

C. The weighted average of time to full recovery of the principal and interest payments on a bond at a present-value basis

D. The weighted average of time to full recovery of the principal on a bond at a present-value basis

➡

9. **The duration of a zero coupon bond is:**

   A. less than its maturity
   B. equal to its maturity
   C. greater than its maturity
   D. impossible to determine

10. **Regarding duration, please select the TRUE statement(s).**

   A. Other things being equal, the shorter the maturity, the longer the duration.
   B. Duration can measure the bond price sensitivity.
   C. Other things being equal, duration is positively related to coupon payment.
   D. Other things being equal, duration is positively related to GRY.

Chapter four

Investing in Equities

In Chapter 2 we discussed the basic characteristics of equity securities and how they are issued and traded on stock exchanges. Here we examine ways in which we can analyse and assess the investment merits of a company's shares. The questions that investors are interested in seeking answers to include:

- What is the fair price for a share and how can we calculate it?
- What are the key financial ratios relevant to an analysis of the investment prospects of a company?
- What yardsticks should be employed to compare one share with another?
- Are there ways to establish the investment value of an equity market?
- How can equity markets in different countries be compared with one another?

In this chapter we first apply the discounted cash-flow technique to estimate the fair price of a share. We then go on to describe the most commonly used relative valuation techniques.

Learning Objectives

After reading this chapter you should:

- Understand the Dividend Discount Model (DDM) and be able to use the model to estimate the fair value of a share
- Use the DDM as an analytical tool to infer market expectations regarding long-term dividend growth and expected market returns
- Be familiar with the price earnings ratio (PER) and its application to share valuation
- Be aware of relative valuation techniques as an approach to share valuation.

DISCOUNTED CASH-FLOW TECHNIQUE

The analysis of bonds in Chapter 3 showed how the fair price of a bond could be calculated using the discounted cash-flow technique. The basic underlying principle is that the price of any security can be determined by its estimated value. This estimated value may be calculated using the discounted cash-flow technique. In the case of bonds this technique can be applied relatively easily, because the expected cash flows from bonds are known precisely. Equation 4.1 expresses the concept more generally:

$$\text{Today's Value of a Security} = \sum_{t=1}^{n} \frac{\text{Expected Cashflows}}{(1+r)^t}$$

[*Equation 4.1*]

where:

Cash flows = future cash flows resulting from ownership of the asset;

r = the appropriate interest rate or expected rate of return used as the discount rate;

n = number of periods (usually years) over which the cash flows are expected.

It is worth examining again **Example 3.3** (reproduced below), where the discounted cash-flow technique was applied to estimating the price of the **3.25% Treasury 2009**.

Example 3.3 Calculating the Present Value of a Government Bond, 3.25% Treasury 2009

| Interest | | | €3.25 | €3.25 | €3.25 | |
| Redemption Amount | | | | | €100 | |

```
       +----------+----------+----------+--------->
    19th April    2007       2008    18th April   Time
    2006                              2009
```

To calculate the present value we need to decide on a rate of discount, in this case r = 3%

Cash flows	Year	Cash Flow	Present Value Calculation	PV of end Payment
	2007	3,25	$\frac{3.25}{1.03}$ =	3.16
	2008	3.25	$\frac{3.25}{(1.03)^2}$ =	3.06
	2009	103.25	$\frac{103.25}{(1.03)^3}$ =	94.49
				100.71

In this example, cash flows are received over the next 3 years and the esti-mated price of the bond has been calculated using a discount rate of 3%. This approach applies to bonds of any maturity, so for a 50-year bond there will just be more calculations. However, financial calculators or interest tables make such calculations fast and accurate.

For other securities, such as equities, the valuation approach expressed in Equation 4.1 can also be applied. However, compared with bonds there is a major obstacle to using this technique – the cash flows that are expected to be generated from ownership of shares are unknown. They are expected cash flows with a high degree of uncertainty, rather then the definite income flows generated by bonds. Therefore, the future expected stream of investment income from an equity has to be estimated from an analysis of the underlying business and an assessment of prospects for the overall economy. This is a very difficult task and, not surprisingly, several approaches have been devel-oped to estimate the value of company shares. There is no one approach that answers all the questions, and most investors and investment analysts apply several techniques in their quest to value company shares. In this chapter we discuss the three most commonly used approaches to share valuation:

i)   The traditional discounted cash-flow technique based on the dividend discount model (DDM)
ii)   The price earnings ratio (PER) or Earnings Multiplier approach
iii)   Relative Valuation Techniques.

THE DIVIDEND DISCOUNT MODEL (DDM)

Discounted cash-flow techniques require two key pieces of information to work effectively:

- the future stream of income that is expected to be generated by a security and its timing;
- a discount rate (r) that is used to calculate the present value (PV) of each cash flow.

We leave until later in this chapter the question of what discount rate to apply. First, let's tackle the thorny issue of estimating the future stream of income that we expect the equity security to generate. Fortunately the DDM provides us with a solution that is conceptually well grounded and is relatively easy to implement once we make some simplifying assumptions. The critical premise underlying this model is that the only cash flows that are relevant to investors in company shares are dividends. At first glance this may seem like an unrealistic assertion, as most investors probably look at equity investment in terms of achieving capital growth. In other words most investors think of the prospective return from equity investment in terms of the holding period return (HPR). For any security this is defined as:

$$\frac{(\text{Sale Price} - \text{Purchase Price}) + \text{Investment Income}}{\text{Purchase Price}}$$

and is usually expressed as a percentage.

Of course the big problem is trying to estimate the future sale price of a security. The DDM looks at the question of share valuation from an altogether different angle. It views a share in terms of a very long holding period – in fact it addresses the issue based on the viewpoint that a company share generates a stream of cash flows that will stretch out to infinity! Conceptually this is in fact correct; unlike bonds, equities have no terminal or redemption date. As long as the underlying business thrives, shares in a company exist for ever. If we also assume that an investor holds shares for a very long time, then the only investment return that such an investor can expect to receive is the future stream of dividend payments from the company. This assumption is not as unrealistic as it may seem at first blush. A substantial proportion of the money invested in the stock market comes from investors that have a very long investment time horizon. Pension funds, insurance companies and many private investors would fall into this category. The DDM does go a step further than the very long term and assumes that the dividend stream from an equity stretches to infinity. We will see that this assumption enables us to use a mathematical equation that simplifies enormously the task of estimating the fair value of a share. In a practical sense, extending the time horizon to infinity is not too troublesome. This is because the present value of income due to be received in (say) 50 years' time is tiny. So while the model does include these theoretical, faraway payments, the fact is that most of the estimated value of a share is accounted for by dividends expected to be received over the first 20 to 25 years.

Therefore dividends, as the only cash payment a shareholder receives from a company, are the foundation of valuation using the discounted cash-flow technique. The DDM equation (4.2) is conceptually exactly the same as the approach used to value bonds and may be written as:

$$\text{Fair Value of a Share} = \sum_{t=1}^{n} \frac{D_t}{(1 + r)^t}$$

[Equation 4.2]

where:

$D_1, D_2 \ldots D_n$ = dividends expected to be received in each future period; r = the discount rate: the rate used is often referred to as the required rate of return. There are two differences compared with bonds:

- The dividend stream is uncertain, and where a company gets into financial difficulty no dividend at all may be paid.
- Because company shares have no terminal date, equation 4.2 indicates that investors are dealing with infinity.

The latter issue is in fact less troublesome than it may seem, as we alluded to above. This is because the present value of a dividend expected to be received a long time into the future is very low. For example, imagine we are analysing Bank of Ireland and we estimate that the dividend to be received in 50 years' time is €10 per share. Assume a discount rate of 10% and the present value of this dividend is only 9c! (Bank of Ireland's dividend in 2005 was a little under 50c per share):

Example 4.1   Present value of Dividend to be Received in 50 Years

$$PV = D_{50}/(1 + r)^{50} = 10/(1.1)^{50} = 10/(111.1) = .09$$

Therefore, we know that in any analysis the dividend income to be received over the first 15–25 years will account for the lion's share of the estimated intrinsic value of an equity. Detailed analysis of a company and its prospects can yield reasonably accurate forecasts of dividends over the first 3–5 years, particularly for long-established companies with a record of steady and stable growth in dividend payments. However, any forecasts of dividend payments beyond this timeframe will be subject to huge margins for error.

The DDM enables investors to get around this seemingly intractable problem by making assumptions about the expected long-term growth rate in dividend payments. The starting point is the most recent dividend paid by a company, which is known. Then an investor or analyst attempts to estimate the future growth rate in that dividend. The simplifying assumption is made that a company will grow its dividend at a *constant* rate of growth. This assumption is not as far removed from practice as it seems. Many companies seek to grow their dividend payments at a stable long-term rate that is in line with the long-term rate of growth of the underlying business. Also, because we are dealing with infinity, even companies that are currently growing rapidly will eventually converge on some long-term sustainable rate of growth. The DDM model is usually framed in terms of three different growth scenarios, namely:

- No Growth
- Constant Growth
- Variable Growth.

No-Growth Model

If we have a company where we expect no growth in the dividend stream, we can represent the dividend stream as:

Figure 4.1 No-Growth Dividend Stream

$$\text{Value of a share} = \frac{D_0}{1 + r} + \frac{D_0}{(1+r)^2} \quad \cdots \quad \frac{D_0}{(1+r)^n} \quad \infty$$

To estimate the intrinsic value of the share we can calculate the present value of each expected dividend by dividing each payment by $(1+r)^t$ and then summing all of these payments. The No-Growth dividend model is essentially a fixed perpetual income stream. Fortunately, there is a simple equation to estimate the present value of a perpetuity that can be applied to this infinite stream of constant cash flows as follows:

$$\text{Value of a share} = \frac{D_0}{r}$$

where:
D_0 = constant dividend payment;
r = the required rate of return, which is used as the discount rate.

Therefore, the estimated value of a share which has just paid a dividend of €1 that is expected to remain constant to infinity, can be calculated as €1/r. If we assume that 10% is the required rate of return, this results in a fair price for this company's shares of €1/0.1 = €10.

This model is of little practical benefit, since it is the ability of equities to grow their dividend over time that makes them an attractive investment. However, when we assume that dividend payments grow at a constant growth rate out to infinity we get an altogether more interesting equation.

Constant-Growth Model

When we assume that a company will grow its dividend at a constant growth rate into the future, we can then represent the expected flow of dividend payments as follows:

Figure 4.2 Constant-Growth Dividend Stream

$$\text{Value of a Share} = \frac{D_0(1+g)}{(1+r)} + \frac{Do(1+g)^2}{(1+r)^2} + \frac{Do(1+g)^3}{(1+r)^3} \quad \cdots \quad \infty$$

where:
D_0 = the most recent dividend paid;
g = projected constant rate of growth in the dividend.

From this equation we can see that the next dividend to be received is projected as last year's dividend multiplied by one plus the assumed growth rate. Each subsequent dividend can be estimated by multiplying the previous payment by $(1 + g)$. We can calculate the present value of each dividend by dividing each cash flow by $(1 + r)^t$ and then summing each present value. While the cash flows in the model go to infinity, we may take (say) 50 years as a cut-off given that we know the faraway cash flows will have very little value today. Fortunately we don't have to calculate the value of a share in this painstaking way, as the constant growth DDM simplifies to the following equation:

$$\text{Value of a share} = \frac{D_1}{r-g} \qquad \textit{[Equation 4.3]}$$

where:
D_1 = the dividend expected to be received at end-year one;
r = the discount rate;
g = growth rate of future dividends, which is assumed to be constant.
Note: r must always be greater than g.

This equation is also 'more correct' than doing lengthy hand calculations, as it includes all dividend payments expected to be received to infinity. As long as the assumption regarding the dividend growth rate is reasonably accurate, then equation 4.3 provides a simple and conceptually elegant valuation tool.

Example 4.2 AIB Fair Value

AIB has just paid a dividend of 60c per share and investors expect dividends to grow at a constant long-term rate of growth of 9% per annum. For investments of AIB's risk level investors require a return of 12% per annum. Using the constant growth DDM to estimate the value of a share in AIB we have:

$$\text{Share Value} = \frac{D_1}{r - g}$$

where:
D_1 = the dividend expected to be received one period from now, which may be calculated as last year's dividend (D_0) multiplied by the assumed growth rate $(1 + g)$ and the estimated value per AIB share is:

$$\frac{60c\,(1 + 0.09)}{0.12 - 0.09} = €21.80$$

Estimating the Discount Rate

So far we have not discussed how we estimate the discount rate (r). For government bonds r could be quite easily established from the current level of gross redemption yields on bonds of a maturity similar to the bond in question. For equities the issue is far more problematic, since the variability of expected returns associated with equity securities means that there is no equivalent of the GRY for equities. The approach adopted by most investors is to think in terms of that long-term rate of return that an equity needs to generate if it is to reward an investor for the risk taken. Equity investment involves risk that must be rewarded through a commensurately higher rate of return. In principle, companies can be ranked in terms of their risk level. For example, most investors would assign a lower degree of risk to AIB than they would to (say) a small oil-exploration company. We can think of that rate of return which compensates investors for the investment risk taken as the required rate of return. A starting point in estimating r can be the long-term historical returns achieved by the overall equity market. For example, over the very long term equity markets have delivered average annual returns of approximately 10% per annum. If we assume that AIB has a risk level higher than the market as a whole we may assign a required rate of return of 12% to AIB. This then becomes the appropriate discount rate to use in the DDM.

Advantages and Usage of the DDM

The constant-growth DDM is theoretically sound and requires only three inputs – the most recent dividend paid, the appropriate required rate of return and an estimate of the future growth rate in dividends. The DDM is used extensively by investment analysts and investors, although it is usually used in conjunction with other models. For many analysts the assumption that dividends will grow at a constant rate of growth to infinity is too restrictive. They often fine-tune this assumption by modelling different rates of growth for different sub-periods. For example, an initial period of high growth may be assumed if a company is at an early stage of its development, and after a period of (say) 5 years a constant growth rate closer to the market average may be assumed. This is referred to as the Variable Growth Model. It allows analysts to refine their growth forecasts, but it exhibits the same advantages and disadvantages as the basic constant-growth model.

Disadvantages of the DDM

The drawbacks of the DDM hinge around the fact that the estimate of fair value that the model produces is extremely sensitive to the values input for r and g. To get some feel for this let's go back to Example 4.2, where we used inputs of 9% for g and 12% for r for AIB. In practice the values chosen for these variables will be subject to substantial judgment on the part of the investor. Let's assume that in this case we are told that any values for r and g within a range of +/–1% would be reasonable. Let's reduce g to 8% and increase r to 13%. These are apparently quite small adjustments in variables that are, after all, subjective estimates. Plugging these new figures into the DDM now results in a very different estimate of fair value for AIB:

$$\text{Share Value} = \frac{60c \ (1 + 0.08)}{0.13 - 0.08} = €12.96$$

It is instructive to establish what happens to the estimate of fair value when we increase g by 1% and leave r at 12%:

$$\text{Share Value} = \frac{60c \ (1 + 0.10)}{0.12 - 0.10} = €33.00$$

The apparently small changes to our input values have resulted in a very wide price range. This highlights the key weakness of the DDM, which is that it is not robust. In other words, small changes to the estimates of r and g can lead to disproportionately large changes in the estimates of fair value. In itself this does not give sufficient cause to discard the model as a valuation tool; rather it emphasises the need to expend substantial effort in estimating the inputs that go into the model.

The DDM as an Analytical Tool

Like any theoretical model the DDM has its flaws, particularly if the objective is to get a precise estimate of the fair value of a share. However, it is a very flexible model and the basic equation can be easily manipulated to help answer a variety of questions concerning individual equities and the market as a whole.

What is the Market Saying about r?

We can manipulate the basic DDM equation to enable us to infer the required rate of return that is built into current market levels, once we assume a value for the growth rate (g).

$$r = D_1/MV + g$$

[Equation 4.4]

Returning to AIB, if the share price today is €18 and we estimate dividend growth of 8% per annum, we can derive the required rate of return based on the market price of the shares using equation 4.3:

$$r = \frac{60}{1800} + .08 = .03 + .08 = .11 \text{ or } 11\%$$

If the assumption regarding g is correct, then investors who buy shares in AIB at €18 can expect to receive a long-term rate of return of 11%. This equation can also be used to infer what the expected return is on the overall equity market. Given the information below for the overall Irish equity market, using equation 4.3 we can estimate the expected long-term rate of return implied by the current level of the market.

ISEQ Overall Index – Current Data
Prospective Dividend Yield (D_1/MV) = 3% or .03
Constant Growth Rate of Dividend = 7% or .07

where MV now is the current level of the index and D_1 is the aggregate level of dividends expected to be paid next year.

$$r = .03 + .07 = .10 \text{ or } 10\%$$

Again, confidence in the estimated value for r depends on how valid the assumption regarding g turns out to be. For the overall equity market the assumed value for g is normally based on an assessment of the long-term rate of growth in nominal GDP. In Ireland's case the medium-term potential real rate of growth is considered to be 5% and inflation has been running in a 2–3% range for a long time. On the basis of this macroeconomic information the assumption that dividends paid by Irish companies will grow by 7% per annum seems reasonable.

What is the Market Saying about g?

In order to answer this question we can rearrange the DDM equation to give:

$$g = r - D_1/MV$$

[Equation 4.5]

To solve for g we must make an assumption about r. Usually analysts estimate r on the basis of the very long-run historical average annual rate of return delivered from an overall equity index. Let's assume that on the basis of our historical investigation of returns we believe that it is reasonable to expect a long–term rate of return of 10% per annum from the Irish market. We also learn that the prospective dividend yield (D_1/MV) is 3%, and armed with these two items of information we can now use equation 4.4 to generate a value for g:

$$g = .10 - .03 = .07 \text{ or } 7\%$$

This indicates that the current level of the Irish equity market implies that dividends will grow at a long-term rate of growth of 7% per annum.

DDM: How It Is Used

ESTIMATE FAIR VALUE OF AN EQUITY	• Assume required rate of return. • Assume constant growth rate in dividends.	• Compare 'fair price' with market price.	• Assumptions may be varied to check for 'reasonableness'.
ESTIMATE GROWTH RATE IN DIVIDENDS (g) IMPLIED BY CURRENT MARKET LEVELS	• If g is high relative to historical norms, it suggests investors may be disappointed as actual growth reverts to historical norms – signals that market may be too high.	• If g is low relative to historical norms, it suggests that market may be too low and could be due a rise.	
ESTIMATE EXPECTED RETURN (r) IMPLICIT IN CURRENT MARKET PRICES	• Constant growth rate in dividends must be assumed. • Current level of market is input.	• If r is high relative to historical norms, it indicates that the share or market offers above-average long-term returns.	• If r is low relative to historical norms, it indicates that current prices are high, thus offering poor future returns.

In summary, the DDM provides a solid conceptual framework whereby assumptions can be tested in a rigorous way and a variety of information can be gleaned based on market prices. The DDM is an extremely useful analytical tool but is most effective when used in conjunction with other valuation tools.

THE PRICE EARNINGS RATIO (PER) OR EARNINGS MULTIPLIER

The PER was defined in Chapter 2 and is reproduced below:

The Price Earnings Ratio (PER)

The most commonly used convention for measuring and comparing company valuations is the Price Earnings Ratio or PER.

A company may be expected to generate a stream of profits into the future. The shareholder is a part-owner of that stream of profits.

Earnings per share is a measure of the amount of profit after tax earned in a financial year, which is attributable to each share issued by the company.

The PER is a profit-based measure of the company's perceived worth that relates share price to earnings per share.

With ABC plc's share price at 200c and EPS of 12c in its most recent financial year:

Price Earnings Ratio: $\dfrac{200c}{12c}$

$= 16.7$ times

The PER is the best-known and most widely used valuation technique. Analysts, company executives and active private investors are comfortable with earnings per share (EPS) and PERs. Despite its more widespread use the conceptual framework for the Earnings Multiplier model is not as solidly based in economic theory as is the DDM. The P/E Model is based on a simple identity:

$P = EPS \times PER$ 　　　　　 where:

　　　　　　　　　　　　　P = current market price;

　　　　　　　　　　　　　E = most recent 12-month earnings;

　　　　　　　　　　　　　EPS = earnings per share.

Therefore, the price of a share is viewed as the product of two variables:

i)　　EPS
ii)　　PER

Investment analysts will often use the model to establish a price target for a company's shares. First, EPS are forecast for (say) the next two years. This forecast will usually be based on a detailed analysis of the company's historical performance and an assessment of its prospects over the next 2–3 years. The second step is to then apply a forecast PER to these EPS estimates, which results in a target price for the shares in one year's and two years' time.

Example 4.3 Forecasting AIB's PER

You are an investment analyst in a stockbroking firm and after lengthy analysis you forecast EPS for AIB as follows:

	Last Year (actual)	This Year (forecast)	Next Year (forecast)
EPS (c)	130	144	150

The current market price of AIB's shares is €18 and, armed with this information, you calculate AIB's PER as:

$$1800/130 = 13.9$$

This is sometimes referred to as AIB's historic PER. You now assume that AIB will trade on the same PER this time next year and in two years' time. Therefore, you put a price target on the shares of:

Price Target in year 1: $EPS1 \times PER1 = 144 \times 13.9 = €20.02$
Price Target in year 2: $EPS2 \times PER2 = 150 \times 13.9 = €20.85$

The degree of confidence that can be attributed to these price targets depends on the accuracy of the EPS forecasts and the validity of the assumption regarding the PER that is attributed to AIB. The degree of error of EPS forecasts increases with time and varies enormously from company to company. Greater confidence can be placed in forecasts for long-established companies such as AIB that operate in relatively stable business sectors. In contrast, forecasts for a small technology company may be subject to a very wide margin of error. Overall market PERs expand and contract depending on investors' expectations regarding overall economic and market developments. PERs for individual companies are influenced by these overall market trends and by the ebb and flow of investors' assessment of the prospects for each individual company. Therefore, forecasting the PER that will apply to AIB in one year is usually more difficult than forecasting AIB's EPS! Analysis of historical trends and an assessment of where we are in the economic cycle is one way to tackle this forecasting problem (see Chapter 8). Analysis of these macro trends would then need to be combined with a historical and peer-group analysis of the particular company.

What Factors Determine the PER?

Most investors intuitively realise that the PER should be higher for companies whose earnings are expected to grow rapidly. Figure 4.3 lists the top ten Irish quoted companies and we can see how the PER for Bank of Ireland is 12.2 and for Ryanair 16.7. Other things being equal, this indicates that investors expect Ryanair to grow its EPS at a faster rate than BOI and are therefore prepared to pay a price for Ryanair shares that represents a much higher multiple of its current earnings.

Figure 4.3 Top Ten Irish Quoted Companies

Company	Share Price (€c)	Market Capitalisation (shares in issue * share price) € million	Price Earnings Ratio 2005
Allied Irish Banks	1,712	14,826	13.5
Bank of Ireland	1,281	13,015	12.2
CRH	2,090	10,956	10.7
Ryanair	695	5,243	16.7
Irish Life and Permanent	1,435	3,860	11.6
Anglo Irish Bank	1,107	3,576	18.1
Kerry Group	1,765	3,290	13.0
Elan Corporation	837	3,223	N/a
Grafton Group	819	1,919	10.8
Independent News and Media	231	1,715	14.3

In the AIB example above we used the current or historic PER as our estimate of the future PER to generate a price target for AIB. However, we are still faced with the question as to whether the current price and PER of AIB is appropriate. Compared with the DDM an apparent advantage of using the PER is that we don't have to estimate or assume values for growth (g) and the required rate of return (r). Ironically, in order to try to understand what factors determine a company's PER it is in fact instructive to derive the PER from the constant-growth DDM.

First, we can think of the value of a share today as a function of forecast earnings per share and the prospective PER. A share price is a function of its future performance and not its historical returns, so we therefore must look to the future to estimate share values. Since we are considering a stock with a constant growth rate we can calculate next year's expected earnings as:

$$E_1 = E_0 (1 + g)$$

Now instead of expressing the current market price as:

$$P = E * PER$$

where:

P = current market price,
E = most recent 12-month earnings per share,
we can express it slightly differently as:

$$P = \text{value of stock today} = E_1 * P/E_1$$

We are now estimating the current value of the share in terms of forecast EPS and the 1-year prospective PER. We can compare this value with the current market price in order to determine whether the shares should be purchased or sold. In order to establish the 'fair value' of a share in this way we must establish a value for the prospective PER. In the AIB example above we simply used the historic PER as our estimate of future PERs. Clearly we need to do more than this, so let's start with the constant-growth DDM equation, which as we've seen is the foundation of valuation of equity securities:

$$\text{Value of a share (P)} = \frac{D_1}{r - g}$$

[*Equation 4.6*]

where:

D_1 = the dividend expected to be received at end-year one;
r = the discount rate;
g = growth rate of future dividends.

Remember that this equation provides us with an estimate of the value of a stock today. Dividing both sides of this equation by expected earnings (E_1) we get:

$$\frac{P}{E_1} = \frac{D_1/E_1}{r - g}$$

[*Equation 4.7*]

The left-hand side of Equation 4.7 is nothing other than the prospective PER, and the right-hand side allows us to focus in on those factors that determine the prospective PER, which are:

i)   the *expected* dividend payout ratio (D_1/E_1)
ii)   the *estimated* required rate of return
iii)   the *expected* growth rate in dividends.

Looked at in this conceptual framework we can see that the PER is a function of the above three variables, and holding the relevant other two variables constant, the following relationships should hold:

i)   The higher D_1/E_1 (the expected payout ratio), the higher the PER.
ii)   The higher the expected growth rate, the higher the PER.
iii)   The higher the required rate of return, the lower the PER.

While the above relationships do hold, it must be emphasised that these three variables interact with one another in terms of their impact on the PER. When a firm raises its payout ratio it usually improves sentiment towards the stock and leads to an expansion in the PER. However, if the rise in the pay-out ratio results in the firm investing less, then this will lower its prospective growth rate. A lower g will lead to a contraction in the PER and a lower share price! By the same token, when a firm tries to increase its prospective growth rate by investing in risky projects it should lead to an expansion in its PER. However, in this scenario investors will demand an increase in the required rate of return, which will act to lead to a contraction in the PER! We can see that, just like the DDM, the key variables that influence a firm's prospective PER are g and r.

   Therefore, while the Earnings Multiplier approach to share valuation may be intuitively easier to grasp than the DDM, the actual estimate of share value is critically dependent on the assumptions made regarding expected returns and forecast growth in earnings. Because of these difficulties many investors and investment analysts concentrate on relative valuations rather than absolute valuations.

Relative Valuation Techniques

Because of the difficulty in forecasting PERs and the consequent unreliability of resultant share-price targets, the investment community often assesses the prospects for a share relative to the company's average PER in the past, and to the average PER of a peer group of companies. Applying this approach involves analysing additional variables to those in the previous example. Example 4.4 stays with AIB and we can see that the object of the exercise is to establish whether AIB at its current share price is a BUY, HOLD or SELL.

Example 4.4 Forecasting AIB's Share Price

From the previous example you know that AIB at its current market price of €18 is trading on a historic PER of 13.9. You have gleaned the information below from various market sources:
Historic PERs for:

	AIB	**UK and Irish Bank-Sector Average**
2 years ago	12.0	13.0
I year ago	11.0	12.0
Current	13.9	14.6
Average	12.3	13.2

It is apparent that AIB is trading on a PER that is significantly higher than its recent historical average. If it were to revert to this average of 12.3, the share price would fall to:

$$Price : EPS * PER = 130 * 12.3 = €16.0$$

However, the PER of the entire bank sector is also trading above its recent historical average. You also note that AIB has in the recent past traded on a PER a little lower than the average bank-sector PER, but is now trading almost in line with this average. Your assessment of the prospects for AIB's share price depends on your judgment of the following:

- Does AIB's recent and prospective financial performance justify a higher PER than its recent average?
- Does it deserve to trade on a PER similar to the average of its peer group?

Perhaps your answer is that AIB's financial prospects are now sufficiently favourable to justify a PER in line with the bank-sector average. This currently stands at 14.6, so your current and one-year target prices for AIB become:

$$Price\ Target\ (Now): EPS_0 * PER_0 = 130 * 14.6 = €18.98$$
$$Price\ Target\ in\ year\ 1: EPS_1 * PER_1 = 144 * 14.6 = €21.02$$

The advantage of this approach is that it is not necessary to make explicit assumptions regarding r and g. The assessment of the appropriate PER is couched in the context of historical analysis of the company and the sector and/or market in which it operates. As well as the relative PER, several other investment ratios are normally analysed; these include Price/Book, Dividend Yield and a variety of cash-flow-related ratios (see Chapter 13).

Inverting the PER to give the Earnings Yield

Investors often express the relationship between a share price and earnings per share in terms of the Earnings Yield. For the AIB example cited here, we now calculate EPS as a percentage of the share price. Above, we calculated AIB's PER as:

$$1800/130 = 13.9, \text{ i.e., Market Price/EPS}$$

and we calculate the Earnings Yield as:

$$130/1800 = .072 \text{ or } 7.2\%, \text{ i.e., EPS/Market Price}$$

The Earnings Yield is useful in that investors can often more easily relate to a percentage rate of return, and it can be compared with rates of return on other assets. The earnings yield can be calculated for individual equities and for equity indices. In particular the earnings yield of an equity index is often compared with the yield on long-term government bonds, and we would normally expect the earnings yield to be significantly higher.

The Earnings Yield can be particularly useful in the context of relative valuation techniques. It is all very well to come to a conclusion that a share is cheap relative to the overall equity market; but what if the market itself is overvalued? One way to assess this is to plot the historical relationship between the Earnings Yield and long-term bond yields. Many analysts believe that there will be a tendency for this relationship to revert to the mean.

SOME CONCLUDING THOUGHTS ON VALUATION

This chapter has covered three approaches to equity valuation:
i)   The Dividend Discount Model
ii)   The Price Earnings Ratio or Earnings Multiplier Approach
iii)   The Relative Valuation Approach.

These are not mutually exclusive and neither are they exhaustive. Each approach has its positives and negatives and those involved in investment analysis will generally use some combination of these techniques. In theory the DDM is the best model, as conceptually the best estimate of the current value of a company's shares is the estimated cash flows to be generated by that company. However, as we saw, any estimate of the company's present value is very dependent on a subjective assessment of future dividend growth and the risk-adjusted rate of return appropriate to the company in question. Because of these difficulties the PER model, when used as a relative valuation technique, has more widespread appeal and is easier to calculate. It has more intuitive appeal and can generate investment conclusions with a clearly articulated logic. The main danger of relying too heavily on relative valuation techniques occurs when the overall market is at a valuation extreme. This occurred at the height of the technology, media and telecom (TMT) bubble when many internet stocks were being sold at extremely high valuations. Investment banks and stockbrokers justified these valuations on the basis that they were 'cheap' compared with other similar stocks. This of course missed the really important reality at the time, which was that these comparator stocks were already ridiculously overvalued. Many investors had their fingers burned during this period, and with the benefit of hindsight the application of the DDM fundamental approach to valuation would have generated warning signals to anyone prepared to take notice.

It should now be clear that just as a tradesman goes to work with a selection of tools, so too must the equity investor and analyst. There are a variety of tools available, and usually each one can play a part in solving the riddle of valuing equity securities. However, they are only tools and the quality of the outputs will depend on the quality of the inputs and the skills brought to bear on the analysis by the investment analyst, fund manager or private investor.

QUESTIONS

---

1. Which of the following statements is FALSE?

  A. The value of a share is the discounted present value of the stream of future earnings attributable to it.

  B. The price of a share results from the interplay of market supply and demand.

  C. Price and Value can diverge dramatically for quite prolonged periods.

  D. At an equity-market peak share prices will tend to be lower than value estimates based on discounted present values.

2. Which of the following statements is FALSE?

  A. Companies with high PERs are usually expected to grow faster than low-PER companies.

  B. Growth investing focuses on stocks that have potential for persistent and high earnings growth.

➡

C. The dividend yield and the price earnings ratio are two commonly used measures of value.

D. Value investing focuses on stocks that are highly rated (they have high PERs) relative to the market.

3. **Please select the FALSE statement:**

A. The discounted cash-flow technique is used to evaluate stocks' prices.

B. Present-value analysis is used to evaluate stocks' prices.

C. The P/E approach is used to evaluate stocks' prices.

D. The profit maximisation approach is used to evaluate stocks' prices.

4. **Which of the following factors is NOT required for the calculation of securities' value in the present-value approach?**

A. The required rate of return

B. The timing of future cash flows paid to shareholders

C. The amount of future cash flows

D. The par value of the shares in issue.

5. **Which of the following dividend discount model formulae is/are correct (where D_0 = last dividend paid, and D_1 = next dividend to be received)?**

A. $D_0 (1+g)/(r-g)$

B. $D_0 /(r-g)$

C. $D_1 /(r-g)$

D. D_1 /g.

   1. A & C only

   2. All of the above

   3. A & B only

   4. A only

6. **C&C Group has just paid a dividend of €1.5 per share. Owing to the increasing popularity of cider drinking, C&C expects to see a future growth rate of 10% per year. Given an average market required rate of return of 15%, what is the estimated current price of C&C?**

A. €33

    B. €30
    C. €4
    D. €53.

7. **If C&C trims its future outlook from a 10% growth rate to a 5% growth rate, what is the impact on its valuation? (Assume other things hold constant.)**

    A. Stock price drops by 50%, that is, the new price is €16.50.
    B. Stock price remains the same.
    C. Stock price drops by about 52.27%, that is, new price is €15.75.
    D. Stock price increases by 50%, that is, new price is €49.50.

8. **Regarding ordinary shareholders, which of the following statement(s) is/are TRUE?**

    A. Their shares entitle them to a guaranteed dividend return.
    B. They are senior to bondholders in the event of the company going bankrupt.
    C. As the owners, shareholders may be described as the residual claimants on the assets of the company.
    D. Limited liability means that shareholders are not responsible for the debts that a company takes on and therefore they cannot lose more than they paid for their shares.

        1. All of the above
        2. C & D only
        3. A, C & D only
        4. B & D only

9. **The current dividend on a stock is 10c per share, growing at 10% p.a. What is the price of the stock if the discount rate is 12%?**

    A. 550c
    B. 500c
    C. 110c
    D. 85c

Chapter five

The Retail Investor's Choices

This chapter discusses the alternative of indirect investing used by many investors. With indirect investing the investor pools his assets with those of others to create a single pool of money, which is then managed by professional investment managers in accordance with a well-defined investment strategy. A key point about indirect investing is that the investor is not directly responsible for the asset, although he is exposed to the same market risk as if he did hold the asset directly; he also reaps whatever investment return those assets generate (less management fees and expenses). In Ireland the life assurance unit-linked funds offered by life assurance companies form the backbone of the industry. Latterly, the emergence of mutual funds – called open-ended investment companies or OEICs – has occurred as a result of EU Investment Services Directives. Once an OEIC is regulated in one EU country it can be sold throughout the EU. The basics of how these collective investment schemes (CIS) are priced is discussed. The role of investment advice and ensuring that individual investors are sold investment funds appropriate to their particular circumstances is a key issue that is addressed in this chapter.

Learning Objectives

After reading this chapter you will:
- Understand the basic mechanics of pooled investment funds or collective investment schemes (CIS)
- Be aware of the advantages of indirect investing
- Be able to distinguish between unit-linked funds, OEICs, unit trusts and investment trusts
- Have a broad understanding of how the price of unit-linked funds and unit trusts is calculated, and how the price of shares in OEICs is calculated
- Understand exchange-traded funds
- Have an awareness of structured products that offer capital guarantees
- Understand the difficulties faced by investors in matching individual investment objectives with appropriate investment products.

In most economies the dominant form of investment is indirect, and Ireland is no exception in this respect. Direct investing involves purchasing securities in the stock market and holding the title to these securities as share certificates or through a nominee account with a financial institution. Indirect investing usually involves placing money with a financial institution that then invests that money on a collective basis on behalf of all of its clients. The essential elements of indirect investing are the same irrespective of any particular jurisdiction and may be summarised as:

- Regulated financial institutions such as banks, insurance companies, investment management companies develop suites of investment products for sale to individuals, companies, pension funds, charitable trusts, etc.
- Each product (or suite of products) is normally structured as a separate entity that allows the institution to collect assets from a large number of clients and to create a clearly identifiable pool of money for investment.
- The investment strategy applied to this 'pool of money' is normally clearly set out in the relevant prospectus or trust deed, depending on the precise legal structure. In addition, a key function of any promotional literature and advertising will be to communicate that investment strategy clearly to potential investors.
- Clients who invest money on this 'pooled basis' will receive a 'pro rata' interest in the investment returns achieved by the relevant investment manager. If the relevant fund produces an investment return of 10% each and every investor will enjoy the same 10% return (after management charges). Likewise if the value of the fund falls by (say) 5%, every investor will suffer the same decline in the value of their particular investment.
- The legal and regulatory structure varies across different product types and across jurisdictions. However, the essential elements are the same, i.e., a large number of investors commit differing amounts of funds to collective investment vehicles. The sponsoring financial institution then invests the entire pool of funds in line with the relevant investment strategy.

ADVANTAGES OF INDIRECT INVESTING

- **Diversification:** Indirect investing will nearly always achieve much greater diversification than can be achieved through investing directly in the markets. Such pooled portfolios should therefore be more efficient than portfolios created by individual investors. In other words they should achieve similar or superior returns but with much lower levels of risk.
- **Access to a much wider range of markets and asset classes:** For example, a single commercial property investment may involve an investment of millions of euro, which is way beyond the scope of most investors

including smaller financial institutions. A pooled fund that invests in property provides even the smaller investor with the opportunity to gain exposure to property markets. Other examples include specialist emerging market funds and funds that specialise in a particular sector, such as biotechnology.

- **Ease of Administration:** Even small direct-equity portfolios will consist of several shares where the individual investor must keep track of dividends received, profits and losses from share trading, etc. Tax returns can quickly become very laborious and expensive to collate. Indirect investing eases this administrative burden dramatically.
- **Tax Efficiency:** The tax treatment of pooled funds in Ireland is now quite favourable. Indirect investing is now at least as tax-efficient as direct investing, and in some situations it may be more so.

COLLECTIVE INVESTMENT SCHEMES (CIS)

For the retail investor there is a bewildering array of investment schemes that deliver the ability to gain exposure to the investment markets through the indirect investing route. Such investment products may be referred to as Collective Investment Schemes. The legal and regulatory framework governing these schemes has evolved over many years in developed countries. In Ireland the legal and regulatory framework has become quite sophisticated, with changes being primarily driven by the need to implement EU-wide directives. The Table below sets out the main institutional categories of products available to Irish-based investors.

Types of Scheme	Key Characteristics
Unit-Linked Funds (Life Assurance Companies)	• Assets held by life assurance company • Company actuary creates units that match various 'pools' of assets • Units are priced at net asset value (NAV) • Units are purchased at an 'offer' price and sold or redeemed at a 'bid' price • Open-ended
With-Profits Funds (Life Assurance Companies)	• Assets held by life assurance company • Company actuary decides on an annual return and a return that is payable only at the final maturity date of a policy • Returns depend on the investment performance of the with-profits fund, but such returns are effectively 'smoothed' over the life of a product ➡

UCITS which are Undertakings for Collective Investment in Transferable Securities	• Can be either an investment company or a unit trust • Must be open-ended • Key benefit is 'EU Passport'
UCITS – Open-Ended Investment Company (OEIC)	• Investment company that invests in securities • Price of shares is determined by NAV • Single price is calculated • Open-ended
UCITS – Unit Trusts	• Established under a trust deed • Trustee responsible for safeguarding and custody of the assets • Price of units is determined by NAV • 'Bid' and 'offer' prices are calculated • Open-ended
Investment Trusts	• Term 'trust' is misleading as they are companies that invest in securities, not trusts • Closed-ended • Shares normally quoted on the stock market.

The legal, tax and regulatory structures determine the precise nature of investment funds on offer in a particular country. The marketplace in Ireland is similar to that in the UK, where insurance companies and banks tend to dominate the market. There is somewhat greater diversity in the UK, where the unit trust industry is much larger than in Ireland and also there is a significant investment trust industry.

Unit-Linked Life Insurance Investment Funds

These are manufactured and marketed by life assurance companies and information on these funds is published regularly in the press. From Exhibit 5.1 it can be seen that each company offers a diverse range of funds based on varying investment strategies. For example, Bank of Ireland Life lists twelve different funds that offer retail investors a choice regarding the type of investment exposure that they can access.

Exhibit 5.1 Unit-Linked Funds Performance Tables

IRISH DOMESTIC FUNDS (Net) All prices quoted in euro

	Cat Code	Bid Price cents	Offer Price cents	Yr to Date %	5 Yr Perf %
ACORN LIFE					
Cautiously Mgd	FX	101.10	106.40	2.60	-
Deposit	CA	243.30	256.10	1.19	11.19
Managed Growth	MG	436.80	459.70	14.75	-6.98
Managed	MB	416.60	438.50	12.21	1.72
AIB					
AIIP	MB	318.00	334.70	18.35	-11.57
ARK LIFE					
2002	FX	311.53	327.92	3.23	11.56
2003	MC	257.53	271.08	4.24	6.16
Assured	CA	196.44	206.77	0.49	8.71
Balanced	MB	286.53	301.61	13.29	-6.70
Capital Gtd 1	GU	187.92	197.81	0.44	5.98
Capital Gtd 2	GU	185.39	185.39	-0.19	1.89
Capital Gtd 3	GU	189.69	189.69	0.02	3.17
Cash	CA	142.33	142.33	0.10	3.69
Dynamic	MG	274.29	288.72	15.19	-15.50
Euro Zone	EE	95.54	95.54	12.68	-26.59
Guaranteed 2002	GU	132.46	132.46	0.91	14.14
Guaranteed 2003	GU	131.87	131.87	1.20	12.76
Guaranteed 2004	GU	129.22	129.22	0.98	17.11
Guaranteed 2005	GU	127.71	127.71	2.32	21.62
Managed	MB	180.68	180.68	12.36	-11.23
Money	CA	170.11	170.11	0.85	8.57
PEP Managed	GE	243.30	256.10	9.40	-3.12
PIP Managed	MB	182.74	192.35	12.35	-11.25
Secure	CA	138.08	145.34	0.10	3.87
Special Inv 2	GE	234.97	234.97	9.40	-3.11
Special Invest	GE	332.16	349.64	10.09	0.57
Steadfast	FX	239.35	251.94	3.41	12.80
BANK OF IRELAND LIFE - UNIT FUNDS					
Cash	CA	240.40	253.10	0.60	7.34
Equity	GE	454.30	478.20	12.39	-9.92
European	EU	377.70	397.60	13.21	-20.89
Far East	FA	276.80	291.40	26.42	-16.03
Fixed Int	FX	451.40	475.10	3.31	28.76
Intern'l	IN	356.20	374.90	12.28	-18.84
Man Security	MC	246.80	259.80	3.14	12.05
Managed Grth	MB	513.60	540.60	10.69	10.19
Managed Opp	MG	500.40	526.70	11.19	3.94
Nth American	US	487.00	512.70	4.98	-15.19
PEP Fund	SF	192.50	192.50	11.66	45.50
Property	PR	712.80	750.40	7.45	40.34
CANADA LIFE					
Balanced Equity	GE	1387.70	1460.80	17.05	-8.33
BIAM Managed	MB	792.30	834.00	11.19	13.66
BIAM Master Client	MB	793.70	835.50	11.18	13.69
Cash	CA	397.30	418.30	0.67	7.59
European Equity	EU	345.60	363.80	16.12	-11.46
Focus 15	SF	112.40	112.40	17.33	-32.89
Gilt & Bond 1	FX	299.80	315.60	3.44	28.45
Gilt & Bond B	FX	302.57	318.50	3.44	29.77
Gilt	FX	942.90	992.60	3.46	28.45
Growth Man	MB	975.50	1026.90	13.78	4.98
HI Growth Man	GE	301.70	317.60	17.07	-8.34
Inter'l Equity	IN	397.20	418.20	16.72	-11.53
Irish Equity	IE	632.20	665.50	10.70	36.69
Leading Co's	GE	400.70	421.80	17.04	-8.33
Leading Cos B	GE	438.33	461.40	17.05	-0.14
Managed 1	MB	729.80	768.30	13.81	4.98
Money	CA	357.01	375.80	0.64	7.08
Pacific Equity	FA	275.40	289.90	16.52	7.44
Passive Equity 3	IN	95.40	95.40	21.07	
Property 1	PR	485.90	511.50	9.20	48.38
Property	PR	650.00	684.30	9.19	48.34
With Profit	WP	159.50	159.50	0.00	10.29
CGU IRELAND					
Cash Fund	CA	145.10	145.10	0.55	7.50
Euro Equity	EE	155.40	155.40	16.14	-15.42
Fixed Interest	FX	203.50	203.50	4.36	55.60
Guaranteed	GU	123.50	123.50	2.40	-10.11
International	IN	127.00	127.00	17.05	-27.63
Irish Equity	IE	120.40	120.40	9.85	-12.12
Managed Fund	MG	146.30	146.30	13.32	-3.18
UK Equity	UK	122.10	122.10	16.95	-12.34
With Profit	WP	170.20	170.20	0.41	14.96
COMBINED					
Managed	MB	389.80	410.30	11.07	4.00
EAGLE STAR					
Balanced	MB	406.00	418.50	11.30	7.03
Dynamic	MG	453.60	467.60	14.38	-1.45
Investment	MB	1533.70	1614.40	12.61	4.50

	Cat Code	Bid Price cents	Offer Price cents	Yr to Date %	5 Yr Perf %
Performance	MB	421.20	434.20	12.75	0.58
Secure	CA	247.50	255.10	0.63	9.77
FIRST ACTIVE					
Cash	CA	311.46	327.85	0.81	10.63
Equity	GE	680.03	715.82	15.21	-8.97
Managed	MB	678.34	714.04	13.56	4.98
FRIENDS FIRST					
Cash 2	CA	267.25	281.32	0.60	9.29
Cash	CA	311.46	327.85	0.81	10.63
E-Fund	SF	37.57	39.55	5.21	-70.84
Fixed Int 2	FX	413.10	434.84	4.04	31.37
Fixed Interest	FX	637.10	670.63	4.26	33.34
Managed 2	MB	468.49	493.15	13.32	3.87
Managed	MB	678.34	714.04	13.56	4.98
Ord Share 2	GE	440.98	464.19	14.96	-9.76
Ordinary Share	GE	680.03	715.82	15.21	-8.97
With Profit	WP	392.10	412.80	2.56	19.61
Property 2	PR	741.42	780.44	12.98	61.79
Property	PR	843.39	887.78	13.22	63.70
SP. INV	PR	202.98	213.66	13.96	30.79
Stewardship	GE	325.35	342.47	17.37	-0.18
With Profit 3	WP	210.50	221.60	1.74	16.90
With Profit 4	WP	151.60	159.60	1.27	17.03
GRE LIFE IRELAND LTD					
Deposit	CA	237.39	250.39	0.76	8.65
Equity	GE	379.52	399.46	10.12	-8.17
Gilt	FX	438.82	461.80	4.09	31.11
Managed	MG	383.21	403.40	9.10	-1.27

■ HIBERNIAN
an AVIVA company

HIBERNIAN LIFE & PENSIONS	Cat Code	Bid Price cents	Offer Price cents	Yr to Date %	5 Yr Perf %
Hib (NU) Cash	CA	304.38	304.38	1.51	19.58
Hib (NU) Equity 1	GE	2323.82	2323.82	0.00	-23.97
Hib (NU) Equity 2	GE	1446.89	1523.05	13.18	-7.15
Hib (NU) Fixed Int	FX	308.82	325.07	3.67	37.48
Hib (NU) Global	IN	293.43	308.87	16.74	-16.82
Hib (NU) Irish Fund	IE	499.84	526.15	8.20	31.04
Hib (NU) Irish Property	PR	244.07	244.07	20.33	51.94
Hib (NU) Managed 1	MB	1998.92	1998.92	10.59	5.82
Hib (NU) Managed 2	MB	1079.69	1136.51	10.59	5.96
Hib (NU) Managed 3	MB	391.75	412.36	11.42	7.90
Hib (NU) Managed 4	MB	355.28	373.98	11.21	6.40
Hib (NU) Money	CA	226.12	238.03	0.67	13.70
Hib (NU) Predator	IN	267.82	281.91	17.04	-18.30
Hib (NU) Property 1	PR	1026.71	1080.75	0.00	28.04
Hib (NU) Property 2	PR	871.75	917.63	17.84	54.60
Hib (NU) SIF	SF	500.80	527.16	6.83	29.22
Hib (NU) UK Property	PR	192.04	192.04	8.44	31.24
(NU) With Profit	WP	175.30	175.30	0.69	13.79
Aggressively Man	MG	314.02	330.55	12.59	-0.64
Balanced Managed	MB	929.46	978.38	11.37	3.03
Balanced	MB	310.76	327.11	11.37	3.05
Cash	CA	404.47	425.75	0.64	8.76
Caut Mgd	MC	291.25	306.57	5.41	14.81
Continental Europe	EU	330.70	348.11	16.09	-18.16
Equity	GE	1329.29	1399.26	14.45	-6.00
Euro Banks	GE	148.56	156.38	18.58	9.84
Euro Equity	EE	173.03	182.14	14.37	-17.08
Euro Managed	MB	180.08	189.56	11.42	-4.73
Expert Man	MB	289.67	304.92	11.36	3.02
Gilt	FX	1098.26	1156.06	3.60	33.72
Global Man	IN	329.86	347.22	23.17	-20.69
Global Technology	SF	38.28	40.30	6.98	-63.73
Global Telecoms	SF	80.81	85.07	10.88	-48.39
HI-Gov Sec.	FX	388.10	408.53	3.59	33.95
HI-Growth	MB	354.36	373.01	11.37	3.01
Index Link	SF	348.17	366.49	2.01	21.79
International Eq	IN	551.19	580.20	17.19	20.70
Irish Equity	IE	665.88	700.92	7.97	31.72
Japanese Equity	JE	96.14	101.20	29.28	-35.67
Laser Capital	FX	633.36	666.70	7.79	33.98
Laser Deposit	CA	256.28	269.77	0.64	9.35
Laser Prop	PR	1051.50	1106.84	23.45	57.83
Latin American Eq	SF	178.21	187.58	43.26	25.31
Managed S 2	MB	168.79	177.67	11.19	1.92
Pacific Basin Eq	FA	335.84	353.52	19.18	-1.02
Precision Portfolio	MG	143.24	150.78	16.13	-7.45
Property	PR	512.90	539.89	23.43	60.51
Secure	GU	176.90	186.30	4.19	20.86
UK Equity	UK	333.77	351.33	16.16	-18.19
US Equity	US	521.01	548.43	16.43	-29.31

	Cat Code	Bid Price cents	Offer Price cents	Yr to Date %	5 Yr Perf %
IRISH LIFE					
3yr Guar. 4	GU	285.80	300.80	3.87	7.98
3yr Guar. 5	GU	260.60	265.90	3.18	4.13
5yr Guar. 4	GU	293.10	308.50	4.97	10.44
5yr Guar. 5	GU	267.00	272.40	4.29	6.47
5yr Guar. 6	GU	267.10	267.10	4.13	5.44
Active Man 4	MB	688.90	725.20	12.78	9.88
Active Man 5	MB	335.20	342.00	12.06	5.83
Active Man 6	MB	327.40	327.40	11.86	4.73
Active Man SIA	SF	416.80	438.70	10.01	30.67
Blue Chip 1	GE	830.30	874.00	15.26	-8.04
Blue Chip 2	GE	1688.80	1777.70	16.05	-2.61
Blue Chip 3	GE	1703.20	1792.80	16.05	-2.56
Cash 3	CA	459.80	484.00	0.85	8.75
Cash 4	CA	459.80	484.00	0.85	8.75
Cash 5	CA	221.40	225.90	0.18	4.78
Cash 6	CA	182.80	182.80	0.05	3.72
Cautious Man 4	MC	219.90	231.50	4.61	21.47
Cautious Man 5	MC	211.70	216.00	3.95	15.33
Cautious Man 6	MC	205.00	205.00	3.74	14.04
Celticscope	IE	139.60	139.60	5.36	5.01
Deposit	CA	347.20	350.70	0.66	7.55
Europascope	EU	127.30	127.30	13.86	-24.22
European 4	EU	336.00	353.70	15.59	-11.93
European 5	JE	307.90	314.20	14.84	-15.14
European 6	EU	330.00	330.00	14.58	-16.08
Eurozone 50	EE	132.40	132.40	13.75	
Far East 4	JE	170.70	179.70	30.03	13.04
Far East 5	IE	155.80	159.00	29.16	8.89
Far East 6	JE	221.80	221.80	28.88	7.70
G I B 5 Year	GU	131.70	131.70	0.84	
Globalscope	IN	76.90	76.90	13.59	-35.78
HI-Income 3	FX	4514.60	4752.20	3.89	31.54
HI-Income 4	FX	4514.60	4752.20	3.89	31.54
HI-Income 5	FX	361.50	368.90	3.25	26.70
HI-Income 6	FX	292.60	292.60	3.03	25.38
Inter'l Equ 4	IN	678.20	713.90	17.84	-12.90
Inter'l Equ 5	IE	272.50	278.10	17.09	-16.05
Inter'l Equ 6	IN	283.90	283.90	16.88	-16.97
Inter'l Man 4	MB	334.60	352.20	14.39	2.28
Inter'l Man 5	MB	305.90	312.10	13.61	-1.13
Inter'l Man 6	MB	309.50	309.50	13.45	-2.15
Irish Equ SIA	IE	619.40	652.00	10.38	37.78
Irish Equity 4	IE	1613.00	1697.90	9.04	27.29
Irish Equity 5	IE	406.20	414.50	8.34	22.63
Irish Equity 6	IE	469.90	469.90	8.15	21.34
Managed 1	MB	3649.60	3841.70	13.03	11.25
Managed 2	MB	1393.60	1466.90	12.78	10.19
Managed 3	MB	1374.50	1446.80	12.78	9.84
Managed 4	MB	1374.50	1446.80	12.78	9.84
Nth American 4	US	439.40	462.50	14.65	-23.20
Nth American 5	US	402.10	410.30	13.94	-25.99
Nth American 6	US	421.20	421.20	13.75	-26.84
Pv Inv Aggressive	MG	134.40	134.40	13.71	-8.36
Pv Inv Balanced	MB	142.50	142.50	11.59	-1.29
Pv Inv Cautious	MC	147.50	147.50	7.19	7.26
Prop Inv Fund	PR	285.40	285.40	7.29	34.11
Property Gro 1	PR	1409.90	1484.10	8.41	42.37
Property Gro 2	PR	1409.90	1484.10	8.41	42.37
Property Gro 3	PR	1405.80	1479.80	8.42	42.40
Property Gro 4	PR	1405.90	1479.80	8.42	42.40
Property Gro 5	PR	619.90	632.60	7.73	37.25
Property Inv 2	PR	270.90	270.90	7.29	34.01
Property Inv 3	PR	239.30	239.30	7.31	34.04
Property Inv 4	PR	196.40	196.40	7.32	34.04
Property Inv 5	PR	174.80	174.80	7.31	33.92
Property Mod 1	PR	1153.50	1214.20	8.73	45.89
Securescope	MC	137.20	137.20	3.78	5.42
Stable Man 4	MC	383.10	403.30	4.59	19.90
Stable Man 5	MC	278.40	284.10	3.95	15.57
Stable Man 6	MC	229.70	229.70	3.75	14.28

MoneyMate

Managed funds typically invest in a mix of equities, bonds, property and cash. Property funds invest in a variety of investment properties. Information on the types of property invested in, for example offices or shops, is not presented here, but again is readily available. The summary information in the exhibit does not include the asset split of these funds, but this information is readily accessible from the respective companies. The information included with each fund is a bid price and an offer price, together with the historical price performance of each fund. For example, the following information appeared for the Bank of Ireland Managed Growth Fund on 11 November 2005:

	Bid Price	Offer Price	Year-to-date Return %	5-year Return %
Managed Growth Fund	513.6	540.6	10.69%	10.19%

The principles behind the determination of these unit prices are the same for all unit-linked funds. Taking the Managed Growth Fund as an example:

i)   The life company ring-fences the monies that are collected from the sale of policies to investors.

ii)   The company's fund managers invest the assets in accordance with the stated investment strategy contained in the policy documents and the marketing literature.

iii)   The market value of these assets is calculated, usually on a daily basis. The total value of the portfolio is divided by the total number of units allocated to investors to give the net asset value (NAV) per unit. Adjustments are made to this NAV to take account of buying costs, stamp duties, etc. associated with the buying of securities. The offer price of the units is this adjusted NAV per unit, which is the price that an investor must pay to invest in the fund. A bid price is also calculated which is normally 5% less than the offer price; it represents the price at which units can be redeemed. This spread can be viewed as part of the profit margin to the life company. Generally, a high proportion of this spread covers marketing and sales costs, including sales commissions to sales forces and intermediaries.

iv)   When new funds are received the actuary creates new units and allocates these to the new investors on a pro-rata basis at the offer price. When investors wish to cash in their units the company redeems the units at the quoted bid price and then cancels the units. Other than in exceptional circumstances, investors can enter and exit the fund at the current NAV because of this open–ended feature of unit-linked funds.

Individual investors will normally purchase units in a unit-linked fund through a variety of products sold by the life company. Such products fall into two main categories:

i)   single-premium investment bonds
ii)   recurring-premium, long-term savings plans.

As the name suggests, single-premium investment bonds are appropriate where an investor, who could be an individual or a corporate entity or a charity, has a lump sum to invest. Usually, such bonds offer the prospective investor the ability to allocate the investment monies amongst the life office's suite of funds. The number of units purchased will be a function of the amount of money invested and the price of the units on the date that units are allocated.

Table 5.1 Investing in ABC Equity Fund

	Price of units at:	Number of units purchased
Launch	€1.00	1,000
End-year one	€0.90	1,111
End-year two	€0.95	1,053
End-year three	€1.15	870
Cumulative units		4,034
Average Cost per unit		€0.99
Value of investment at end-year three	4,034 * €1.15	€4,639

The purchaser of a recurring-premium policy contracts with the life office to pay a fixed premium on a regular basis, which is usually monthly but may be quarterly or annually. After expenses the premiums are invested in the chosen fund(s). Table 5.1 illustrates what happens with a recurring-premium investment of €1,000 per annum into a notional unit-linked fund. The same annual investment of €1,000 purchases a different number of units each year, depending on the price of the fund at the time of purchase. In the illustration the price of the fund has declined in the first year, which means that at end-year one the value of the initial investment will have fallen to €900. However, the investor is now investing at a low point in the cycle and his second €1,000 investment purchases more units. Over the four years the average cost per unit works out at €0.99. In this example regular investment has worked in the investor's favour. This is referred to as pound cost averaging and is a potential benefit of regular investment in volatile markets. More units are bought at low prices than at high prices, so that the average purchase price is less than the average price of the units over the particular time period. As long as the long-term trend in equity markets is positive then investors in recurring-premium policies will eventually benefit.

Special Savings Investment Accounts (SSIAs)

In 2001 the Irish government introduced SSIAs to encourage the savings habit. Financial companies created a range of SSIA regular contribution products with the maximum monthly contribution capped by legislation at

€254 per month. The exchequer contributed 25% to each account every month for a term of five years. Investors could choose from a wide range of products but the three core categories were variable-rate interest deposit funds, fixed-rate interest deposit funds and equity market-linked deposit funds. Initially the equity-backed products underperformed owing to falling equity markets in 2002 and 2003. However, equity markets recovered in 2004 and 2005 and investors in equity products benefited from pound cost averaging. By August 2005 equity-linked SSIA's had pulled well ahead of deposit-based SSIAs (Exhibit 5.2).

Exhibit 5.2 SSIAs and Pound Cost Averaging – Equity SSIAs Beating Cash Accounts

Laura Slattery, 03/08/2005

People who opened Special Savings Incentive Accounts (SSIAs) linked to the equity markets are on track to receive a higher sum than those who opted for deposit accounts.

New figures from Bank of Ireland show that savers who contributed the maximum sum of €254 to an equity SSIA since May 2001 have a 9 per cent higher fund than those who took out a variable-rate deposit SSIA.

People who chose the riskier option of Bank of Ireland's equity Growth Fund are also 5 per cent better off than those who opted for a fixed-rate SSIA at an interest rate of 4 per cent.

The Growth Fund maximum contribution savers had a balance of €18,534 as of July 1st, compared to a balance of €17,645 in the fixed-rate accounts and €16,990 in the variable-rate accounts. These accounts will mature next May.

The balances include the Government bonus of €1 for every €4 saved and are net of charges, but do not show the effect of exit tax.

SSIA holders who opened their accounts closer to the scheme's deadline in April 2002 will have been rewarded to an even greater extent if they chose an equity-linked account over deposit ones.

The Growth Fund is outperforming fixed-rate accounts by 8 per cent and variable-rate accounts by 12 per cent.

Equity SSIAs opened later in the scheme are performing better than those opened earlier as they would have avoided equity market weakness in 2001 and 2002.

The figures confirm a sharp turnaround in the fortunes of equity-based SSIAs versus cash deposits. At the end of June 2002, fixed-rate cash SSIAs that had been open for at least a year were worth 8 per cent more than equity-based equivalents.

"Today's figures back up our message that equities offer greater potential for good returns than cash over time," said Gareth McQuillan, Bank of Ireland Life's head of marketing.

However, figures released by Eagle Star last week indicate that SSIA savers who opted for its equity 5 Star 5 fund are on course to receive an even greater windfall on maturity. ➡

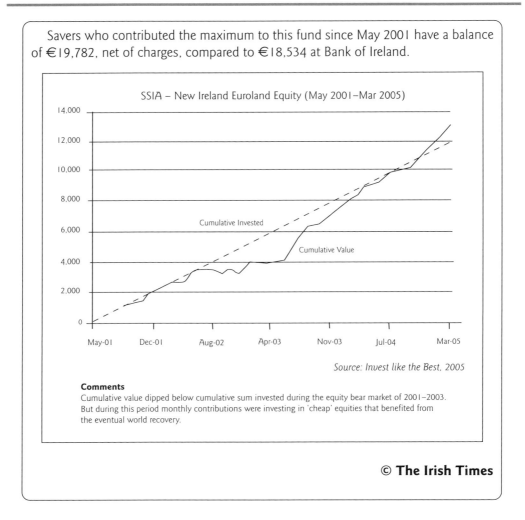

Savers who contributed the maximum to this fund since May 2001 have a balance of €19,782, net of charges, compared to €18,534 at Bank of Ireland.

SSIA – New Ireland Euroland Equity (May 2001–Mar 2005)

Cumulative Invested

Cumulative Value

Source: *Invest like the Best, 2005*

Comments
Cumulative value dipped below cumulative sum invested during the equity bear market of 2001–2003. But during this period monthly contributions were investing in 'cheap' equities that benefited from the eventual world recovery.

© **The Irish Times**

With-Profits Funds

This type of life assurance policy formed the backbone of the industry in both the UK and Ireland up until the early 1980s. Throughout the 1980s and 1990s unit-linked funds and unit trusts gained in popularity as the preferred routes to gain exposure to the stock markets. Nevertheless, substantial funds continued to be invested in with-profits products up until recent years. These funds take pooling of investment return and risk to its logical extreme. Unit-linked funds allow each individual investor to 'identify' their assets on a daily basis by multiplying the number of units that they hold by the published price.

> An investor holds 1,270 units in the Irish Life International Managed Fund 6. The bid price today is 467.30 (cents) and the encashment value is: $1,270 * 4.673 = €5,934.71$

This is not the case for a with-profits fund, as there is not a current value attributable to each policyholder. Rather, the actuary declares an annual percentage return called a bonus, which accrues to the with-profits policy-holders. This is paid only when the policy matures. The actuary will also declare a terminal bonus each year that is paid out on policies maturing in that particular year. Typically the terminal bonus accounts for a very high proportion of the total return accruing to such policies. The advantage to investors of such policies is that investment returns are smoothed over time. Their opaque structure is a major disadvantage. Many investors are not aware that the returns depend on the pool of assets within the with-profits fund and on the overall performance of the life assurance company as a business. This is because the with-profits funds of life assurance companies are used to support the ongoing development of the business. Instead of capital from shareholders, many life assurance companies rely on the capital strength of the with-profits fund. The equity bear market in the early years of the millennium and lower prospective investment returns have created major solvency issues for such funds and have resulted in much lower annual and terminal bonuses across the industry. In the UK the long-established Equitable Life was forced to drastically cut bonuses (returns) to its policy-holders in order to remain solvent. Equitable Life had problems specific to it that made its predicament far worse than most other life assurance companies. Nevertheless, the entire with-profits sector of the market suffered badly as a result of the equity bear market of 2000–2003.

Exhibit 5.3 An A–Z of with-profits investment
Laura Slattery – 23/01/2004

With-profits are usually capital guaranteed investment policies that spread the returns over the term of the investment. Some returns made in good years will be held back to compensate for bad years.

The returns are paid by way of annual bonuses, but these are not guaranteed until the tenth anniversary of the policy (or the seventh anniversary in the case of Irish Life's with-profits bonds). Policyholders will also be promised a terminal bonus on the maturity of with-profits policies. Alongside 10-year single premium bonds, with-profits policies with a term of up to 25 years may be taken out as a pension or an endowment policy to pay off a mortgage.

One firm may have a higher annual bonus rate than another, but that does not mean it is a better policy. A high annual bonus rate could just mean part of the

➡

terminal bonus has been brought forward: the returns will be smoother, but they will not necessarily be any greater. If the annual bonuses declared equal or exceed investors' share of the fund profits, there will be no terminal bonus.

But if bonus rates fall even lower, the danger is that deposit accounts and other cautious investments will start to look more attractive.

An early exit penalty called a market value adjuster (MVA) is sometimes applied to stop a stream of policyholders from leaving when markets are down.

MVAs, which have been as high as 15 per cent in recent years, are subject to ongoing review and can be applied or increased at a later date. This makes with-profits unattractive to investors looking for flexibility.

According to financial adviser Mr Ian Mitchell, MVAs have altered the whole face of and justification for with-profits investment. Their now "almost ubiquitous" presence, coupled with retrospective reductions of previous years' bonuses by some UK firms, means it is a misnomer to call the policies "with-profits" at all, he argues.

With-profits investments arose traditionally from mutual companies, where investors took a bet on the performance of the company itself. Standard Life's with-profits policies still work like this, with investors receiving "mutuality bonuses". However, the company is under pressure and has admitted it may consider demutualising.

With-profits funds at non-mutual companies today are ringfenced, so policyholders are not exposed to any solvency problems the company might have.

The biggest scandal involving with-profits so far has been the Equitable Life debacle. Around 20,000 members of the troubled UK mutual company saw their with-profits pensions repeatedly cut so that Equitable could pay the bonuses it had guaranteed to former policyholders in the UK. Many policyholders here had believed the Irish funds were ringfenced.

Other insurance companies stressed that it was the poor business performance of the mutual company that pushed it over the edge, rather than the nature of with-profits.

Concern about the health of with-profits also arose two years ago when Canada Life closed its with-profits business, warning that new customers would only end up subsidising the over-generous bonuses awarded to existing policyholders. Last year, Scottish Provident, estimated to have up to a 10 per cent share of the total with-profits sector, closed its Irish operation to new business.

© **The Irish Times**

Mutual Funds

In Ireland the main form of mutual fund is an open-ended investment company (OEIC), which is a company whose purpose is to invest in other companies. An OEIC then sets up a series of funds in which investors buy shares. The open-ended nature of its capital structure means that its capital can be increased and decreased by issuing and redeeming shares. The key features of an OEIC are:

- It has a corporate form.
- It can have several different classes of share.
- A single price is calculated based on the net asset value of the relevant portfolio of securities.
- The OEIC has an Authorised Corporate Director (ACD), who is responsible for operating the company in accordance with the regulations and with the OEIC's instrument of incorporation.
- The OEIC must also have a Depositary, who is responsible for the safe keeping of the scheme's assets.
- The ACD and the Depositary must be independent of each other.

The regulations pertaining to OEICs require the ACD to prepare and maintain a prospectus giving information about the constitution, objectives and operation of the OEIC. Information concerning the personnel responsible for running the OEIC must also be kept up to date and be available to investors and potential investors. The prospectus must also include a description of investment policies and the arrangements for the management of the OEIC's investments. The ACD acts as the seller and buyer of shares and it can act in either of two capacities:

i)   It can act as an agent between the OEIC and the investor; or
ii)   It may deal directly with the investor and hold the shares in what is called a 'box'. Shares will normally be held in the box for a short period of time and will either be sold to another investor or will be sold back to the OEIC for cancellation.

The price at which shares are sold or purchased is the single mid-market price, which is normally quoted on a daily basis.

There are three types of OEIC permitted:

- Securities companies, which invest in transferable securities
- Warrant companies, which have powers to invest in warrants beyond the 5% limit imposed on securities funds
- Umbrella companies, which have at least two sub-funds that permit shareholders to switch all or part of their investment from one sub-fund to another.

Unit Trusts

A unit trust is constituted by a trust deed. The trustee owns the assets of the trust and is therefore responsible for the custody and safe keeping of the assets held by the trust. This role is normally taken by a bank or an insurance company. As custodian of the assets the trustee maintains a register of unitholders and generally oversees the management of the trust fund. A professional investment manager will be appointed to invest the funds in securities in accordance with the investment objectives of the trust. The trustee must be independent of the investment manager. The trustee has the role of protecting the interests of the unitholders and ensuring that the manager manages the assets in line with the investment strategy stated in the trust deed. Like OEICs, unit trusts are open-ended and therefore inflows and outflows involve the creation and cancellation of units in the trust.

When an investor contributes money to the fund he receives a number of units in the fund, with the price of the units determined by the total value of the funds under management in the trust divided by the number of units in issue.

Authorised Unit Trusts

Only unit trusts that are authorised by IFSRA are permitted to advertise. Unauthorised unit trusts are legal but can be marketed only to professional investors. All authorised unit trusts are governed by a trust deed which covers the detailed running of the trust. It will include the maximum management fees that can be paid to the various service providers to the trust, including fund-management fees. The precise method of calculating the price of units will be detailed as well as the provisions enabling new investors to join. The trust deed will also include some limitations on the investments made by the fund manager. For example, there is a maximum of 10% of the net asset value of a trust that can be invested in unquoted securities.

Pricing of Unit Trust Units

The value of a unit at a particular time is determined by the net asset value (NAV) of the trust. The NAV is based on the market value of the securities held by the trust less the market value of any liabilities. If a trust has a market value of €20m, with 20 million units in existence, then the NAV per unit would be €1 (i.e., €20m divided by 20m units). If the value of assets were to double to €40m, then the NAV per unit would also double to €2 per unit, provided that there was no change in the number of units in issue. Bid and offer prices of units are quoted for a trust. Expenses such as administration costs, dealing costs, stamp duties, sales commissions, etc. have to be taken into account when calculating the price of units. These expenses are reflected in the spread between the bid and the offer price. Units in unit trusts are purchased from the managers at the offer price and sold back to the managers at the lower bid price.

Investment Trusts

Investment trusts are not a feature of the Irish market but Irish investors can invest in investment trusts that are listed on the London Stock Exchange. As with unit trusts and OEICs, investment trusts allow investors to pool their funds in order to benefit from economies of scale and portfolio diversification. However, the term 'trust' is in fact misleading, as they are companies rather than trusts. An investment trust is a company that is set up to invest in securities. Just like any quoted company, an investment trust sells shares to the public for cash, and this cash is then used to create investment portfolios. The flow of funds into the trust (or investment company) is limited by the number of shares sold at its initial public offer. The capital raised from this sale of shares is exactly the same as the capital raised by any company that goes for an IPO. The only difference is that the capital of the investment trust is invested in other companies (usually, but not always, other quoted companies). The board of the investment trust will appoint a fund manager, and other service providers such as a custodian, to provide fund management and related services to the trust. Post the IPO prospective new investors can purchase shares in the trust only on the secondary market. Unlike OEICs, investment trusts cannot create new shares to satisfy new demand. Therefore, the flow of funds into the company is limited by the number of shares that have been issued, and as such they are 'closed-ended funds' in contrast to the open-ended structure that pertains to OEICs, unit trusts, and indeed unit-linked life assurance funds.

If investors wish to exit the investment trust they can sell their shares only on the secondary market. One consequence of being closed-ended is that the price of the shares in any investment trust is determined by the interaction of buyers and sellers at any one time. Investment trusts publish their NAV per share on a regular basis, and investors pay close attention to this figure. However, unlike OEICs this NAV acts as a reference point for the price of the shares in an investment trust, and does not determine the price at which shares actually trade. The shares in an investment trust can trade at a discount or a premium to this NAV per share, depending on the balance of supply and demand in the secondary market at any point in time. In fact investment trusts often trade at a discount to NAV, although sometimes they can trade at a premium. Exhibit 5.4 presents the information on investment trusts (investment companies), which is published on a daily basis in the *Financial Times*.

Exhibit 5.4 Investment Companies Listed on the London Stock Exchange

INVESTMENT COMPANIES

	Notes	Price	Chng	52 week high	52 week low	Yld	NAV	Dis or Pm(-)
CONVENTIONAL TRUSTS & VCTs								
3i	...........†s	805	−7	*815	634	1.9	676.3	−19.0
AbnAsian	...♣	269$\frac{1}{2}$xd	−1$\frac{1}{2}$	272$\frac{3}{4}$	188$\frac{1}{4}$	1.3	262.7	−2.6
Wt	....	168$\frac{3}{4}$	−1$\frac{1}{4}$	172	102	−	−	−
AbnGthVCT1	.	52	......	52	47	1.1	74.4	30.1
AbnGthOpsVCT		82$\frac{1}{2}$	+$\frac{1}{2}$	**82**$\frac{1}{2}$	71	1.2	97.2	15.1
VCT 2		100	......	100	100	−	95.8	−4.4
AbnNewDn	♣s	433$\frac{1}{2}$	+1$\frac{1}{4}$	452$\frac{1}{4}$	305$\frac{1}{2}$	0.9	426.1	−1.7
AbnNewThai	♣	124$\frac{1}{4}$	......	124$\frac{1}{2}$	96$\frac{3}{4}$	1.1	135.0	8.0
Abf Sml	......†	590	−3$\frac{1}{2}$	602$\frac{1}{2}$	484	1.9	638.3	7.6
AbsoluteRetPf		108$\frac{1}{2}$	......	109$\frac{3}{4}$	101$\frac{3}{4}$	−	102.7	−5.7
ActiveCap	...♣	108$\frac{3}{4}$	......	127$\frac{1}{4}$	101$\frac{1}{4}$	−	127.0	14.4
AdvDvpMk	..♣	261	+1$\frac{1}{4}$	261$\frac{3}{4}$	175	0.2	284.1	8.1
AdvFcsPf	...♣	106	......	112$\frac{1}{4}$	99	−	111.6	5.0
Adv UK	......♣	177	......	177	136	1.3	188.0	5.9
AIM Dist	...♣s	60$\frac{3}{4}$	......	61	51	−	75.2	19.2
AIM VCT	......s	58$\frac{1}{2}$	......	59$\frac{1}{2}$	50$\frac{1}{2}$	−	70.9	17.5
AIM VCT 2	..	73$\frac{1}{2}$	......	83	72$\frac{1}{2}$	4.8	86.7	15.3
Albany	......♣†	254$\frac{1}{2}$	......	258	210	3.2	302.6	15.9
Alliance	...♣†	3212	+12	**3212**	2640	2.3	3670.6	12.5
AllDres2nd	.♣	153	......	153	139$\frac{1}{2}$	−	161.9	5.5
2nd '09	....	112	......	112$\frac{1}{2}$	96	−	129.8	13.7
AlliDres'10	.♣	88	......	88	77$\frac{3}{4}$	−	106.8	17.6
Alt Asts Rd P.		110	......	110$\frac{1}{2}$	100	−	108.4	−1.5
AIS Stg Hdg	..	122$\frac{3}{4}$	......	127$\frac{3}{4}$	113$\frac{1}{2}$	−	119.3	−2.9
Altin $	....	£27$\frac{11}{16}$	+$\frac{3}{2}$	£28$\frac{1}{16}$	£24	−	3005.5	7.8
Am Opp	......♣	118$\frac{1}{4}$	......	119	93	−	127.4	7.2
Amerindo	...♣	16$\frac{1}{2}$	......	17	14	−	19.1	13.7
Anglo & Overs		97$\frac{1}{2}$	......	102	93$\frac{1}{4}$	−	103.2	5.5
Art AIM	......♣	85	......	97$\frac{1}{2}$	85	−	93.4	9.0
Art Aim VCT2		95	......	106	95	−	99.1	4.1
Art Alpha	......	192$\frac{1}{2}$	......	217	164	1.1	167.1	−15.2
Atls Japan$	..	1450$\frac{1}{2}$	−2	1465$\frac{3}{4}$	932$\frac{1}{4}$	−	1361.2	−6.6
Aurora	...♣	184$\frac{1}{2}$	......	219$\frac{1}{2}$	171$\frac{1}{2}$	1.6	211.2	12.6
AXA Property	105$\frac{1}{2}$xd	+1$\frac{1}{4}$	106$\frac{3}{4}$	101$\frac{1}{2}$	1.5	−	41
BG Japan	..♣	236$\frac{3}{4}$	−5$\frac{1}{4}$	246$\frac{1}{4}$	143$\frac{1}{2}$	−	232.9	−1.7
BG Shin	......♣	234$\frac{3}{4}$	−1$\frac{1}{2}$	238	143	−	231.4	−1.4
Bankers	...♣†	329$\frac{1}{4}$xd	−1$\frac{3}{4}$	331	267$\frac{1}{4}$	2.4	370.2	11.1
BrngEmEu	.♣	525$\frac{1}{2}$	−2$\frac{1}{4}$	593	295$\frac{1}{2}$	0.4	552.2	4.8
Baronsmd	....	90$\frac{1}{2}$	......	93$\frac{1}{2}$	81$\frac{1}{2}$	14.9	99.0	8.5
VCT C	....	90	......	95	90	1.7	95.6	5.9
VCT 2	....	102$\frac{1}{2}$	......	102$\frac{1}{2}$	91$\frac{1}{2}$	10.2	115.8	11.5
VCT 2 'C'	..	92$\frac{1}{2}$	......	95	92$\frac{1}{2}$	2.2	97.9	5.5
VCT 3	........†	100$\frac{1}{2}$	......	101$\frac{1}{2}$	91$\frac{1}{2}$	4.7	114.1	11.9
VCT 4	........†	96$\frac{1}{2}$	......	97$\frac{1}{2}$	89	4.5	109.5	11.9
BGI End	....	158$\frac{1}{2}$#	......	158$\frac{1}{2}$	154	−	160.6	1.3
II	....	92$\frac{1}{2}$	......	92$\frac{1}{2}$	82$\frac{1}{2}$	−	101.1	8.5
III	....	70	......	70$\frac{1}{2}$	55$\frac{1}{2}$	−	73.8	5.1
BioscnceVCT	♣	52	......	80	45	1.0	79.8	34.9
Blue Plt E Fin	♣	100	−$\frac{1}{4}$	106$\frac{1}{2}$	51$\frac{1}{2}$	0.7	125.5	20.4
Blue Plt G&I Uts	.♣	1417$\frac{1}{2}$	+5	1587$\frac{1}{2}$	930	1.6	1978.6	28.4
Blue Plt WW	♣	113$\frac{1}{2}$xd	+2	126	63$\frac{1}{2}$	1.2	150.3	24.5
Brit&Am	...♣s	101$\frac{1}{2}$xd	......	108	87$\frac{1}{2}$	5.3	121.2	16.2
Brit Ast	......♣	124$\frac{3}{4}$	−1$\frac{1}{4}$	127$\frac{3}{4}$	105	4.3	136.2	8.4
Brit Emp	...♣s	414$\frac{1}{2}$	+$\frac{1}{2}$	**414**$\frac{1}{2}$	293	0.5	385.1	−7.6
Ln '13	......t	245	......	250	213	4.0	−	−
Brit Prt	....♣†	154	−1	157$\frac{3}{4}$	129$\frac{1}{2}$	2.3	161.1	4.4
BSCVCT	......s	77$\frac{1}{4}$xd	......	77$\frac{1}{4}$	64$\frac{1}{2}$	4.9	93.9	17.7
BSC C share	.	95$\frac{1}{2}$	......	95$\frac{1}{2}$	95$\frac{1}{2}$	−	95.1	−.4
BSTCVCT	......	47$\frac{1}{2}$	......	48$\frac{1}{2}$	43$\frac{1}{2}$	5.3	56.4	15.8
BSTCVCT2	...	70	......	82	69$\frac{1}{2}$	7.1	80.5	13.0
Brunner	....♣†	352$\frac{1}{2}$	−$\frac{1}{2}$	353$\frac{1}{4}$	281	2.3	0413.6	14.8
Caledna	...♣	1778	−10	1788	1260	1.6	1831.2	2.9
Can Gen C$	♣	992	+6	1121$\frac{1}{2}$	606$\frac{1}{4}$	1.2	1158.3	14.4
Wts C$	.....	695$\frac{1}{4}$	+2$\frac{3}{4}$	822$\frac{3}{4}$	355$\frac{1}{4}$	−	−	−
Candover	....†	2000	−2	2022	1496	2.3	1656.3	−20.8
Cap Gr	........s	1995	......	2087$\frac{1}{2}$	1795	0.5	1821.7	−9.5
Chameleon Tst	121$\frac{1}{2}$	......	121$\frac{1}{2}$	104$\frac{1}{2}$	0.2	118.1	−2.9	

The final column of information is the discount or premium that the company's price is trading at relative to the net asset value (NAV) per share. This is calculated by dividing the share price by the NAV. The first company listed is the venture capital company 3i, whose share price was 805p and whose NAV was 676.3. In this case the shares were trading at a premium of 19.0%.

There is no single satisfactory explanation to explain why investment trusts usually trade at either a discount or a premium to NAV. In fact usually such companies trade at a discount, as can be seen from Exhibit 5.4. (Note that by convention a discount is a positive number and a premium is a negative number.) The incidence of tax may provide part of the explanation. Under London Stock Exchange and UK Revenue rules investment trust companies must limit their investment in any one company to 15% of total assets. As long as the trust satisfies the rules as set by the Revenue, it achieves 'approved' status. As a consequence of this gains made by the trust are exempt from capital gains tax. However, the income of the company is subject to corporation tax, and dividends paid by the trust company to its shareholders are taxed in the hands of shareholders in the normal way. In contrast the tax treatment of OEICs is more favourable, in that the OEIC itself pays neither capital gains tax nor income tax. Rather, the investor in an OEIC is taxed at a composite rate of tax on the total investment gains made at the point of encashment. The recent investment performance of a trust also impacts on the discount to NAV. If a trust is going through a period of underperformance, this will often manifest itself in a relatively high discount to the published NAV per share. Another issue concerns the accuracy and timeliness of the NAV figure. In the case of the premium to NAV cited above for 3i, it may be due to an NAV figure that was calculated on 'old' valuations. While investment trust companies usually trade at a discount, there are occasions when they trade at a premium. Specialist trusts in areas of keen interest may trade at a premium as the demand for shares exceeds supply. For example, trusts focusing on emerging markets have in the past traded at a premium to NAV at times when investors were scrambling to gain exposure to such markets. Direct investing in these markets is often restricted and very expensive, and specialist trusts may be the only viable way to gain investment exposure.

Exchange-Traded Funds (ETFs)

Like investment trusts, these are shares in investment companies that are bought and sold on stock exchanges in exactly the same way as ordinary shares are traded. An exchange-traded fund (ETF) is an index fund holding a diversified portfolio of securities, priced and traded on public stock exchanges. ETFs are technically closed-ended companies, but they operate an unusual process to ensure that the shares always trade very close to the NAV of the fund. Special trading rights are granted to selected institutions by the company sponsoring the ETF. If the ETF share price is lower than the NAV per share, an ETF institutional investor can buy ETF shares and turn them in to the sponsoring company for an equivalent amount of underlying stocks, which the institution can then sell for an immediate profit. If the ETF share price is greater than the NAV per share, the process is reversed. The institutional investor sells the ETF back to the sponsoring company and buys the underlying stocks on the market for a lower aggregate price. The underlying stocks can then be delivered to the sponsoring company instead of actual shares in the ETF. This trading mechanism has the effect of ensuring that ETFs do not suffer from the disadvantages of closed-ended funds. While they are technically closed-ended, they can effectively operate as if they were open-ended funds.

Attractions of ETFs

ETFs invest on a passive basis and therefore the fund-management charges are much lower than those for actively managed funds. Annual expenses range from as low as 0.09% to 0.99% per annum, and as such ETFs have some of the lowest expense ratios among registered investment products. Annual expenses are deducted from dividend payments, which are typically paid on a semi-annual basis. Stockbroking commissions are payable by the investor on purchase/sale, as ETFs are traded in exactly the same way as ordinary shares. Because they are quoted on stock exchanges trading prices are available on a continuous basis. They are likely to be of interest to the more sophisticated private investor who may use them as a complement to direct investing. For example, an Irish-based investor might invest (say) 50% of his portfolio directly in the Irish equity market, with the balance invested overseas in a range of ETFs.

Exhibit 5.5 New Investment Opportunity on the ISEQ
Laura Slattery, 06/05/2005

A diversified portfolio limits investors' losses in the event of a much-fancied share crashing unexpectedly, but buying a range of shares individually or investing in a unit-linked fund can be an expensive business for small stock market players.

But now the Irish Stock Exchange has set up a new mechanism that gives investors diversification in a single, low-cost transaction: an exchange traded fund (ETF).

Investors can place their bets on the 20 most-liquid and largest-capped equities on the Iseq index via one single security. It is, broadly speaking, a 20 for the price of one kind of deal.

The main advantage of the Iseq 20 ETF, which is itself listed and traded on the Irish Stock Exchange, is that investors gain exposure to each of the shares without having to fork out for the fees, commissions and stamp duty associated with buying each share individually.

➡

They can also beat the annual management charges of 1 to 1.5 per cent payable on a managed fund and avoid all kinds of hidden charges buried within the terms of some index-tracking products.

The charge on the ETF is 0.5 per cent, which covers all management fees and operating expenses.

The only additional cost is the normal commissions charged by the stockbroker or intermediary selling the ETF, which usually arrive at about 1 per cent.

Although this means investors won't be able to avoid taking an upfront hit, as they may be able to do on a managed fund, there are still good savings to be made from buying in numbers.

Buying one share of the Iseq 20 ETF currently costs around €12. An investor purchasing 1,000 shares will, therefore, pay €12,000, plus 0.5 per cent or €60, then a possible stockbroker fee of €120 (1 per cent). The total cost of buying the 1,000 shares is €180, meaning the fund will have to rise in value by more than 1.5 per cent before investors can actually make any money.

However, if an investor was buying 1,000 shares in a single stock priced at about €12 each, they would pay the 1 per cent stockbrokers' commission and a 1 per cent stamp duty, meaning their typical total trading cost would be 25 per cent higher at €240. And as the exposure would be limited to a single share with unpredictable fortunes, the investment would also be much more of a gamble.

ETFs are tax efficient. Individual investors pay tax at a rate of 20 per cent on dividends, compared with a possible 42 per cent on dividends paid out by regular shares.

Although the ETF acts like a fund, it trades like a share. This means that prices and trading volumes are published in real time on the Irish Stock Exchange website, giving investors more transparency than they could expect from other index trackers, which only give one opening and one closing price each day.

Although the Iseq 20 ETF is the first ETF to be based on the Irish stock market, the concept was introduced in the US and Canada more than a decade ago. At the end of last year, there were 336 ETFs listed on 29 exchanges worldwide.

Trading in ETFs has grown rapidly, with the assets under management in European-based ETFs mushrooming by 66 per cent in 2004.

Bank of Ireland Asset Management buys and manages the underlying stocks on the Iseq 20 ETF, while NCB is the promoter.

Tom Healy, Irish Stock Exchange chief executive, believes there is clear demand for an ETF based on the Irish market.

The fund attracted reasonable volumes of money during its first full week of trading, according to Peter Duff, director of NCB Investment Services. Up to €500,000 was invested on a daily basis with the money mostly coming from private clients.

Some investors may be wary of placing too much cash in the ETF on the basis that the Iseq index is dominated by a handful of large stocks capable of sinking the entire index into negative territory if they have a bad day.

> And there is no geographical diversification. In other words, they may be spreading their eggs over several baskets, but all the baskets are being stored in the one warehouse.
>
> According to NCB, Iseq 20 ETF investors are buying Europe's best economy in a single share.
>
> "The Irish market has become one of the strongest performing markets over time and we would expect it to continue to outperform," says Mr Duff.
>
> "You would have to be happy that you want exposure to the stock markets in the first place but, if you do, the Irish market is one of the best places to be."
>
> © **The Irish Times**

ETFs are now available on a broad range of stock markets and specific sectors within the larger markets. In 2005 there were approximately 350 ETFs available with an estimated $275 billion of assets. They enable investors to gain a tailored investment exposure on a real-time basis and at a lower cost than many other forms of investing. Well-diversified portfolios can be created with just a few selected ETFs, but of course these investments are subject to market risk and the consequent fluctuation in value.

Structured and Capital-Guaranteed Investment Products

In Ireland these are often generically referred to as 'tracker bonds', and the typical structure is as follows:

- The product itself is a straightforward deposit account and therefore the investor deposits funds with the financial institution.
- As with a normal deposit account the capital is guaranteed. Unlike a normal deposit account the capital is guaranteed only as long as the funds are held on deposit for a pre-specified period of time, which usually ranges from 3 years to 6 years. Early encashment will be subject to penalties.
- The investment return is not a rate of interest, but a return that depends on the performance of a particular stock-market index or a composite of indices.
- At the end of the life of the product the investor receives his original capital plus the investment return, the latter depending on stock-market performance.
- Deposit interest retention tax (DIRT) applies to the return achieved in the same way as if it were normal interest on a deposit.

In order to create these products, financial institutions utilise derivative markets. A typical tracker bond consists of two underlying components:

i)   A zero-coupon bond that has a term exactly matching the term of the tracker bond;

ii)   An option that is purchased from an investment bank and that promises to pay out a return at the end of the term based on the performance of a predefined stock-market index.

These products have proved to be very popular with retail investors and the financial industry has proved to be adept at designing innovative products. There is now an almost bewildering array of such products in the marketplace.

Hedge Funds

Hedge Funds have grown in popularity amongst high-net-worth investors over the past decade. Whilst they are still largely the preserve of the very wealthy investor, hedge fund retail products have started to move into the mainstream. Minimum investment amounts of €100,000 or higher are typical for these products, although in some markets products are available with minimum investment amounts as low as €10,000. The typical hedge fund that is available to retail investors is a 'Fund of Funds'. As such the manager invests only in other hedge funds, which controls the risk but of course also limits the potential upside. The investment objectives of these funds differ from those of 'long only' funds in two key respects:

- The return objective is normally an absolute return and not a relative return.
- A wide array of investment assets and investment strategies are encompassed within a typical retail hedge fund. In contrast traditional investment products usually limit their investment to a well-defined and often narrow set of assets and/or markets.

Management fees in the hedge-fund universe are much higher than for traditional funds. The underlying hedge funds typically charge an annual management fee of 2% of funds under management plus a performance fee equal to 20% of returns generated. A 'Fund of Funds' hedge fund will have charges that vary but are typically 1% of funds under management plus a performance fee equal to 10% of returns generated. Despite the recent higher profile of hedge funds and moves by regulators to allow private investors access to such funds, for the foreseeable future the traditional collective investment schemes will continue to absorb the lion's share of retail investment monies.

INVESTMENT DECISION MAKING FOR THE PRIVATE INVESTOR

Individuals who invest directly in the stock market are a minority – the overwhelming majority of the investing public invest indirectly using some of the products described in this chapter. In fact in Ireland the main form of direct investing occurs in the property market. Rapid growth in the economy, dating from the early 1990s, has spawned a significant number of high-net-worth individuals. Many of them have sufficient funds to purchase investment properties either individually or through syndicates. Many smaller investors have become involved in the buy-to-let residential property market. Despite the growing popularity of direct investing in property, investing indirectly in securities accounts for the lion's share of investing in the Irish and other developed economies.

For the private investor the type of investment vehicle used – a unit-linked fund, an OEIC or a unit trust – is relatively unimportant, since there is now

Table 5.2 *Matching Products to Investor Requirements*

Investment Requirements and Constraints	Investment Product Categories
Regular Income Required	Deposits Low-Risk Managed Funds Structured Products Paying Regular Income
No Tolerance for Capital Fluctuation	Deposits Capital-Guaranteed Products
Some Capital Fluctuation Acceptable	Most Collective Investment Schemes
Short Time Horizon and Premium on Marketable Investments	Deposits Money Market and Bond Funds Low-Risk Managed Funds
Medium Time Horizon and moderate requirement for Liquidity/Marketability	Most Collective Investment Schemes
Long Time Horizon and Capacity for Illiquid Investment	Most Collective Investment Schemes Structured Products with long investment period (up to 7 years) Hedge-Fund Products

a level playing field as far as tax is concerned across the different structures. Of far greater importance is the investment strategy being pursued, and the fund managers who are best equipped to deliver the targeted, risk-adjusted returns. Therefore the starting point for any investor is an assessment of their investment goals, investment time horizon and tolerance for risk. Once this step has been completed, the investor is then faced with a wide array of investment choices that include all the product structures already discussed. In addition, there are also deposit-based products and hybrid products that combine capital guarantees with exposure to stock markets, including absolute return-focused hedge funds. Table 5.2 illustrates in broad terms the link between an investor's particular requirements and constraints, and the categories of investment products that are capable of meeting those goals.

THE MECHANICS OF INDIRECT INVESTING

Most investors accept that direct investment in stock markets is a risky business and requires a considerable amount of skill and time to be successful. What is often not properly appreciated is that indirect investing can also involve high levels of risk, since most investment products are built upon underlying investment strategies that are exposed to market risk. Therefore, the majority of private investors require professional advice to help them choose the right products to match their specific requirements. The financial services industry, however, is geared to sell financial products, with impartial advice sometimes coming a poor second. The inherent conflict in combining advice and sales has resulted in a high proportion of investment products being sold through investment intermediaries. Such intermediaries normally sell the products of many different financial institutions and, at least in principle, are in a position to offer impartial advice. Unfortunately this hasn't always worked to the best interests of the individual investor, as intermediaries are generally rewarded through commission payments from the financial institutions. This creates a bias in the system whereby intermediaries push those products that offer the highest rates of commission. In the UK there have been a number of high-profile investigations by the regulators into the mis-selling of investment products relating to endowment policies and personal pensions. Many of the UK's leading life insurance companies are still faced with substantial compensation claims relating to the mis-selling of personal pension products in particular.

In Ireland the same issues arise concerning the difficulty in getting appropriate and impartial investment advice, although there have not been the same mis-selling scandals as in the UK. Nevertheless, the industry has been forced to become more consumer-friendly over the years through initiatives largely driven by pressure from regulators/legislators and consumer groups. The key areas in which changes have come about include:

- **Transparency:** Commission and charges must now be clearly set out before a product is sold.
- **Cooling-Off Period:** After signing up to a product consumers now have a cooling-off period, during which they are entitled to change their mind with no financial penalty.
- **Fee-Based Advisers:** Many intermediaries now offer their clients the option of paying a fee for advice and commission-free (or very low-commission) products.

The establishment of a single regulator for the financial services industry in Ireland has been a key development in improving the investment landscape, particularly from the consumer's point of view. The Irish Financial Services Regulatory Authority (IFSRA) was established in May 2003 and regulates the manufacturers of financial products (banks, insurance companies, etc.) and the distributors of such products (insurance brokers, mortgage brokers, investment advisers, etc.). Despite the extensive advances achieved in the development of the Irish financial services industry, there are still many instances whereby clients of such institutions feel that the products that they were sold have not delivered the expected returns. Some of this reflects a general over-optimism that still pervades both the industry and its clients after the high-return decades of the 1980s and 1990s. It also reflects the inherent tension between the sales process, which must extol the virtues of a product to make the sale, and the need to set out clearly the risks associated with those expected investment returns. The equity bear market in the early years of the millennium led to a very difficult environment for the once-dominant life assurance companies (Exhibit 5.6).

Exhibit 5.6 Life Insurers face wait before regaining status as rock-solid investments

Investor 01/11/2002

In time there is a good chance that many life insurers will regain the mantle of being safe and attractive investments

Life insurance and the companies that sell such products have been in existence for a long time. The original rationale for buying life insurance was to ensure that there would be a lump sum available to meet funeral expenses when the time came. However, it wasn't long before life insurance companies developed products that combined long-term savings plans with protection plans. Today's life insurance companies have long been far more dependent on savings, investment and pension products than on pure life insurance.

➡

From a stock market investment perspective, life insurance companies have traditionally been viewed as rock-solid investments compared with most other sectors of the market.

Recent developments across the sector must be causing many investors to reappraise their view of these companies. This has been the worst year ever for the sector across Europe. For example, the UK life insurance sector has dropped by 42 per cent over the past 12 months compared with a fall of 22 per cent in the overall market as measured by the FTSE All Share index. These companies have been hit hard by falling equity markets, which have affected life assurers' financial position on two fronts.

Firstly, the fees charged on investment products are based on a percentage of the market value of the assets under management. Clearly, falling markets lead to lower fund values, which in turn lead to lower revenues.

The prolonged equity bear market has therefore created substantial downward pressure on the fees earned by the life sector. For a company such as Irish Life & Permanent (IL&P) this has represented the main drag on its revenues. However, IL&P has been able to offset much of this negative influence through strong growth in sales of new products.

The second channel through which falling equity markets have affected life companies is through the direct impact on their capital bases. Many companies sell investment products where the life company takes much of the investment risk onto its own balance sheet. Therefore, when equity markets fall as sharply as they have in recent years, such companies may be forced into raising fresh capital from shareholders. In extreme cases, a company may be brought to the brink of insolvency.

An example of this is Equitable Life in the UK, which had made promises to its policyholders that it could not meet because of the decline in the value of its assets.

However, most UK firms have been able to protect their capital bases by cutting bonus rates to policyholders, and many have trimmed holdings of equities or hedged against further falls. Some companies such as Legal & General have shored up their capital bases through rights issues. The accompanying table provides information on IL&P and the main quoted UK life insurers. IL&P enjoys a higher investment rating than its UK counterparts. It trades on a price-earnings ratio (PER) of 10.4 compared with 9.5 and 8.6 for Legal & General and Prudential, which are two of the stronger UK life assurers. The weakest company shown is Britannic, which trades on a PER of only 5 and offers an enormous dividend yield of 17.7 per cent. A yield as high as this clearly implies that the market anticipates a very sharp cut in Britannic's dividend payment.

The higher rating enjoyed by IL&P can in part be explained by the better growth prospects of the Irish economy and the fact that IL&P is now a well-diversified financial company.

However, the key factor that differentiates Irish Life from the UK life sector is that the Irish company sells only unit-linked type investment products.

These products mirror market performance for policyholders and don't need propping up with extra capital as with-profit policies do. Lower equity markets will mean lower management fees, but the firm's capital base remains intact.   ➡

> Until equity markets enter a sustained new bull market those life companies with weak capital positions will find the going very difficult. Ultimately, demand for the products that life insurers offer is likely to grow strongly on a medium to long-term view.
>
> Across the globe there is a large gap between the amount that consumers actually save and what they need to save in order to provide for retirement. So in time there is a good chance that many life insurance companies will regain the mantle of being safe and attractive long-term investments.
>
> © **The Irish Times**

THE FUTURE FOR RETAIL INVESTMENT PRODUCTS IN IRELAND

Unlike in the US, where there is a long tradition of direct investment in the stock market by individuals, direct investment in stocks and shares by Irish individuals is still a minority activity. Indeed, even in the US investment volume through vehicles such as mutual funds has long eclipsed direct investment by individuals in the stock market. Trends in Ireland are likely to mirror those in Europe, where the bulk of stock-market-related investment occurs through collective investment schemes. EU directives will be important in determining the legal and regulatory framework, and in widening consumer choice through the encouragement of cross-border competition. For the individual investor distinguishing between the array of investment and savings products on offer will remain a daunting task. The key role of investment intermediaries and product providers in properly advising clients will become even more important in the future. With the increased focus on investing for the future, the savings and investment marketplace in Ireland is certain to thrive.

SUMMARY

- As an alternative to purchasing financial assets themselves, all investors can invest indirectly, which involves the purchase of shares in an investment company or units in a unit trust or unit-linked life assurance fund.
- Collective Investment Schemes are classified as either open-end or closed-end, depending on whether the number of shares or units are fixed or constantly changing.
- In Ireland the bulk of indirect investing occurs through open-end investment vehicles such as OEICs, unit-linked life assurance funds and unit trusts.   ➡

- The key benefits of indirect investing include:
  - diversification
  - ease of administration
  - tax efficiency.
- For open-ended investment vehicles investors buy and sell shares or units at the net asset value, which is determined by the current market value of the securities held by the investment company or trust.
- Capital-guaranteed products, which combine exposure to stock markets and/or bond markets with guarantees on the original capital investment, now attract large inflows of funds from private investors.
- For the very wealthy, hedge funds offer an alternative to traditional equity and bond funds. Regulators in several jurisdictions are now moving to allow hedge-fund products access to the wider retail investment market.
- For private investors, matching their specific requirements to the appropriate investment products usually requires expert financial advice.

QUESTIONS

1. **Regarding fund types, which of the following is TRUE?**

   A. An investor in a unit-linked fund receives units in proportion to his/her contributions.
   B. The investor in a unit-linked fund is exposed to the market risk associated with the underlying assets.
   C. Many large pension funds prefer to invest on a segregated fund basis, as it enables the fund managers to construct dedicated, customised portfolios.

      1. A and B only
      2. All of the above
      3. B and C only
      4. None of the above

2. **In assessing the suitability of an investment strategy for a client, an investment manager will be concerned with the client's:**

   A. Attitude to Growth versus Security
   B. Existing liabilities
   C. Investment time horizon
   D. Pattern of cash inflows and outflows

1. A & B
2. A, B & C
3. All of the Above
4. B & C

3. With reference to Exhibit 5.5, list the advantages of using the ISEQ Exchange-Traded Fund to invest in the Irish stock market compared with an Irish equity unit-linked fund. What are the disadvantages of the ETF?

Chapter six

Investment, Investors and Risk

This chapter distinguishes between the investor, the gambler and the speculator. It examines the different sources of investment return. The important concept of risk is introduced and what risk means to different investors is explored. The concept of risk as defined and measured by Markowitz is examined, and is extended to the implications for portfolio construction.

Learning Objectives

After reading this chapter, you will be able to:
- **Define investment, investors, risk and return**
- **Recognise the characteristics and requirements of investors and their importance as a first step in determining investment policy**
- **List the various types of investment risk**
- **Explain Markowitz's important contribution to the definition and measurement of risk**
- **Calculate the return and risk of individual securities and of portfolios**
- **Explain the importance of correlation and covariance of assets in measuring a portfolio's risk**
- **Differentiate between naïve diversification and Markowitz diversification**
- **Describe Markowitz's efficient frontier and its role in the construction of optimal portfolios.**

Investment is the process whereby consumption is deferred and resources are set aside to build a store of future value and to earn a return. Individuals invariably have short-, medium- and long-term financial commitments and goals. In the short term we must house, feed and clothe our family and ourselves. Our medium-term aspirations may be to educate our children, provide for family healthcare and generally improve our quality of life. In the long term we may need to repay a house mortgage or ensure a comfortable life in retirement. Organisations have a similar mix of financial objectives. A limited company, in the short term, must meet its obligations to its suppliers and workforce. Over the medium term it may be required to pay down debt and pay dividends to shareholders. Its long-term objective might be to generate growth and higher returns for its shareholders. A charity might, in the short term, require to generate steady or rising distributions to those who depend upon it for income whilst, in the medium to long term, preserving the value of its capital. A pension fund will be concerned with meeting its long-term obligation to provide pensions to existing and future pensioners, but will also be focused on its short-term statutory requirement to meet solvency standards. Prudent financial management, at the individual and organisational levels alike, requires that current and future needs are recognised, anticipated and provided for.

INVESTORS

An investor makes a commitment of resources now in anticipation of future reward. In effect, the investor will forgo current consumption in the expectation of generating a future increase in value. In attempting to generate this future increase in value the investor must live with uncertainty. The value he or she realises on the investment will depend on what someone else will pay for it in the future.

This uncertainty is evident in the frequently erratic path followed by the investment markets. The markets are subject to short-term fluctuations, to cyclical patterns that reflect the business or economic cycles and to secular, or long-term, trends that may be driven by changes in demographics, in inflationary expectations or in corporate profitability. In sharp contrast the biblical servant in the Parable of the Talents simply buried the talents (the money) in the ground and eventually returned them to his master. There was no expectation of return or reward. This was not investment. There are also important distinctions between the investor and the gambler:

i)   The gambler is prepared to lose all his stake in the pursuit of high and rapid rewards. The investor abhors the prospect of losing all his investment. For the investor it is essential to prevail and to meet his obligations or objectives.

ii)   Typically, when the gambler places his bet he is committed, unable to change his mind or withdraw. The investor will reserve the right to change his mind, to alter his position, perhaps withdraw his position altogether if economic, investment or business conditions change.

The speculator straddles the ground between the investor and the gambler. The speculator adopts a high-risk, short-term approach to investment in the pursuit of rapid gains. This appetite for risk and his short-term perspective distinguishes the speculator from the investor.

INVESTMENT RETURN

Components of Investment Return

There are three sources of investment return:

- investment income
- capital return
- currency return.

Investment Income

Investment income is the recurring payments receivable by an investor on his investment. Included in investment income are:

- interest on bank deposits
- interest on debt instruments (government securities, corporate bonds)
- dividends on ordinary shares (the annual payment made to shareholders out of profits by companies)
- rents on properties.

Investment income is the most reliable stream of investment return. It is recurring, forecastable and relatively stable. It normally grows over time as profits and dividends on ordinary shares and rents on property rise in response to rising economic activity. It is always positive, never negative.

Capital Return

The capital component of return refers to the appreciation or depreciation (rise or fall) in the value of the investment over time. The capital value of bank deposits is fixed. The capital value of the other investment assets – bonds, equities and property – fluctuates in response to changes in monetary, economic or business conditions. An improving investment environment – lower inflation, lower interest rates, better economic growth, better corporate profitability – will tend to boost capital growth and vice versa. The capital component of investment return is non-recurring, unreliable and difficult to predict and volatile. It may be positive or negative.

Currency Return

Where the investor invests only within his or her domestic country or currency bloc (e.g., an Irish investor who invests only in euro-denominated assets), he enjoys only the two streams of return discussed earlier – investment income and capital return. This investor is not exposed to currency gain or loss. Where the investor invests outside his domestic currency (e.g., an Irish investor who invests in sterling-denominated UK assets), he generates a third stream of return: currency gain or loss. The outcome here is dependent upon the performance of the external currency – in the example, sterling – against the domestic currency, the euro. If sterling rises against the euro, a currency gain results. The currency component of investment return is non-recurring, unreliable, difficult to predict and often volatile. It may be positive or negative.

Inflation

In providing a fund, through investment, to meet future obligations or liabilities the investor must account for inflation. Inflation means that the costs of education, healthcare and retirement will be higher in the future than they are today. The focus of the investor therefore, is on generating a real return on his investment i.e., an increase in the value of the investment after inflation has been allowed or accounted for.

Compound Interest

If inflation is the enemy of the investor, he or she has a powerful ally in compound interest. Compound interest generates a steady progression in the value of an investment over the long term. Assume an investor commits €1000 to an investment at a return of 4% per annum compound:

Table 6.1 The Power of Compound Interest

Opening Investment	€1000.00
After 1 year	€1040.00
After 2 years	€1081.60
After 5 years	€1216.65
After 10 years	€1480.24

The power of compound interest, of course, does not work on zero, reinforcing the investor's abhorrence of a permanent loss of capital, in contrast to the gambler's willingness to put all his bet at risk.

INVESTORS: DIFFERENT DRIVERS

Investors react in different ways to changes in the economic or investment environment. It is this difference in reaction that 'makes the market', with some investors wishing to buy and others wishing to sell in reaction to new information.

The reaction of investors to market developments is driven by:

i)   Their different liabilities
ii)   Their different time horizons
iii)   Their different requirements for income
iv)   Their different needs for protection against inflation
v)   Their different requirements to generate real returns above inflation
vi)   Their different base currencies
vii)   Their different requirements for liquidity
viii)   Their different tax and regulatory regimes to which they are subject
ix)   Their different exposures to transaction costs
And, finally but importantly:
x)   Their different attitudes to risk.

INVESTORS: COMMON CHARACTERISTICS

Investors are not a unique species, highly logical and cold-bloodedly rational. Like the rest of us, they are human beings and they share our emotional and physiological characteristics. Amongst those common characteristics which have implications for the manner in which investors approach investment are:

i)   *A tendency to stick with existing beliefs*
        Beliefs tend to be based on the degree to which information is available – media mentions, rumour, chat. We tend to overvalue data which supports our beliefs and underweight contrary information.

ii)   *Conservatism*
        Investors tend to be fearful of the unknown or the new. They prefer the familiar to the unfamiliar. They seek protection in the herd.

iii)   *Myopia*
        Investors tend to use horizons which are over-focused on the short term. Specifically, their tendency to extrapolate recent events into the future is a particular weakness.

iv)   *Hindsight*
        Investors are inclined to remember the occasions when they beat the market, but not their unsuccessful transactions. Winners are attributed

to their own skill and expertise, losers to poor advice. Past events always look inevitable after the event.

v)   *Loss Aversion*
      Investors, not unnaturally, hate to lose. They are heavily focused on book cost and will often defer for as long as possible the date of realisation of a loss. They sell winners too early, hold losers too long. Losses have a greater impact than gains of a similar magnitude.

vi)   *Excessive Optimism*
      Investors are inclined to be overconfident in their own or in analysts' forecasts. They often exaggerate their ability to control events and they tend to have excessively optimistic expectation of likely future long-term returns.

Investors, in their approach to investment, are complex. At times they may be contradictory and confusing. Their reactions to new information will depend on their different drivers, but also on their psychological characteristics. Their reactions are often unpredictable.

Risk Defined

The dictionary defines risk as 'hazard danger, exposure to mischance or peril'.

Investment, as a forward-looking activity, is concerned with the uncertain future. The uncertain future will include the possibility that events that are damaging to the financial well-being of the investor may occur. Investors will attempt to account for these uncertainties and to protect themselves against them in the investment strategies they develop. In the mid-1970s, for example, Irish investors were concerned with protecting their investments from the risk of sustained high inflation. In the late 1970s and early 80s, the weak state of the national finances and fears of financial collapse were a major concern for investors. In the early 1990s the focus was on currency devaluations. More recently, in sharp contrast to the situation of the mid-1970s, investors have been concerned that persistent disinflation might lurch into deflation.

Common Concepts of Risk

A survey of investors in the US showed that investors' attitudes to risk varied. The following concepts of risk emerged:

* Risk is the chance of losing some of my original investment.
* Risk is the chance that my investment will not keep pace with inflation.
* Risk is fluctuation in value.
* Risk is not having enough money to meet investment goals.

This last response is important, because it establishes a link between the riskiness of the investment and the consequences for the investor if investment objectives are not met.

The following definition of Investment Risk emerges:

> *'Investment risk is the likelihood of not having sufficient cash with which to make essential payments.'*

Investor Attitudes to Risk

Risk is subjective. The investor's time horizons, requirements and objectives will be key influences on his or her attitude to risk. A strategy which is entirely prudent for a long-term investor may be totally inappropriate for an investor with short-term time horizons. Risk is multi-faceted. For example, within a single pension fund the attitudes to risk of the different participants will vary. The employee will be concerned that the pension fund is properly invested, so that it will be in a position to pay his pension or retirement in ten or twenty years' time. The employer may have the additional concern that the fund's investments perform well in the short term, thus reducing employer contributions into the fund. Meanwhile, the investment manager of the fund's portfolio will attempt to meet the requirements of both employee and employer, while at the same time attempting to generate competitive returns to manage the risk of losing the client.

Investors' attitudes to risk are inconsistent. Investors may be more tolerant of taking a risk when attempting to avoid a loss than when trying to make a profit. The investor's recent experience can be a factor in his or her attitude to risk. If the most recent experience was satisfactory, the investor may take on more risk because, in a sense, he or she is playing with 'house money'. An unsuccessful recent experience may cause the investor to adopt a very cautious attitude to risk subsequently. Risk is therefore complex. Not only does it vary from investor to investor, but even for one single investor it will vary as his or her time horizons and objectives change and according to his or her purpose and recent experience.

Types of Risk

Investors are concerned with the uncertain future. Risk, therefore, is an ever-present and unavoidable feature of the investment process. No listing of types of risk can be comprehensive. Risk by its very nature is unpredictable and surprising. It catches us unawares. Unexpected events outside the boundaries of our previous experience occur. The financial markets are surprised, unsettled and shocked. Risk takes many forms. The following listing simply illustrates various types of risk encountered by investors in recent years. By definition other risks, not currently anticipated or discounted by financial markets, will shock and confuse us at some point in the future.

Systemic Risk

This is the risk of system-wide collapse: for example, the Japanese financial system in the 1990s. The collapse of a huge hedge fund, LTCM, in 1998 threatened the collapse of the US Treasury Bond market, the world's most liquid and most transparent market.

Specific Risk

This is overexposure to individual investments: for example, the unavoidable overexposure by Irish pension funds to leading Irish companies prior to the introduction of the euro. As soon as Ireland adopted the euro, pension funds moved to reduce this risk by diversifying their Irish equities across euro-denominated equity markets.

Currency Risk

This risk is that of exposure to currency loss, e.g., the sterling devaluation of 1992 and the Asian currency crisis of 1998.

Counterparty Risk

The risk of collapse of a counterparty, i.e., a bank or stockbroker. Even when the investor may be protected by government guarantee or compensation scheme from eventual loss, the inability to access cash or securities may cause financial difficulties.

Default Risk

The risk that the issuer of a bond may default on its obligation to pay interest or reply capital. For example, the default by Russia on its domestic debt in 1998.

Credit Risk

Credit risk is the additional risk taken on by the investor in the search for higher returns when investing in a corporate bond rather than a government bond. If the credit rating of the issuer disimproves, the bond value will suffer: for example, the downgrading of General Motors' debt in 2005.

Market Risk

This is the unavoidable exposure to the uncertainty of the market, and is the uncertainty that the investor must embrace in the search for higher returns. The other types of risk may be diversified away. The investor has to live with market risk.

Risk Measurement: Volatility

The discussion so far has emphasised the multi-faceted nature of investment risk. It may therefore come as a surprise to learn that nowadays investment theory and practice focus on quite a narrow, albeit all-embracing, concept of risk. This concept of risk is built upon work carried out by a statistician, Dr Harry Markowitz, in the 1950s. Markowitz defined risk as volatility or fluctuation in prices, as indeed did some of the respondents to the survey discussed above. He further concluded that, by using Normal Distributions and Standard Deviations, the spread of returns on an asset around their average could be measured and quantified.

Therefore, for the first time, there were now available hard numbers to measure the two elements of investment: return numbers, which had long been available, and now risk numbers based on volatility. Investors could address both risk and return in a quantified way and examine the trade-offs between them. Markowitz's insights, together with the availability of greatly improved computing power, enabled us to prove some of the basic concepts which heretofore we had instinctively understood:

- Diversification controls risk.
- The higher the expected return, the higher the risk.

Markowitz's insights were key building blocks in the development of a more scientific and sophisticated approach to investment management. Volatility as a measure of risk has the attraction that we instinctively feel that uncertainty should be associated with something whose value jumps around a lot over a wide range. However, volatility has some inherent limitations; it is not a comprehensive measure of risk. Using data from the past can be dangerous; forecasting the future is unreliable. Importantly, volatility is an asset-based measure. It tells us nothing about the consequences for the investor of fluctuations in values.

Nevertheless, despite these limitations, volatility has become the standard measure of risk in the investment business today and has wide application in portfolio construction.

INVESTMENT OBJECTIVES AND RISK

It is clear from the discussion so far that risk is an integral part of investment. Investment is a two-handed process; it is about risk and return. Investment objectives, therefore, must embrace both the risk and return dimensions of investment. A single-minded focus on return alone is insufficient. Investment is not about the maximisation of returns, getting the best possible return. Investment, rather, is about the optimisation of returns, the maximisation of returns subject to an acceptable or appropriate level of risk.

In the next section we set out the key building blocks of the Markowitz approach to measuring risk and to constructing diversified investment portfolios.

CALCULATING EXPECTED RETURNS AND RISK

In analysing investment opportunities investors need to think explicitly about a security's distribution of probable returns. By assuming that the distribution of these potential returns is a normal distribution, investors can benefit from the statistical properties of the normal distribution. The normal distribution is a cornerstone of modern portfolio theory, although it is important to recognise that the actual distribution of a security's returns may not be normal. Active institutional investors and hedge-fund managers who use sophisticated mathematical models carry out ongoing analysis of the pattern of security returns. Such studies have shown that it is often the case that the pattern of returns is not normal. For example, the one-day fall on 19 October 1987 in the US stock market was an event that supposedly had a tiny statistical probability of occurring. The statistical models would have predicted that such an event should occur only once in several hundred years. There have in fact been many more instances of these extreme events in investment markets than would be predicted by the normal distribution. While there are some caveats, the key advantage of the normal distribution is that it is a two-parameter distribution that is fully described by the mean and the variance (or standard deviation). For any security we can calculate its expected return, which is the single most likely outcome for its particular distribution. It is extremely difficult to predict the future probability distributions of returns for securities. In practice we rely on historical data to provide us with an estimate of these future returns.

Table 6.2 Calculation of Expected Return and Standard Deviation for ABC plc

Observations (1)	Returns (R$_i$) (2)	Probability (one in five for each) (PR$_i$) (3)	Weighted Returns (2*3) (4)	(R$_i$-ER) (5)	(R$_i$-ER)^2 (6)	(R$_i$-ER)^{2}pr$_i$ (7)
20%	.20	.2	.04	.116	.01346	.002692
-2%	-.02	.2	-.004	-.104	.01082	.002164
10%	.10	.2	.02	.016	.00026	.000052
8%	.08	.2	.016	-.004	.00002	.000004
6%	.06	.2	.012	-.024	.00058	.000116
		= 1.0	=.084(ER)			=.009724 (Variance)

Standard Deviation = $(.009724)^{1/2}$
=.0986

Table 6.2 gives a detailed example of the mechanics of calculating the expected return and variance/standard deviation based on historical data. We are given return information for ABC plc for the past five years and from these we can readily calculate the average annual return by summing each return and dividing by the number of years. This gives an average annual return of 8.4%. We can also consider the data in terms of a probability distribution, which enables us to calculate the expected return as well as other statistical measures such as variance and standard deviation. In this example we have in effect assumed that each annual return has an equal probability of occurring in the future. Columns 2–4 calculate the expected return based on this probability distribution using the formula:

$$E(R) = \sum_{i=1}^{n} R_i \, pr_i$$

where:

E(R)	=	the expected return on a security
R$_i$	=	the return in period i
pr$_i$	=	the probability of ith return
n	=	number of possible (or historical) returns.

We can see that the probabilities sum to 1.0 and the expected return is .084 or 8.4%. Columns 5–7 calculate the variance of returns, from which we can calculate the standard deviation which computes to .0986 or 9.86% based on the formulae:

$$\text{Variance of returns} = \sigma^2 = \sum_{i=1}^{n} [R_i - E(R)]^2 \, pr_i$$

$$\text{Standard Deviation} \quad \sigma = \sqrt{\sigma^2}$$

We can now use this information to generate a picture of the range of likely future returns. In doing this we are assuming that the patterns of the past, as represented by these statistical measures, will be repeated in the future. Using the statistical information that we have calculated for ABC plc, Figure 6.1 shows how we can use the standard deviation (SD) of returns to generate a picture of what we can say about the future.

Figure 6.1 Expected Returns for ABC plc

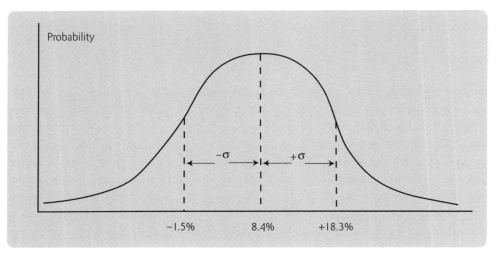

Now we see that two-thirds of the time we can expect the annual return from ABC plc to lie within a range of −1.5% to +18.3%, which is given by the E(R) +/− 1SD. If we expand the range of returns to E(R) +/− 2SD, we can be confident that returns will lie within this range 95% of the time. Even at one SD, the range of returns is wide and highlights how difficult it is to forecast point estimates of security returns with any degree of accuracy. However, the key application of this statistical approach is not in predicting future returns, but in creating a framework for making rational investment decisions.

Figure 6.2 The Risk-Averse Investor

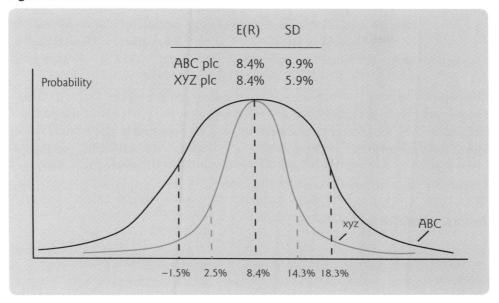

	E(R)	SD
ABC plc	8.4%	9.9%
XYZ plc	8.4%	5.9%

Figure 6.2 illustrates a key assumption that underlies portfolio theory, namely that investors are risk-averse. On the basis of the historical return information available for another stock – XYZ plc – we now have return/risk information for two stocks. The same analysis as applied to ABC results in finding that XYZ has an E(R) of 8.4%, the same as ABC's, but it has a lower SD of 5.9%. Armed with this information we can forecast next year's return for XYZ as lying within a range of +2.5% to +14.3%, with a 66% chance of being correct. This is a much narrower range than that for ABC as is illustrated in Figure 6.2. Both companies have the same E(R) but XYZ is the lower-risk investment. Investment theory states that investors are risk-averse and therefore they will always choose XYZ over ABC. In a rational investment world investors will take on the higher-risk ABC only if its expected return is greater than XYZ's. In a well-functioning market investors would sell ABC's shares, thus driving down the price and increasing its E(R) to the point where it offers a return that compensates investors for its higher risk level.

Portfolio Return and Risk

The approach described above for assessing individual securities can also be applied to portfolios. The E(R) and SD may be calculated for any portfolio of securities, and this information can then be used to compare the relative investment merits of various portfolios. The E(R) of a portfolio is the weighted average of the E(R) of the portfolio constituents.

Table 6.3 Calculation of Portfolio Expected Return and Standard Deviation

	Investment €	Portfolio Weights	E(R)	Standard Deviation	Weighted Portfolio Return
	(1)	(2)	(3)	(4)	(2)*(3)
CRH	5,000	.5	.11 (11%)	.12	.055
AIB	2,500	.25	.10 (10%)	.10	.025
Ryanair	2,500	.25	.12 (12%)	.15	.030
	10,000	1.00			=.110 (11%)

Imagine that you have invested €10,000 in three companies as set out in Table 6.3 and the expected portfolio return is 11%. Algebraically, the E(R) for any portfolio is:

$$E(Rp) = \sum_{i=1}^{n} W_i \, E(R_i)$$

where: $E(Rp)$ = expected return of the portfolio
W_i = portfolio weight of ith security
$\sum W_i$ = 1.0
$E(R_i)$ = expected return of ith security
n = number of securities in the portfolio.

The calculation of portfolio return is therefore relatively straightforward and, irrespective of the number of securities and their respective weights, it is calculated as the weighted average of those security expected returns.

Calculating Portfolio Risk

In Table 6.3 we are also given information about the SD of Ryanair, CRH and AIB, respectively. We could try to estimate the SD of the portfolio as the weighted average of the portfolio constituents, but this would in fact be incorrect. This is because there is another dimension that must be taken into account when calculating portfolio variance or standard deviation. This dimension revolves around the extent to which the individual stock returns move in tandem with one another, or otherwise. For example, if we find that Ryanair performs well when CRH and AIB perform poorly, we would expect this to dampen down the volatility of the portfolio. On the other hand, if the patterns of returns for the three companies were exactly the same, then the volatility of the portfolio would be equal to the weighted average of the SDs of the three stocks. Therefore, the interrelationships between the stocks that make up a portfolio can reduce portfolio volatility.

Random Diversification

Investors have intuitively known for years that spreading investments across a range of securities reduces risk. Random or naive diversification refers to the act of randomly diversifying without regard to investment characteristics such as expected return and risk. An investor adds to his portfolio by simply randomly adding stocks to it. The good news is that in fact this will substantially reduce portfolio risk with a relatively small number of holdings. Figure 6.3 illustrates how portfolio risk declines very rapidly as the portfolio expands from one stock to several stocks.

Figure 6.3 Random Diversification

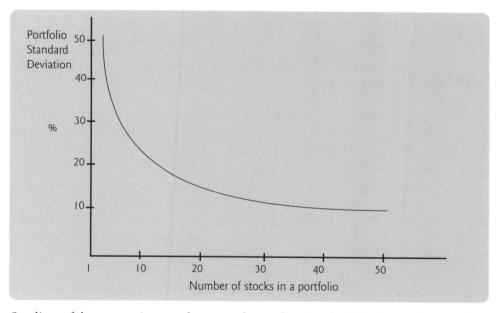

Studies of large equity markets, such as that in the US, have shown that approximately 50% of portfolio standard deviation is eliminated with as few as ten stocks, randomly selected. However, as more stocks are added the marginal portfolio risk reduction becomes smaller and smaller. In fact most of the diversification benefits are achieved when a portfolio consists of approximately 30 stocks. Such a portfolio will then have a level of risk that is quite close to that of the overall equity market. Studies of the US equity market have shown that this risk level equates to an annual standard deviation of approximately 20%.

Efficient Diversification

Markowitz's statistical analysis enabled investment theory, and eventually investment practice, to move forward by advancing our understanding of the true nature of portfolio risk. As we saw earlier, Markowitz's analysis distilled the key investment characteristics of any security into two variables – expected return and SD (a measure of risk). The investment characteristics of portfolios may also be described by these two variables. However, to calculate portfolio SD one additional piece of statistical information needs to be gathered. This additional variable measures the interrelationship between the securities that make up a portfolio. The covariance between two securities is a statistical measure that quantifies this interrelationship. An adjustment is often made to this to give the correlation coefficient between two securities, which is a statistical measure of the relative co-movements between security returns. It is bounded by +1.0 and –1.0, making it relatively easy to interpret. If we have two securities A and B, the correlation coefficient may be written as ρ_{AB} (ρ pronounced 'rho').

ρ_{AB} = +1.0 = perfect positive correlation
ρ_{AB} = −1.0 = perfect negative (inverse) correlation
ρ_{AB} = 0.0 = zero correlation.

With perfect positive correlation, the returns of A and B have a perfect, direct linear relationship. In other words, stocks A and B have identical return patterns. Combining these two securities into a portfolio will result in NO diversification benefits whatsoever. With perfect negative correlation, securities A and B have a perfect inverse relationship with one another. When A's return is high, B's is low and vice versa. Now combining these securities into a portfolio will eliminate risk completely. With zero correlation there is no relationship between the security returns. In this case there is statistical independence and combining the two securities will lead to a significant reduction in risk.

In the real world, returns from securities are rarely zero or negatively correlated. For example, a sharp rise in interest rates will tend to cause bond prices to fall and will dampen the share prices of most companies. Therefore, the correlation coefficient between two equities quoted on the same stock exchange will usually be much higher than zero. In fact studies have shown that the value of the correlation coefficient between pairs of stocks quoted on the same market has a value of approximately 0.5. This is sufficiently far away from a value of 1.0 to deliver diversification benefits to equity portfolios. The correlation coefficient between stocks in the same sector would be higher again. For example, in the Irish market we would expect Bank of Ireland and AIB to have a higher correlation coefficient than Bank of Ireland and Ryanair. However, in all cases we would expect the correlation coefficients to be significantly less than 1.0. The calculation of portfolio risk must take account of the interrelationship between each pair of securities. In the case of a two-security portfolio the formula for measuring portfolio risk is:

$$\text{Portfolio Risk} = \sigma_p = \left[W_A^2\sigma_A^2 + W_B^2\sigma_B^2 + 2(W_A)(W_B)(P_{A.B})\sigma_A\sigma_B \right]^{1/2}$$

When we are dealing with a small number of securities Markowitz mean-variance analysis can be applied with relative ease, always remembering that usually the values are based on the assumption that the historical data provides a good guide to the future. However, the model becomes very complex for a large number of securities because of the large number of covariances that have to be calculated. If the model has to deal with 250 securities, the number of unique covariances will be 31,115! Irrespective of the availability of computing power, analysts are unlikely to be able to directly estimate such a large number of correlations. To get over this problem Markowitz suggested using an index to which securities are related as a means of reducing the number of covariances required.

One of Markowitz's key contributions to portfolio theory is his insight about the relative importance of the variances and covariances. If the number of securities in a portfolio is large, the contribution of each security's own risk to total portfolio risk will be small. In fact the covariances between securities will have a greater impact on portfolio risk.

Efficient Portfolios

Markowitz's approach led investors to focus on the trade-off betweeen risk and return and led to the concept of the *efficient portfolio*, which is defined as that portfolio that has the smallest risk for a given level of expected

Figure 6.4 The Efficient Frontier

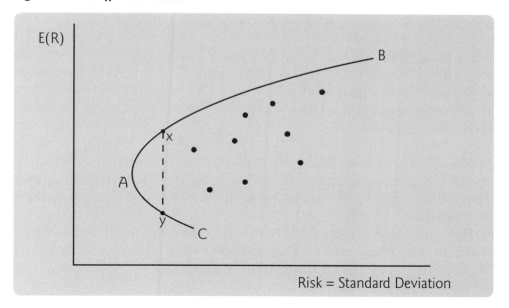

return, or the largest expected return for a given level of risk. First we need to list the possible portfolios that can be derived from a given set of securities. Figure 6.4 illustrates the opportunities available, which we can see are very numerous.

Only those portfolios that lie on the line segment AB – the efficient frontier – need to be considered. The reason for this may be illustrated by examining the portfolio at point X compared with point Y. Investors will *always* choose X over Y because X offers a higher expected return for the same amount of risk as Y. This is true for every portfolio on the curve AB. We can say that any portfolio on the curve segment AB is preferable to any portfolio below the curve. Portfolios above this curve are unattainable.

CONCLUDING COMMENTS

Markowitz's contribution to investment theory and portfolio management is enormous. As a result of his insights the business of asset management has become more quantitative and scientific. The importance of the conceptual link between risk and return is now at the forefront of the mind of even the novice investor. Risk is no longer a fate before which we are powerless, but has become a choice, rather than a fate. We can manage risk, deal with it, shape and engineer it. We can now use risk to construct portfolios, aiming to maximise return whilst minimising risk. Central to investment is the construction of efficient portfolios, which are designed to deliver the highest expected return for any given level of risk, or the lowest level of risk for any given expected return.

Diversification is the key to controlling risk. Granny was right: 'Don't put all your eggs in one basket.' Portfolios may be diversified:

- across asset types (bonds, equities, property, cash)
- across currencies (euro, sterling, dollar, yen)
- across regions or countries
- across industrial or market sectors
- across a range of securities.

Markowitz, with his hard numbers, confirmed our instinctive understanding that diversification reduces risk. He went further: by establishing that investors can achieve an optimum position by efficiently diversifying their investments.

The next chapter provides a more detailed analysis of Markowitz's portfolio theory, and also presents the best-known capital market theory, namely the Capital Asset Pricing Model (CAPM).

SUMMARY

- An investor makes a commitment of resources in expectation of future reward.
- Understanding the requirements and characteristics of investors is the first step in formulating investment strategy.
- Investment is a two-handed process; it is about risk and returns.
- Investment risk is the likelihood of not having sufficient cash with which to make essential payments.
- Markowitz defined risk as volatility and measured it in hard numbers using normal distributions and standard deviations.
- The return of a portfolio is the weighted average of the expected return of the securities in the portfolio.
- Markowitz demonstrated that the risk of a portfolio is not, however, the weighted average of the risk of the securities in the portfolio, but is affected by the covariance or the correlation between the securities in the portfolio. The lower the correlation, the lower the risk.
- Markowitz demonstrated that diversification controls risk.
- Markowitz led investors to the concept of the efficient portfolio, that portfolio which has the smallest risk for a given level of expected return or the largest expected return for a given level of risk.
- Efficient portfolios sit on Markowitz's efficient frontier.

QUESTIONS

1. **With regard to total risk, which of the following statement(s) is/are TRUE?**

   A. Market risk is part of total risk.
   B. Market risk is not diversifiable.
   C. Systematic risk is also called market risk.

   1. All of the above
   2. None of the above
   3. A & B only
   4. A & C only

2. **Please select the TRUE statement(s):**

   A. Realised returns help investors form expected future returns.
   B. Realised returns help investors assess the performance of their portfolios.

   ➡

C. A probability distribution contains a set of likely outcomes and their associated probabilities.
D. The sum of these probabilities equals 1.

   1. A, B & C only
   2. All of the above
   3. B, C & D only
   4. C & D only

3. Which statement(s) is/are FALSE regarding diversification?

A. Random diversification chooses only securities with positive dividend yields
B. Random diversification can completely eliminate market risk.
C. As the number of securities held in a portfolio increases, the marginal benefit of diversification significantly decreases.
D. A large number of securities (at least 100) are required to achieve substantial diversification benefits.

   1. None of the above
   2. A, B & C
   3. A, B & D
   4. B & D

4. Which statement(s) is/are TRUE regarding portfolio risk?

A. Portfolio risk takes only individual security risk into consideration.
B. Portfolio risk takes only covariance between securities into consideration.
C. Portfolio risk takes both individual security risk and covariance between securities into consideration.
D. Portfolio risk is totally independent from the investment weight of the securities held in a portfolio.

5. Markowitz defines an efficient portfolio as one that:

A. Has the smallest risk for a given level of expected return.
B. Has the smallest expected return for all levels of risk.
C. Has the largest expected return for a given level of risk.
D. Has the largest expected return and zero risk.

   1. A & B only
   2. A & C only
   3. A, B & C only
   4. A only

Chapter seven

Portfolio Theory

In Chapter 6 we discussed investment risk, and the important concept of Markowitz diversification was introduced. This chapter explores Markowitz diversification further and shows how a concept such as the correlation coefficient can be used to construct portfolios. The concept of the efficient frontier is discussed and the impact on the efficient frontier of introducing a risk-free asset is explored. The separation theorem is also discussed. Building on this analysis, the capital asset pricing model (CAPM) is introduced. The capital market line and the security market line are described and discussed.

Learning Objectives

After reading this chapter you will:

- Understand the Markowitz approach to portfolio construction
- Understand how portfolio return and risk are calculated
- Be aware of the importance to portfolio risk of the covariance or correlation between pairs of securities
- Understand the concept of the efficient frontier
- Be aware of how indifference curve analysis can be applied to show how individual investor preferences interact with the efficient frontier
- Understand the concept of the optimal portfolio
- Be aware of how the single-index model offers a simpler way of establishing the efficient frontier
- Be able to distinguish between market risk and unique risk
- Have developed an understanding of how the introduction of the risk-free asset expands the efficient frontier
- Understand how capital market theory builds on Markowitz portfolio theory to explain how share prices are set in equilibrium.

The final chapter in the book presents information on the historical returns delivered by the various asset categories. These realised returns provide the historical data on which measures of risk such as standard deviation can be calculated. However, when constructing portfolios our concern is with expected returns – in an uncertain world we know that future returns are subject to a wide range of possible outcomes. In Chapter 6 the basic principles underlying the analysis of portfolio risk and return were explored. There we saw that for the purpose of portfolio construction all investment assets can be characterised by just two variables – expected returns and estimated standard deviations of returns.

Before moving on to the selection of optimal portfolios we first recap and extend our analysis of the Markowitz equations first introduced in chapter 6.

The expected return on any portfolio E(Rp) can be calculated as:

$$E(Rp) = \sum_{i=1}^{n} W_i E(R_i)$$

[Equation 7.1]

where: E(Rp)   = expected portfolio return
        W_i = portfolio weight for i^{th} security
        $W(R_i)$ = expected return on i^{th} security
        n   = number of securities in the portfolio.

Note: $$\sum_{i=1}^{n} W_i = 1.0$$

Calculating portfolio risk is not quite so straightforward and symbolically we have:

$$\sigma p^2 \neq \sum_{i=1}^{n} W_i \sigma_i^2$$

[Equation 7.2]

where: σp^2 = portfolio variance
        σ_i^2 = variance of ith security
        W_i = portfolio weight for i^{th} security.

We saw above that the calculation of portfolio return is determined by two variables:

i)   the expected return of each security
ii)   the weight of each security within the portfolio.

To calculate portfolio risk we need to add one more variable: namely the interrelationship between each pair of securities within the portfolio. This is measured by the covariance or the correlation coefficient. These concepts were introduced in Chapter 6 and here we explore them in more detail.

Covariance and Correlation Coefficient

The covariance is an absolute measure of the degree of association between returns for a pair of securities, and we will express it as:

COV_{AB} = the covariance between the securities A and B.

The actual absolute value of the covariance is not easy to interpret and hence the correlation coefficient (ρ_{AB}) is usually used to assess how interdependent the returns are between two securities. The correlation coefficient and covariance are related as follows:

$$\text{Correlation Coefficient} = \rho_{AB} = \frac{COV_{AB}}{\sigma_A \, \sigma_B}$$

[Equation 7.3]

where σ_A, σ_B are the standard deviations of securities A and B, respectively.

This states that the correlation coefficient is the covariance standardised by dividing it by the product of the standard deviations of A and B respectively. The correlation coefficient is a relative measure of association that lies between +1 (perfect positive correlation) and –1 (perfect negative correlation). If we could find pairs of securities that are negatively correlated, it would enable us to reduce portfolio risk to extremely low levels. In the real world this rarely occurs and we normally find that the correlation coefficients among securities usually lies between 0 and +1. For example, if I decide to invest in just two quoted Irish companies, I would ideally like to find two companies with a very low (or negative) correlation coefficient. What I will find is that the typical value of the correlation coefficient between pairs of securities quoted on the same stock exchange will be approximately 0.5. This is because all stocks on (say) the Irish exchange are affected by many of the same variables such as interest rates, the performance of the Irish economy, the impact of the monetary policy of the European Central Bank, etc. Nevertheless, a correlation coefficient of +0.5 is still far enough below a value of +1.0 to deliver significant diversification benefits. In other words, it should in general be possible to combine stocks in such a way as to reduce risk without adversely affecting expected returns.

Calculating Portfolio Risk

Applying the basic Markowitz approach to portfolio construction is complex, and where many securities are involved it is extremely cumbersome. First, let's consider the case of just two securities, A and B. The risk of the portfolio consisting of these two securities is given by the equation:

$$\sigma_P = \left[W_A^2 \, \sigma_A^2 + W_B^2 \, \sigma_B^2 + 2 \, (W_A)(W_B)(COV_{AB}) \, \sigma_A \sigma_B \right]^{1/2}$$

[Equation 7.4]

This equation states that the risk of the portfolio is determined by the sum of the variances of A and B multiplied by their respective portfolio weights (squared), plus a second term consisting of the covariance between A and B, and the portfolio weights and standard deviations of A and B respectively. The risk of the portfolio, as measured by its standard deviation, will be lowered as the covariance reduces or as the correlation coefficient moves downward from +1.0. Therefore, in this simplified two-security case, portfolio risk depends upon the interplay of:

- the risk of each security
- the portfolio weights assigned to each security
- the covariance or correlation between the two securities.

Extending the Analysis to Many Securities

This two-security case can be generalised to many securities and the same mathematical principles will apply. Therefore, portfolio risk can be reduced by combining assets with correlations of less than +1.0, and the smaller the positive correlation the better. The big problem in applying this technique is the exponential rate of increase in the number of covariances as the number of securities is extended. In the case of two securities there are just three variance–covariance numbers, the variances of A and B and the COV_{AB}. The number of covariances grows quickly based on the calculation that there are:

$$[n(n-1)] / 2$$

unique covariances.

With four securities, the number of covariances jumps to six. With ten securities, the number jumps to 45. An investment analyst with a list of 100 securities to choose from must estimate 4,950 unique covariances. As well as the sheer computing power required to calculate these covariances, analysts must decide on what raw data to use. Historical returns are usually used to estimate expected returns, variance, etc., but appropriate data may not be available for all the securities being considered.

Efficient Portfolios

Setting aside the practical issues of estimation and calculation, Markowitz's approach to portfolio selection assumes that all investors evaluate portfolios based on their expected return and risk. Markowitz portfolio theory is based on a small set of assumptions that include:

- a single investment period, usually a year
- no transactions costs and no taxes
- investors base their preferences only on a portfolio's return and risk, as measured by variance or standard deviation.

In Chapter 6 we discussed the concept of efficient portfolios and assuming that we have calculated the efficient set of portfolios (the efficient frontier), we must then select the portfolio most appropriate to us from the efficient frontier. Markowitz's model does not select this optimal portfolio; rather, it produces a range of optimal portfolios from which investors make their choice. The key assumption that investors are risk-averse provides a mechanism

Figure 7.1 Indifference Curves

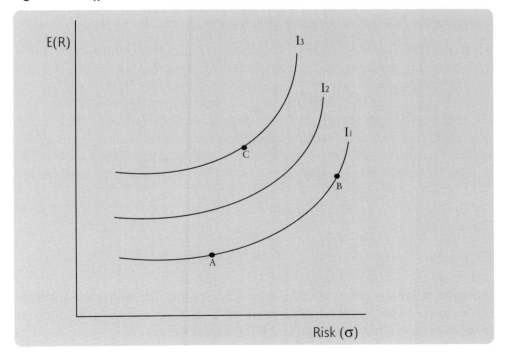

for choosing each individual investor's optimal portfolio. Investors have different attitudes to risk and these preferences can be expressed in the form of indifference curves, which should be familiar to students of economics. A set of indifference curves is shown in Figure 7.1 and each curve represents the set of portfolios that are equally desirable to an investor.

If we think of an investment portfolio in terms of delivering a certain amount of 'wealth satisfaction', then each of portfolios A and B delivers the same amount of satisfaction to this particular investor. Portfolio B has a higher return and higher risk than A, but the investor is indifferent between both. Portfolio C is preferable to both A and B because it is on a higher indifference curve. For risk-averse investors the curve will always be upward sloping, but the shape will vary depending on the differing risk preferences of investors. An investor will choose the portfolio that places him on the highest attainable indifference curve. This occurs at point P in Figure 7.2, which is the portfolio that enables the investor to reach indifference curve I_2.

Figure 7.2 Indifference Curves and the Efficient Frontier

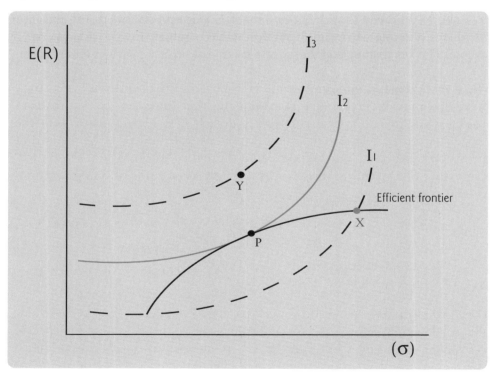

Portfolio X on the efficient frontier is inferior to P, as it leaves the investor on the lower indifference curve I_1. Portfolio Y on I_3 is superior to both P and X, but is unattainable as it is above the efficient frontier.

The Single-Index Model

An alternative and simpler method of obtaining the efficient frontier was developed by William Sharpe. This single-index model relates returns on each security to the returns on a common index. In America this common index may be the S&P 500 index. In Ireland it may be the ISEQ Overall index or a broader European index that includes stocks across Europe, such as the FTSE E300 index. The key advantage of the single-index model is that it reduces dramatically the number of calculations required, because we do not need to calculate the relationship between all pairs of securities being considered. Instead we define each security in terms of its relationship with the market (as measured by the relevant index). The equation for the single-index model is:

$$R_i = \alpha_i + \beta_i R_m + e_i$$

[Equation 7.5]

where: R_i = return on security i
R_m = return on the market index
α_i = that part of security i's return that is independent of market performance
β_i = a constant that measures the expected change in R_i, given a change in R_m
e_i = random residual error.

The β (beta) term is very important as it measures the sensitivity of a stock to market movements. If $\beta_i = 1$, it indicates that the expected return from stock i will equal that of the market index. If $\beta_i < 1$, it indicates that the expected return is less than that for the market; and $\beta_i > 1$ means that the stock's expected return is greater than the expected market return. Remember that in this model returns are framed in terms of a single period, usually one year.

The single-index model divides the returns from a security into two components:

i)   a market-related component represented by $\beta_i R_m$
ii)   a unique component represented by α_i.

The third term in the equation is the error term, which has an expected value of zero. The unique or stock-specific component depends on factors specific to the company in question. Such factors would include the successful launch of a new product, a sudden unexpected event such as a crash for an airline company, etc. For example, the share price of the Irish drinks company C&C performed very strongly in 2005 owing to the successful roll-out of its cider brands in the British market. This was an event that was clearly unique to

C&C, affecting only its share price. Market-related events are ones that affect all businesses and would include a change in interest rates, a change in the rate of corporation tax, or a sudden unexpected event such as a terrorist attack. As well as splitting the expected return into two components, the single-index model also splits risk into the same two components. The total risk for a security thus splits into market risk and stock-specific or unique risk:

$$\sigma_i^2 = \beta_i^2 \left[\sigma_m^2 \right] + \sigma_{ei}^2$$

[Equation 7.6]

Stock Risk = Market Risk + Unique Risk

Unique risk can be eliminated through the construction of a diversified portfolio – leaving market risk, which cannot be reduced. The single-index model makes two important simplifying assumptions:

i)   It assumes that the market index (R_m) is unrelated to the residual error (e_i).

ii)   It assumes that the residual errors between pairs of securities are unrelated to one another. More formally, this is expressed as Cov(e_i, e_j) = 0, for securities i and j.

The upshot of these simplifying assumptions is that the only common influence on each security is the market index. All other factors are random. This now means that the covariance between any two securities (i and j) can now be calculated from their respective betas and the variance of the market:

$$COV_{i,j} = \beta_i \, \beta_j \, \sigma_m^2$$

[Equation 7.7]

This greatly simplifies the task of calculating risk values for securities and portfolios.

Using The Markowitz Model

For the selection of portfolios consisting of individual securities, the basic Markowitz model is very cumbersome. The single-index model is far more practical when applying the model to the selection of portfolios of individual securities. However, the basic model can be applied more readily to the task of asset allocation, where investors are choosing from a limited set of asset categories. For an Irish-based investor such a list could include:

• Eurozone equities
• Eurozone government bonds

- US equities
- Emerging-markets equities
- US Treasuries
- Japanese bonds.

The first step is to decide on an appropriate index for each asset class. Historical data on each of these asset classes is readily available, so that the return and risk parameters for each index can be calculated. Given the relatively small number of assets, a variance/covariance matrix can be generated and the efficient frontier can be calculated. An investor can then decide on the weights for each category depending on their own risk preferences.

Introducing the Risk-Free Asset

The Markowitz analysis involves establishing the efficient frontier based on risky assets. However, investors in most markets have the option of investing in risk-free assets such as short-term government bonds or bills. Introducing the risk-free asset into the Markowitz world leads to some very interesting developments. First, we can define the risk-free asset in terms of expected return and variance. There is certainty about its expected return and consequently the variance of this return is zero. More interestingly, the risk-free asset will have a correlation coefficient of zero with all risky assets. Intuitively, most investors know that cash or near-cash instruments are a good way to protect a portfolio in falling markets. More formally we can see this from the equation that describes the relationship between the covariance and correlation coefficient:

$$COV_{RF, i} = \rho_{RF, i} \, \sigma_i \, \sigma_{RF}$$
$$= \rho_{RF, i} \, (0) = 0$$

[Equation 7.8]

where: $COV_{RF, i}$ = covariance between the risk-free asset and security i
$\rho_{RF, i}$ = correlation coefficient between the risk-free asset and security i
σ_i = standard deviation of i
σ_{RF} = standard eviation of risk-free asset = 0.

One of the key insights of Markowitz portfolio theory was the identification of the relative importance of the covariances (or correlations) between securities. Applying the theory to the practicalities of portfolio construction means that investors seek pairs of securities with correlation coefficients of well below one. The correlations between the securities that make up the portfolio will have a greater impact on portfolio risk than will the size of the variance (or standard deviation) of each individual security. Therefore, a portfolio consisting of mainly very high-risk securities could have a relatively low portfolio risk, as long as the correlations between the securities were very low or negative.

As we noted earlier, the correlation coefficients between stocks will often be approximately 0.5. Yet the risk-free asset has the very desirable attribute of a correlation coefficient of zero with all risky assets! Viewed in this light it is perhaps not surprising to find that introducing the risk-free asset to the Markowitz efficient frontier radically alters that efficient frontier. In effect it expands the frontier as illustrated in Figure 7.3.

Figure 7.3 The Risk-Free Asset Expands the Efficient Frontier

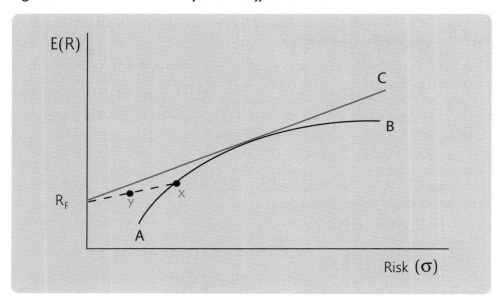

Remember that the efficient frontier consists of those portfolios that deliver the highest E(R) for a particular risk level, or the lowest risk level for a given E(R). The curve AB is the efficient frontier calculated on the basis of Markowitz covariance/variance analysis. R_F has a SD = 0 and a certain E(R) and is therefore represented at point R_F on the chart. Investors can now combine this risk-free asset with any risky portfolio on the efficient frontier. Let's assume that an investor picks portfolio X on the efficient frontier and creates a new portfolio with (say) 90% in portfolio X and 10% in R_F. The new portfolio is represented by Y on the chart. As usual, the E(R) for the new portfolio will be the weighted average return of R_F and portfolio X. If we are given values for the relevant variables, we can calculate the E(R) and standard deviation for the portfolio:

Given: R_F = 3% ; $ER(P_X)$ = 20% ; σ_X = 20%

[Equation 7.9]

$$ER(P_y) = W_{RF} R_F + (1 - W_{RF}) ER(P_X)$$
$$= (.1)(.03) + (.9)(.20) = .183 \text{ or } 18.3\%$$

Because there is zero correlation between R_F and P_X, the calculation for the standard deviation of the new portfolio simplifies to:

$$\sigma_y = (1 - W_{RF}) \sigma_X$$
$$= (.9)(.20) = .18 \text{ or } 18\%$$

[Equation 7.10]

In this case the covariance term becomes zero, because the standard deviation of the risk-free asset is zero. Therefore the standard deviation of any new portfolio combining the risk-free asset with any risky portfolio is the standard deviation of the risky portfolio weighted by its share of the new portfolio. In the example above, 90% of available assets are committed to this risky portfolio which has an SD of 20% and therefore the SD of the new portfolio is (.9)(20%) = 18%.

In this new situation, what will an investor do? Bear in mind that an investor will always seek to get onto the highest possible indifference curve. First, we need to establish the new efficient frontier, now that the risk-free asset is an option. We can choose a variety of portfolios on the original efficient frontier (AB) to give us a wide range of possibilities. Each one can be represented by a straight line from R_F to a point on the efficient frontier, such as (R_FX). However, we will find one line that is preferable to all others, which is the line R_F C on the chart. To see why this is so, look at portfolio (Y) in Figure 7.4.

Figure 7.4 The New Efficient Frontier

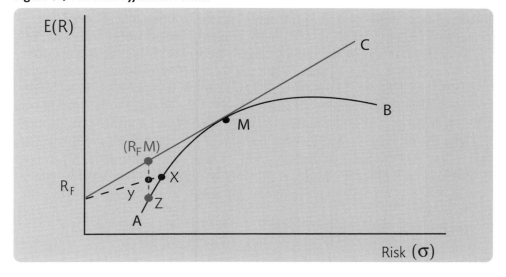

This portfolio is better than portfolio (Z) on the efficient frontier because it delivers a higher return for the same level of risk. However, it in turn is not as good as portfolio (R_FM) on the line R_FC, because this portfolio delivers a higher E(R) than Y, but with the same level of risk. What we find is that the line that is tangential to the curve AB becomes the new efficient frontier. The implication of this is that all investors will choose just one risky portfolio (M), which we will refer to as the market portfolio, and combine that with varying proportions of the risk-free asset. Therefore, an investor with indifference curves I_1, I_2 (Figure 7.5) will choose portfolio (R_FM)

Figure 7.5 The Market Portfolio and the Risk-Free Asset

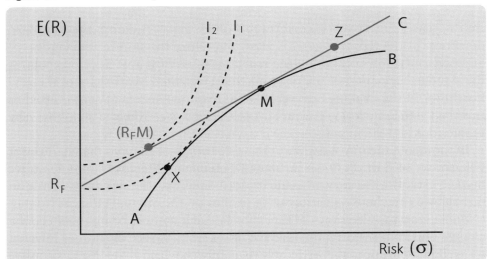

Without the risk-free asset this investor would choose portfolio (X) on the original efficient frontier AB, which is on a lower indifference curve I_1. The line R_FM now replaces AM as the new efficient frontier, where every point is preferable to every point on AM. In this model investors now have only one decision to make – how to split their assets between M, the market portfolio, and the risk-free asset. In theory the market portfolio should consist of all available risky assets. In practice we can think of it as a broad-based index of risky assets. For example, an Irish-based equity investor may consider the FTSE Eurofirst 300 index as his relevant market index. According to this analysis the investor should invest a portion of his assets in a fund that tracks this index, and the balance in short-term Irish government bonds. A cautious investor would allocate a high proportion of available assets to government bonds, whereas an aggressive investor will invest a much higher proportion of assets in M.

Borrowing Possibilities

Allowing for borrowing possibilities leads to the efficient frontier extending from M to C (Figure 7.5). An investor seeking a high-return/high-risk portfolio might choose a portfolio represented by Z. This portfolio lies on the efficient frontier R_FC and is reached by borrowing at the risk-free rate of interest and investing those funds in the market portfolio. Assume that investor Z has borrowed 20% of his investable assets and invested the borrowed funds (on top of available funds) in M. If $R_F = 3\%$, $R_M = 20\%$ and the standard deviation of the market portfolio (σ_M) is 20%, we can calculate the expected return and risk of portfolio Z as:

$$
\begin{aligned}
E(R) &= (-.2)(.03) + (1.2)(.2) \\
&= -.006 + .24 = .234 \text{ or } 23.4\% \\
\sigma_Z &= (1.2)(.20) = .24 \text{ or } 24\%
\end{aligned}
$$

[Equation 7.11]

Investor Z is risk-seeking compared with investor I and can achieve a higher expected return by leveraging his investments, but at the cost of higher risk as measured by the higher standard deviation.

In summary, the introduction of the risk-free asset changes the Markowitz efficient set of portfolios so that the new efficient set is a straight line rather than a curve. Borrowing and lending possibilities enable investors to position themselves anywhere on this line.

The investment decision simplifies to choosing the weightings between the market portfolio (M) and the risk-free asset (R_F). This is sometimes referred to as the **separation theorem**, which states that the investment decision (which portfolio of risky assets to invest in) is separate from the financing decision (what proportion of investable assets to invest in the market portfolio and the risk-free asset, respectively).

CAPITAL MARKET THEORY

The Capital Asset Pricing Model (CAPM)

Markowitz portfolio theory is normative in the sense that it describes how investors should go about the task of selecting portfolios of risky securities. If everyone adopted this approach, then all portfolios would consist of some combination of the market portfolio and the risk-free asset. Portfolios would differ only in terms of the weighting applied to each. Capital market theory tries to explain how security prices would behave under these idealised conditions. The most widely known model is the capital asset pricing model (CAPM). The CAPM is attractive as an equilibrium model, because it can be applied to the job of portfolio construction relatively easily. It does have a number of weaknesses and alternative theories have been developed, the most important of which is arbitrage pricing theory (APT), although here we limit the discussion to the CAPM.

The CAPM was originally developed independently by W. Sharpe, and Lintner and Mossin, in the mid-1960s. The model assumes that each investor diversifies his portfolio according to the Markowitz model including the risk-free asset. The following additional assumptions are made:

- All investors have identical probability distributions for future rates of return. Therefore, investors use the same information to generate the efficient frontier.
- All investors have the same one-period time horizon.
- All investors can borrow or lend at the risk-free rate.
- There are no transaction costs and no taxes.
- Investors are price-takers, capital markets are in equilibrium and there is no inflation.

While these assumptions may appear highly unrealistic, they can be relaxed without causing too much damage to the CAPM's predictions. We take as our starting point Figure 7.6, which replicates Figure 7.4.

Figure 7.6 The New Efficient Frontier

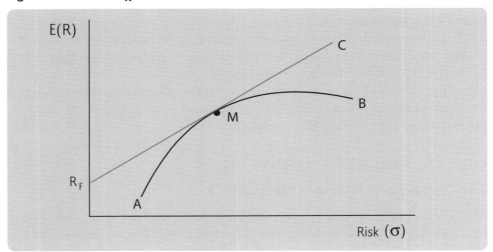

The market portfolio M is a portfolio of all risky assets and is determined by the Markowitz variance/covariance analysis. Because all investors are basing their decisions on the same information, and have identical time horizons, they will all choose the same portfolio of risky assets. In theory this market portfolio should include all risky assets worldwide, with the weight of each determined by its market value. All risk other than market risk is thus diversified away and market risk is quantified by the standard deviation of this market portfolio.

The Capital Market Line and the Security Market Line

The CAPM encompasses two important relationships that are represented graphically in Figures 7.7 and 7.8.

Figure 7.7 The Capital Market Line

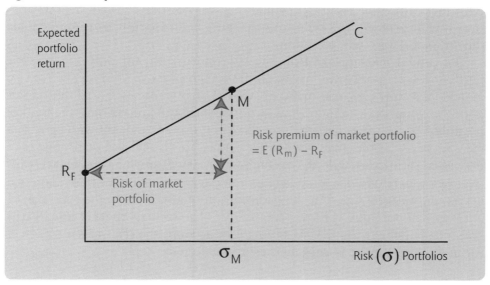

Figure 7.8 The Security Market Line

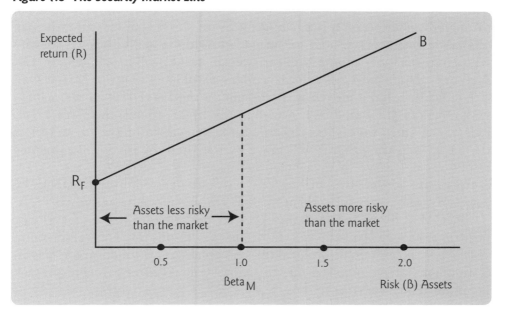

The **capital market** line plots the equilibrium relationship between expected portfolio return and the total risk, measured by standard deviation, of efficiently diversified portfolios. This plots the familiar trade-off between risk and return for efficient portfolios. All combinations of portfolios consisting of the risk-free asset and the risky market portfolio are bounded by the line R_F–C. In equilibrium all investors will end up on the capital market line. This line R_F–C is upward sloping and the slope of the line quantifies the risk/return trade-off. The vertical distance between the risk-free rate and R_F–C at point M in Figure 7.7 equals the excess return above the risk-free rate. If M is proxied by a broad-based equity index, then this distance equals the familiar equity risk premium.

The capital market line plots the risk/return trade-off only for efficient portfolios. It cannot be used to assess the equilibrium expected return from an individual security, because under the CAPM all investors will hold the market portfolio. How does an individual security contribute to the risk of the market portfolio? We can reformulate the expected return/risk trade off with beta, as a measure of risk, rather than standard deviation. This is achieved by relating each individual security's risk to the overall market risk through its covariance with the market portfolio. By using beta as a measure of risk rather than standard deviation, we recognise that the contribution of a security to the total risk of a diversified portfolio is its systematic risk. The **security market line** (SML) graphically depicts the CAPM taking into account the risk/return trade-off for individual securities (and inefficient portfolios).

Beta

Beta is a measure of the systematic risk of a security that cannot be avoided through diversification. It is a *relative* measure of risk that measures the risk of an individual stock relative to the market portfolio of all stocks. A security whose returns move in line with the overall market will have a beta of 1.0. A security that is more risky than the market will have a beta of greater than 1.0, indicating that it moves by more than the market. For example, a stock with a beta of 1.5 would be expected to rise by 15% when the market rises by 10%. A stock that is less risky than the market will have a beta of less than 1.0, indicating that it will move by less than the market. In practice stocks can be ranked by their betas and because the variance of the market is a constant across all securities for a particular period, ranking stocks by beta is the same as ranking them by their absolute systematic risk.

The CAPM formally relates the expected rate of return for any security or portfolio through the expected return–beta relationship. This relationship states that the expected rate of return on an asset is a function of the two components of the required rate of return – the risk-free rate and the risk premium. Thus we have:

$$E(R_i) = R_F + B_i [E(R_m) - R_F]$$

[Equation 7.12]

where: $E(R_i)$ = expected return on asset i
$E(R_m)$ = expected return on the market portfolio
B_i = beta coefficient for asset i
R_F = risk-free rate of return.

This is the equation that underlies the security market line in Figure 7.8. This graphical representation of the CAPM risk/return trade-off illustrates how the theory posits a positive linear relationship between an asset's risk and its required rate of return. The security market line plots risk as measured by beta on the horizontal axis and required rate of return on the vertical axis.

Estimating Beta

Analysis of historical return data is usually the approach taken to estimate beta values for stocks. Once betas for stocks have been estimated, it is relatively straightforward to calculate the beta of portfolios. Historical returns from a stock are plotted against the historical returns from the relevant market index, and the line of best fit is called the characteristic line.

Figure 7.9 Hypothetical Characteristic Line

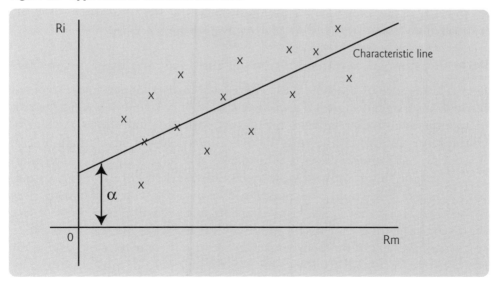

Figure 7.9 shows the characteristic line for a hypothetical stock. In this case annual returns are available for the past 15 years for the stock and the market index, and the returns for each year are plotted on the chart. The characteristic line can be plotted visually or more usually regression analysis

is used to produce the line of best fit. The slope of this line provides an estimate of beta and the intercept on the vertical axis should equate to the alpha of the stock. In equilibrium the alpha of all stocks should equal the risk-free rate of return. Often the characteristic line is calculated using **excess returns**. The excess return is calculated by subtracting the risk-free rate from both the market returns and the stock returns. In this form the intercept with the vertical axis again represents the alpha for a stock and the slope of the line will be the same in both cases. In equilibrium the alpha should now equal zero.

The big problem with beta estimates is that the betas of individual stocks change over time. Unfortunately it is impossible to predict such changes, making beta estimates for individual stocks unreliable. Researchers have found that forecast betas *on average* turn out to be closer to 1.0 than the models predict. This information can be used to adjust beta estimates to make them somewhat more reliable. When it comes to estimating beta for large portfolios the news is somewhat better. In a portfolio of (say) 40 or more stocks the betas of some stocks may be rising while the betas of others may be falling. This averaging effect means that estimates of portfolio betas tend to be more robust than beta estimates of individual stocks.

CONCLUDING COMMENTS

The key conclusions of the CAPM are quite straightforward:

i)   Investors are rewarded for taking extra risk and there is a positive linear relationship between risk and reward.
ii)   The relevant risk for a security is its impact on portfolio risk.

Although the assumptions underlying the CAPM are very restrictive, empirical studies in general support the main predictions of the CAPM. The security market line appears to be linear, indicating that the trade-off between expected return and risk is an upward-sloping straight line. Also, it appears that unsystematic risk does not command a risk premium and therefore the evidence supports the prediction that investors are rewarded only for assuming systematic risk.

The CAPM has proved itself to be a very useful practical tool in the world of investment. It has flaws, such as the fact that the theoretical market portfolio that it is based on cannot be observed. Researchers have developed another model called arbitrage pricing theory (APT), which some argue as being superior to the CAPM. So far neither model has proved itself to be clearly superior, and analysts are likely to continue to work with both and to seek improvements through further research.

SUMMARY

- For the purpose of portfolio construction all investment assets can be characterised by just two variables – expected returns and estimated standard deviations of returns.
- The calculation of portfolio return is determined by the expected return of each security and the weight of each security within the portfolio.
- The covariance is an absolute measure of the degree of association between returns for a pair of securities.
- The correlation coefficient is a relative measure of association that lies between +1 (perfect positive correlation) and −1 (perfect negative correlation).
- In general it should be possible to combine stocks in such a way as to reduce risk without adversely affecting expected returns.
- In the simplified two-security case, portfolio risk depends upon the interplay of the risk of each security, the portfolio weights assigned to each security, and the covariance or correlation between the two securities.
- Applying the basic Markowitz approach to portfolio construction is complex, and where many securities are involved it is extremely cumbersome.
- The key advantage of the single-index model is that it reduces dramatically the number of calculations required, because we do not need to calculate the relationship between all pairs of securities being considered.
- Introducing the risk-free asset to the Markowitz efficient frontier radically alters that efficient frontier and in fact it expands the frontier.
- Introduction of the risk-free asset has the result that *all* investors will choose just one risky portfolio (M), which we refer to as the market portfolio, and combine that with varying proportions of the risk-free asset.
- The separation theorem states that the investment decision (which portfolio of risky assets to invest in) is separate from the financing decision (what proportion of investable assets to invest in the market portfolio and in the risk-free asset, respectively).
- The CAPM assumes that each investor diversifies his portfolio according to the Markowitz model, including the risk-free asset.
- The **capital market line** plots the equilibrium relationship between expected portfolio return and the total risk, measured by standard deviation, of efficiently diversified portfolios.
- By using beta as a measure of risk rather than standard deviation, we recognise that the contribution of a security to the total risk of a diversified portfolio is its systematic risk.

➡

- The **security market line (SML)** graphically depicts the CAPM taking into account the risk–return trade-off for individual securities (and inefficient portfolios).
- Beta is a measure of the systematic risk of a security that cannot be avoided through diversification.
- The equation for the security market line states that the expected rate of return on an asset is a function of the two components of the required rate of return – the risk-free rate and the risk premium.

QUESTIONS

1. Which statement(s) is/are TRUE regarding the Markowitz model?

A. The relative importance of variance of each security increases when more securities are included in a portfolio.

B. If 100 securities are included in a portfolio, 100 covariances are needed to estimate the risk of a portfolio.

C. Adding two securities with a –1 correlation coefficient, with all other things remaining constant, will reduce the risk of a portfolio.

D. In a large portfolio, the covariance terms become less important than the covariance terms in a small portfolio.

1. All of the above
2. C only
3. None of the above
4. A, B and C only

2. Which statement(s) is/are TRUE regarding covariance and correlation coefficients?

A. Covariance measures the relationship between two securities in relative terms.

B. The correlation coefficient ranges in value from –1 to +1.

C. Negative covariance means the returns of two securities move in opposite directions.

D. A correlation coefficient value of 0 indicates there is positive relationship between the returns of two securities.

1. B and C only
2. A and B only
3. A, B and C only
4. None of the above

3. Which of the following statement(s) is/are TRUE?

A. By combining securities with perfect positive correlation with each other, the portfolio's expected return is maximised and risk is minimised.

B. By combining securities with perfect positive correlation with each other, the portfolio's expected return is minimised and risk is minimised.

C. By combining securities with perfect negative correlation with each other, the portfolio's expected return is minimised and risk is minimised.

D. By combining securities with perfect negative correlation with each other, the portfolio's expected return is maximised and risk is minimised.

1. All of the above
2. None of the above
3. A and B only
4. A and D only

4. Which statement(s) is TRUE regarding portfolio risk?

A. Portfolio risk takes only individual security risk into consideration.

B. Portfolio risk takes only covariance between securities into consideration.

C. Portfolio risk takes both individual security risk and covariance between securities into consideration.

D. Portfolio risk is totally independent from the investment weight of the securities held in a portfolio.

5. Markowitz defines an efficient portfolio as one that:

A. Has the smallest risk for a given level of expected return.

B. Has the smallest expected return for all levels of risk.

C. Has the largest expected return for a given level of risk.

D. Has the largest expected return and zero risk.

1. All of the above
2. A & C only
3. A & D only
4. B & D only

6. **Which of the following is/are considered input variables for the Markowitz model?**

   A. Weights
   B. Expected returns
   C. Standard deviations
   D. Correlation coefficients.

   1. None of the above
   2. A, B & C only
   3. All of the above
   4. B, C & D only

7. **Regarding risk, which of the following statement(s) is/are TRUE?**

   A. Systematic risk affects only stocks but not bonds.
   B. Through a well-diversified portfolio, nonsystematic risk can be eliminated.
   C. In the best case, total risk for a portfolio approaches the systematic risk after diversification.

   1. All of the above
   2. None of the above
   3. A & C only
   4. B & C only

8. **Which is the TRUE statement about 'beta'?**

   A. Beta is a measure of total risk, including market risk and issuer risk.
   B. An efficient portfolio has the smallest beta of any other portfolios.
   C. Beta is the slope of the SML (Security Market Line).
   D. A security with a beta of 2 is considered to be less risky than the risk of the benchmark market index.

9. **Which statement(s) about CAPM is/are TRUE?**

   A. CAPM relates the expected return of securities to their relative risk measure, i.e., their beta.
   B. Market risk premium is equal to expected return on the market portfolio less the risk-free rate.
   C. Stocks with higher beta tend to have a higher risk premium than stocks with lower beta.

1. A & B only
2. All of the above
3. B & C only
4. A only

10. **Assume the market expected return and the risk-free rate for the next period are 12% and 4%, respectively. What is the required rate of return for a stock with a beta of 1.8?**

   A. 15.8%
   B. 11.2%
   C. 18.4%
   D. 17.6%.

11. **Stock A has a required rate of return of 18%. If the risk-free rate is 4% and the market risk premium is 11%, what is the beta of stock A?**

   A. 0.79
   B. 1.27
   C. 1.96
   D. 2.12.

Chapter eight

The Real Economy and the Markets

This chapter identifies the central importance of growth and inflation in determining asset prices and in driving both the real economy and the financial markets. The relevance of the economic cycle in influencing the asset allocation decision is discussed. Periods of speculative excess are examined to isolate their common denominators and to identify the insight that there is a difference between price and value.

Learning Objectives

After reading this chapter you will be able to:
- **Recognise the role of future cash flows and inflation in determining asset prices**
- **Describe the development and phases of the economic and investment cycles**
- **Describe the relationship, interplay and linkages between the economic and market cycles and identify their common drivers – growth and inflation**
- **Outline the benefits and limitations of using the economic cycle to inform asset allocation decisions**
- **Recognise the conditions that give rise to periods of speculative excess in markets**
- **Understand that there is a difference between price and value.**

INTRODUCTION

Investment is a forward-looking activity. In determining the value of an asset the focus of the investor is on the cash flows that the asset will generate in the future. In assessing these flows the investor recognises that:

- In the case of certain assets, the future flows are fixed in nominal monetary terms.
- In the case of other assets, the future flows are variable depending, for example in the case of equities, on underlying company profitability or, in the case of property, on rents.
- That inflation must be taken into account when assessing the present value of these future flows.

In the case of fixed-interest securities, e.g., government or corporate bonds, the future flows are fixed, by definition, in nominal monetary terms. They are guaranteed by the issuer of the bond and their payment dates are known with precision as they are set out in the terms of the bond's issue, the prospectus.

Index-linked securities generate flows that are adjusted upwards to account for the prevailing rate of inflation. Here, although the dates of future payments are known in advance, the nominal monetary values of the flows are not as they are subject to the inflation rate. Flows are guaranteed by the issuer.

Inflation, therefore, has a very different impact on the respective values of fixed-interest and index-linked bonds. When inflation rises, on the one hand the value of fixed-interest securities falls, because the present value of the fixed (in monetary or absolute terms) future flows is eroded by rising inflation. The value of index-linked securities, on the other hand, is protected against rising inflation by the adjustment process, which increases the future flows in monetary terms to compensate the investor for higher inflation.

Future flows from cash deposits vary with the level of short-term interest rates. Clearly, investors will attempt to obtain a rate of interest that is higher than the inflation rate so as to earn a real (i.e., after inflation) return on their deposits. The rate of inflation is an important influence on short-term interest rates, and in the long run investors in cash deposits have received a real return on their monies. Nevertheless, there have been quite extended periods of negative real interest rates, i.e., when the inflation rate exceeded short-term interest rates. Clearly, there is little incentive for investors to place monies on deposit at short-term interest rates that are below the prevailing inflation rate. Here, the real value of the investment is being eroded. It would make more sense for the investor to spend his or her money now.

Future flows from investment in equities and property are intrinsically different from those arising in the bond and deposits markets in that they are not guaranteed by the issuer. Equities and property generate flows that reflect growth in profits and rents, respectively.

The flows arising on an equity investment will vary with the underlying profitability of the company. When profits are strong and rising, flows are likely to increase. Contrarily, weak and falling profitability will result in lower flows.

Similarly, rising rents boost the flows from property investment, while lower rents will result in lower flows.

Equities and property are real assets, i.e., assets that have a linkage to the performance of the economy. Over time corporate profits and property rents will reflect developments in the underlying economy. They will respond to growth in nominal gross domestic product (economic output), i.e., to real growth and inflation. Strong economic growth will drive increases in profits and rents – 'A rising tide lifts all boats.' Further, company management and landlords will attempt to protect the real value of profits and rents, respectively, against rising inflation. For example, in periods of rising inflation company management may protect profits from the higher cost of inputs, e.g., raw materials and labour, by seeking cost efficiencies or by raising product prices.

Clearly, therefore, in so far as the value of their assets is concerned – i.e., the present value of the future flows that those assets will generate – investors are deeply concerned with developments in the underlying economy and in particular with growth and inflation.

THE ECONOMIC CYCLE

The central importance of economic growth and inflation as key influences in the determination of asset valuations was discussed above.

Economic activity tends to be cyclical, marked by successive and recurring phases of expansion and contraction. This cyclical pattern tends to be reflected in the activities of businesses – the business cycle – and in developments in financial markets – the investment cycle.

An Idealised Economic Cycle

Figure 8.1 The Economic Cycle

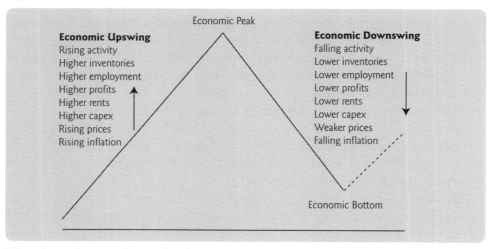

The chart depicts the path of economic activity.

In the opening phase of the cycle (bottom left-hand corner), economic activity is at a low ebb. Business and consumer confidence are low. Profits are under pressure and unemployment is high. Consumer demand and capital investment are weak. Short-term interest rates are in low ground. Earlier falls in interest rates as economic activity softened and demand for money fell have been augmented more recently by cuts in official interest rates, as the authorities attempt to revive the economy. Government expenditure is rising as the authorities compensate for the absence of business and consumer demand. Inflation is low.

Eventually, the economy begins to respond to the new environment of low interest rates and increased government spending. Some companies, encouraged by the availability of cheap money, begin to rebuild their inventory levels, which had been run down during the downturn. They increase their orders to their manufacturing suppliers. When this increased inventory is sold off they further increase their order levels.

Inventories are further rebuilt, production is expanded, workers are rehired. The workers, now back in employment, in turn spend their wages and salaries, further boosting demand. Their more secure financial situation permits them to borrow, perhaps for house purchase, boosting construction demand. Employment increases further as more companies respond to the improving background.

Corporate profitability is now strong as companies benefit from higher volume throughput. Companies also take the opportunity presented by higher demand to increase prices. Strong demand and high levels of profitability and cash flow encourage companies to invest in new production lines, new plants and new factories. Property rents rise in response to rising demand for office, industrial and retail space as companies expand. The workforce also benefits as their bargaining power is increased by lower unemployment levels and strong demand for labour, sending wages and salaries higher.

Higher prices for goods, property and labour inevitably result in higher and accelerating inflation. Finally the authorities, alarmed by the prospect of inflation running out of control, act to dampen the economy by increasing interest rates. Eventually the economy peaks, followed by a peak in the rate of inflation.

Higher interest rates now throw the whole cyclical process into reverse. Companies cut back their inventories, workforce and capital expenditures. Higher unemployment forces the consumer to retrench, further depressing demand. Higher unemployment also eases the pressure on wages and salaries. Lower demand puts pressure on product prices. Corporate profits fall as prices weaken and volume throughput falls. Rents fall as demand for new space evaporates and as excess space becomes available.

The slowdown gathers pace. Inflation and interest rates fall. Eventually the authorities act by cutting interest rates to end the slowdown and reignite the economy. The cyclical process starts over.

An Idealised Investment Cycle

Figure 8.2 below illustrates how events in the real economy are reflected in the financial markets. Again the chart depicts the path of economic activity.

Figure 8.2 The Investment Cycle

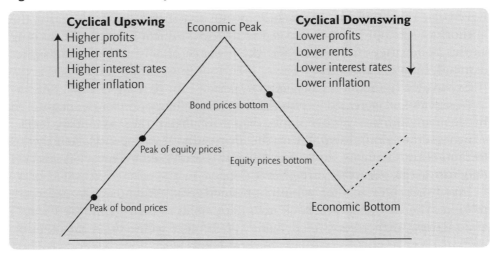

In the early part of the upswing, downward pressure on short-term interest rate ends as the authorities end the series of rate reductions and as demand for money increases. Market expectations are for higher short-term rates in the future. Meanwhile, even at this relatively early stage in the cyclical economic recovery, bond prices, which had been strong during the recession as inflation fell, reach their peak. Bond investors respond quickly, and indeed nervously, to signs of increased activity because they fear that increases in activity will be followed by increases in inflation. Bond investors, ever mindful of the damage inflicted on bond portfolios during the high-inflation 1970s and early 1980s, are extremely sensitive to any signs of emerging inflation. The mechanism driving the bond market is quite straightforward, as discussed in Chapter 3. Bond flows are fixed in monetary terms. The price of a bond is the present value of these future flows. Higher inflation erodes the present value of the future flows, thus depressing the bond price.

In sharp contrast, equity investors respond enthusiastically to evidence of increasing economic activity. They recognise that increased activity results in higher volumes, higher product prices and higher profits. Share prices rise. Property values also benefit as higher profits encourage companies to expand, take additional space and pay higher rents. Here expectations of higher profits and rents are boosting the anticipated future flows from equities and property, thus increasing equity and property values.

Eventually, however, equity and property investors recognise that higher economic activity will result in higher inflation, forcing the authorities to dampen down the economy by increasing interest rates. The equity and property markets reach their peaks. Notice that the equity market anticipates the economic peak and will peak before the peak in economic activity. Equities, in particular, are a forward-looking asset; they are concerned with anticipating economic events.

Finally, the economy reaches its peak, the downturn begins and the cyclical process goes into reverse. The prospect of lower economic activity causes bond prices to bottom and begin to rise, because the bond market associates lower activity with lower inflation. Lower inflation increases the present value of the future flows from bonds.

Equity and property prices, which have been falling since before the peak in the economy, remain weak on expectations of falling profits and falling rents.

Interest rates decline owing to falling demand for money, and fall further as the authorities attempt to foster an economic recovery. Again, the equity market anticipates the economic trough and begins to improve in advance of it. Eventually, the economy reaches its bottom and the cyclical process begins anew.

THE KEY LINKAGES

Economic activity is the driver that the real economy and the investment markets share in common. Economic activity drives growth; growth drives profits and rents. Economic activity drives inflation; inflation drives interest rates. Asset values are the outcome of the flow of future payments (e.g. profits in the case of equities, rents in the case of property), discounted back to present value by a discount factor which rests importantly on interest rates. Central to the relationship are growth and inflation. This relationship is illustrated below.

Figure 8.3 The Economy and the Markets: Key Drivers

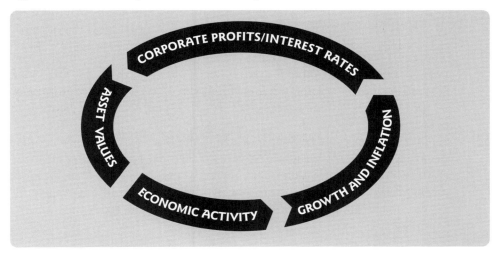

The relationship is outlined further in the figure below.

Figure 8.4 Key Linkages: Economies and Markets

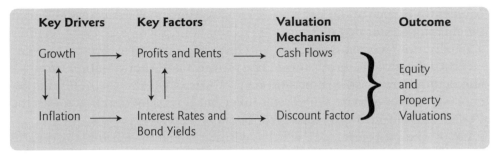

Inflation drives interest rates; interest rates drive bond yields. In fact, bond yields are long-term interest rates.

Equity valuations are derived from the interplay between corporate profits and bond yields. Growth drives the stream of corporate profits. The value of a company is the present value of that stream of future profits restated in today's money by a discount factor which rests heavily on the bond yield. The key element in the discount factor is the bond yield. The lower the bond yield, the lower the discount factor and the higher the present value of the company. The higher the bond yield, the higher the discount factor and the lower the present value of the company. In other words, low bond yields permit investors to attach high valuations to companies, i.e., high price earnings ratios. High bond yields result in low price earnings ratios.

A similar mechanism is at work in the property market. Growth in the economy drives growth in rents. The stream of future rents is discounted back to present value by employing a discount factor, which again is heavily influenced by bond yields. The lower the bond yield, the lower the discount factor, the higher the property valuation and vice versa.

The illustration above also shows that:

i)   There is a trade-off between growth and inflation. For example, in the typical cycle as discussed earlier, economic growth as the cycle expands typically results in higher inflation. This causes the authorities to reduce inflationary pressures by dampening down economic activity.

ii)   Higher interest rates may have a negative effect on corporate profits, because companies typically have borrowings. Higher interest rates result in higher interest charges. Nevertheless, because of the benefits arising from increased volumes of production and enhanced pricing power, corporate profits will rise strongly during the economic upturn.

When the historical data is examined we find there is a very strong linkage between falling interest rates and rising equities. However, rising interest rates are not consistent with falling equities, because at that point in the cycle equities benefit from the strong profits background. Not surprisingly, given the mechanism for determining equity valuations, there is a strong relationship between profits growth and share prices.

The linkages among inflation, interest rates and the valuation of bonds and equities are illustrated below:

Figure 8.5 The Real Economy and the Markets: Key Linkages

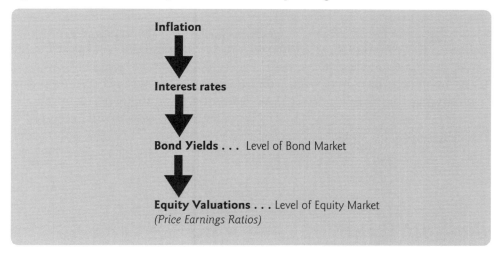

The Price Earnings Ratio is a measure of the stock market's comfort with the quality and growth potential of company earnings (or profits). The higher the price earnings ratio, the higher will be the market's confidence in the company. A price earnings ratio for the stock market as a whole may be calculated by using an index of stock-market prices and earnings.

The price earnings ratio is calculated by dividing the share price by annual earnings per share. The inverse of this calculation, as shown below, displays the very same relationship as an earnings yield.

Figure 8.6 The Price Earnings Ratio and The Earnings Yield

$$\text{Price Earnings Ratio} = \frac{\text{Share Price}}{\text{Earnings per Share}}$$

$$\text{Earnings Yield} = \frac{\text{Earnings per Share}}{\text{Share Price}} \times 100\%$$

By contrasting the very different investment environments of 1982 – at the beginning of the secular bull market in equities and bonds – and of 2000 – when equity markets peaked – the linkages between inflation interest rates, bond yields and equity valuations are clearly shown. High inflation led to high interest rates, high bond yields and high earnings yields (i.e., low equity-market price earnings ratios) in 1982. In sharp contrast a low-inflation, low-interest-rate, low-bond-yield background in 2000 permitted equity valuation to move to high, albeit unsustainable, extremes.

Table 8.1

	United States		Ireland
	1982	**2000**	**2000**
Inflation	6.0%	2.5%	5.6%
Interest Rates	16.0%	6.2%	3.7%
Bond Yields	10.0%	6.2%	5.3%
Earnings Yield	12.5%	3.5%	5.5%
(Price Earnings Ratio)	8.0	28.3	18.1

THE CYCLE AND ASSET ALLOCATION

Given the relationship between the economic and investment cycles outlined earlier in this chapter, it may be worthwhile to consider to what extent, if any, developments in the real economy might be used by investors as a basis for predicting market developments and, in particular, for determining the relative attractions of the different investment assets at a particular point in time.

However, while an idealised cycle was outlined earlier, in practice every cycle is different. The leads and lags between the various cyclical phases and events vary and the sequence of occurrences changes.

Nevertheless, by examining economic and investment cycles in the US between the Second World War and the early 1990s, it is possible to construct a 'Cyclical Clock' as follows:

Figure 8.7 The Cyclical Clock

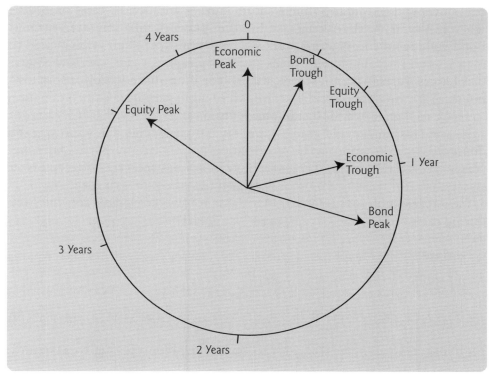

Even in the light of the limitations expressed above, the Cyclical Clock delivers some interesting evidence:

i)   The average cycle has a life of just over 4 years. Within the average cycle there is about 1 year of slowdown and over 3 years of growth. This is good news for investors in real assets, equities and property, which are predicated on growth.

ii) The equity market does indeed perform its role as an anticipator of economic events. The peak of the equity market occurs, on average, about 1 year ahead of the peak in economic activity. The bottom of the equity market occurs, on average, some 6 months ahead of the trough of economic activity.

iii) The sensitivity of the bond market to economic activity, which it associates with movements in inflation, is clearly shown. Shortly after the peak of economic activity, as activity slows, bond prices – which had been weak during the prolonged economic upswing – finally bottom and begin to rise. Similarly, shortly after the economy reaches its bottom and begins to improve, bond prices, which had been strong during the economic downturn, now reach their peak.

iv)   The equity market cycle reflects the economic background. On average, during each cycle equity markets rise for about 3 years and fall for 1. In sharp contrast, bond markets rise for about 1 year and fall (or move sideways) for 3.

It is hardly surprising, therefore, that in the long run equities outperform bonds.

However, because of the limitations outlined earlier, the Cyclical Clock is not a precision instrument and its application is extremely limited in informing the investor as to the appropriate portfolio asset mix at any particular time. Neither is it a reliable tool for timing switches between the different asset classes, i.e., for moving from bonds to equities or equities to cash.

Nevertheless, it does pinpoint that there are two key points for investors during each cycle:

i) The Bond Market Trough

At this point in the cycle, the investor:

•   should be fully invested to take advantage of the coming upswing in markets;
•   should have a short-lived bias to bonds but be preparing to maximise equity exposure;
•   should expect to stay fully invested for the next 2 to 3 years.

ii) The Equity Market Peak

At this point in the cycle, the investor:

•   should adopt a defensive portfolio posture (i.e., cash at maximum permitted);
•   should be bearish (cautious, pessimistic) on equities (i.e., equities at minimum permitted exposure);
•   should be preparing to maximise bond exposure;
•   should be prepared to revert to a fully invested position within 9 to 12 months.

Secondly, the Cyclical Clock does broadly indicate that there is an 'asset of choice' for the different stages of the economic cycle:

•   Cash is king either side of the peak of economic activity.
•   Bonds perform best during the economic downturn.
•   Equities are the asset of choice during a prolonged phase of the economic upswing.

This is illustrated in the figure below:

Figure 8.8 The Cyclical Clock: Asset Strategy

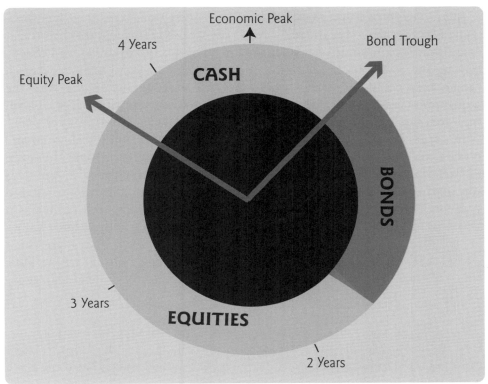

Awareness of the relationship between the economic and investment cycles, as refined by the insights available from examination of the Cyclical Clock, can help the investor to understand, track and interpret economic and financial developments. However, when predicting financial and market out-turns there is no escaping the requirement for judgment. The investor, whether he or she be the Chief Investment Officer of a large fund-management house or a private individual, must make a judgment pinpointing the precise phase of the current economic cycle, determine its implication for the investment assets in the light of the typical developments of the average cycle – as shown by the Cyclical Clock – and adjust for the unique characteristics of the current cycle. Judgment, nerve and courage are required. The position is rarely as clear in practice as it is in theory.

SPECULATION, EUPHORIA, BUBBLES, CRASHES

In Chapter 6 investors are characterised as thoughtful and rational individuals who carefully analyse their requirements and needs and tailor their investment portfolios accordingly. Investors are keenly aware that investment, a two-handed process, is about risk and return. They are focused on optimising, rather than maximising, their investment returns.

In this chapter a framework is outlined which demonstrates that the investment assets are rooted in the real world. The real economy and the investment assets share common drivers. They are linked by a series of causes and effects, actions and reactions, anticipation and outcomes. The interactions between the economy and the investment assets are sensible and logical and the sequence of developments fits comfortably into the cyclical patterns of both the economy and the markets.

Investors do indeed make informed judgments, they employ a systematic process and they act on a rational basis. This is normally the case. However, financial history shows that, periodically, investors are gripped by bouts of speculative fever that may overwhelm their normal thoughtful, rational and systematic approach to investment. During these periods, first enthusiasm and then greed and euphoria develop into a mania that can drive asset values far from the solid ground of the real world. There have been many such episodes throughout history. Some, despite the long periods which have elapsed since they occurred, are indelibly imprinted in financial folklore – notably 'Tulipmania' in Holland during the 1630s, and 'The South Sea Bubble' in Britain in 1720.

Episodes of this vintage do carry lessons and insights for us today, not least in the dangers involved in excessive borrowing. However, our focus in this chapter is on occurrences of more recent vintage: those that took place in the twentieth century.

Figure 8.9 The Dow Jones Index: 1924–1934

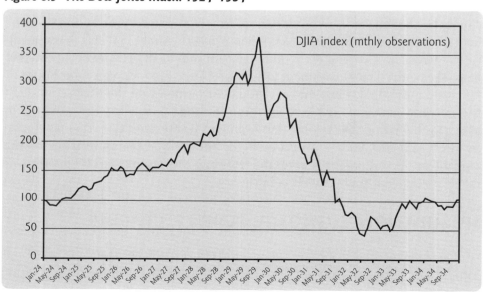

Wall Street: The Great Crash of 1929

Perhaps the speculative episode most firmly embedded in financial folklore is the Great Crash of 1929. Its short-term financial consequences during October 1929 were dramatic enough, but the long-term fallout in the Great Depression of the 1930s was calamitous for the world economy.

Share prices on Wall Street, which had been rising through 1924, 1925 and 1926, accelerated in 1927 and simply charged ahead in 1928 and 1929. Borrowings played a key role in the acceleration, as they invariably do during Bubbles. Investors bought shares 'on margin', using money lent by their stockbrokers, while highly geared investment trusts piled borrowings on borrowings in the fashion of pyramid sales schemes.

A number of the key events during the momentous month of October 1929 are set out below to illustrate their dramatic impact at the time, but also to highlight those elements that tend to recur in Bubbles.

1929

Wed. 2 October   Brokers' loans at new high of $6.8bn. Brokers' loans to investors consistently hit new highs during the run-up to the peak of the Technology Bubble in March 2000.

Wed. 23 October   Heavy selling.

Thurs. 24 October Huge volume of forced selling. Forced selling occurs when the broker, having lent money 'on margin' for the purchase by the client of stocks that have now fallen in price, and in the absence of fresh funds from his client, liquidates the investor's position. Forced selling dramatically changes the dynamics of the market. The typical investor is sensitive to market price; he will be reluctant to sell his stock at a price that is sharply below recent levels. The broker engaged in forced selling is insensitive to price, focused only on raising cash. Forced selling hugely accentuates market downside.

A consortium of bankers, in an effort to steady investors' nerves and share prices, support the market by investing $240m.

In 1929 this operation had its desired effect but only for a few days. It failed to turn the market. However, in 1974/5 a consortium of insurance companies successfully stabilised and turned round the UK market after its huge fall of 1974.

Fri. 25 October   Market steady in large volume.

Sat. 26 October   Market steady in large volume, but weak towards close.

Mon. 28 October   Share prices routed.

Tues. 29 October   Massive forced selling in huge volume.

Wed. 30 October   Companies increase dividends. The 'Great and Good'
                     rally round in an attempt to allay investor fears by
                     pointing to the health of business and of the economy.
                         Again, in October 1987 after the large one-day fall in
                     the US market, many of the major US corporations
                     announced share buy-backs.

As mentioned earlier, the debacle of the Great Crash of 1929 was followed
by the global suffering of the Great Depression of the 1930s. The shock
suffered by the financial and economic systems from the stock-market
collapse was exacerbated by poor economic management.

The Crash of 1987

The foundations of the 1987 Crash, in typical Bubble fashion, were built on
debt. The 1980s were the era of the Leveraged Buy Out (LBO), whereby
financiers or 'corporate raiders' employed highly borrowed investment

Figure 8.10 The Dow Jones Index: 1983–1993

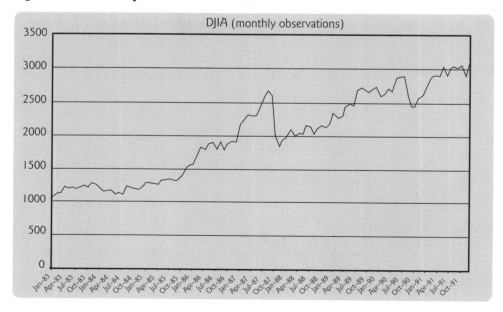

vehicles, often financed with a significant element of High Yield or 'Junk' bonds, to acquire quoted companies. The period culminated in the extraordinary events of the takeover of RJR Nabisco, memorably described in the book '*Barbarians at the Gate*'.

At the peak of the corporate raiders' influence, no company seemed to be too large to be safe from the threat of takeover. Upon acquisition the acquired company would be 'run for cash', with the new owners focusing on EBITDA – Earnings Before Interest, Tax, Depreciation and Amortisation – rather than on the shareholders' typical focus on earnings. Asset-disposal proceeds and cash flows were applied in debt reduction, with a view to eventual relisting of the company to provide an exit for the raiders. Market valuations moved to a cash-flow basis from the normal earnings basis. The key to valuation was 'private market value' – the price a raider funded by debt could afford to pay to buy the company.

Share prices continued their strong rise into 1987, until finally a sustained rise in bond yields (i.e., long-term interest rates) forced a more sober reappraisal of valuation.

Figure 8.11 US Treasury 10-Year Bond Yield: 1985–1987

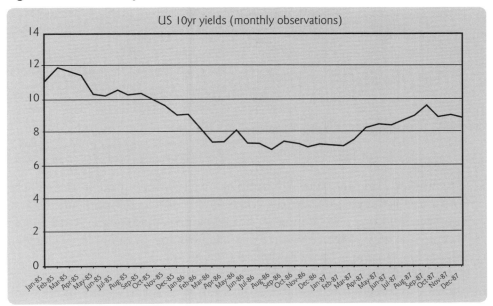

Prices collapsed, falling by 22.6% in a single trading day on 19 October 1987. The decline in prices was ratcheted downwards by derivative-based strategies, including program trades and portfolio insurance, which spewed out sell orders in an unprecedented fashion.

Thankfully, on this occasion a more robust and sophisticated financial and economic infrastructure, and timely corrective action by the monetary authorities in the US and elsewhere, helped to avoid longer-term economic repercussions.

The Technology Bubble

The technology bubble and, in particular, the mania for investment in internet and dotcom companies may be traced back to the Netscape Initial Public Offering (IPO) of August 1995. The price of Netscape shares rose by 108% on the day of the IPO, valuing the company at $2.2bn. However, it was not until late 1998 that the really explosive phase of the bubble kicked in with dramatic rises in the share prices of technology, media and telecommunications (TMT) companies.

Figure 8.12 The NASDAQ Index: 1998–2001

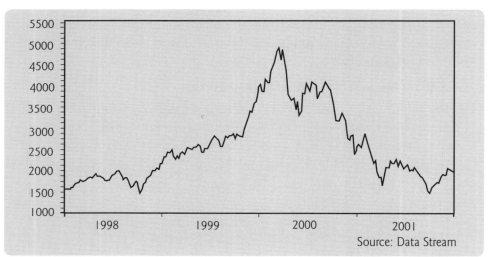

Source: Data Stream

The technology mania, like all bubbles, was based upon a real-world opportunity. In the past decade the convergence of telecommunications and computer technology via the internet has transformed, through e-mail and e-commerce, the way in which we live our business and personal lives. Further revolutionary change is likely in the next few years.

However, during 1999 and into early 2000, investor enthusiasm for technology and technology-related stocks ran well ahead of any likely real-world benefits. Investors, again as in the 1920s, used margin debt and other borrowings to fuel their demand. Nor was the phenomenon restricted to private investors. Institutional investors and corporate managements also leapt on the bandwagon. Demand for stock well outstripped supply. The supply imbalance was exploited by the investment houses as they introduced ever more fragile technology stocks to the market. They curtailed supply and magnified hype by issuing to the public only a very small proportion of total stock, thus further exacerbating the supply imbalance.

At the peak of the bubble, in March 2000, TMT valuations had reached absurd levels. There was simply no way that these companies could grow at the rates implied for the lengths of time implied by their valuations.

Table 8.2 Peak Valuations: 10 March 2000

	Price/Earnings	Price/Sales
Old 'Old Industrials'	12.6	0.6
Old 'New Industrials'	69.2	7.3
New 'New Industrials'	N/A	85.7
NASDAQ	147.1	11.0
S+P 500	28.3	2.1

Source: Paine Webber

Old Old: Dow, GM, Ford, etc
Old New: Intel, IBM, Microsoft, etc
New New: Amazon.com, Ebay, etc

In a timely and insightful review, Ed Kerschner of Paine Webber contrasted the valuation of twenty old 'old industrial' companies, i.e., 'smokestack America' companies – such as Dow Chemical, General Motors, Ford, etc. – with twenty old 'new industrial', i.e., the long-standing and well-established leading technology companies – such as IBM, Intel, Microsoft, etc. – and with twenty new 'new industrials' – the more recently issued technology newcomers such as Amazon.com, E-Bay, Siebel, etc. The comparisons, as shown in the table above, were stark and his conclusions unavoidable. The valuations of the old 'new industrials' at best were extremely demanding, while valuations of the new 'new industrials' were simply foolish.

By coincidence, on the very day on which Kerschner's review was issued, the Nasdaq index peaked at 5048.6. Over the next two years and seven months it retraced its earlier gains, falling by 78% to its low on 9 October 2002.

Bubbles: Common Denominators

i)   Bubbles invariably begin with a profitable real-world opportunity, for example the riches of South America or the potential of the internet.

ii) Human nature is a common and consistent factor:
– during the bubble phase, greed and euphoria;
– during the crash phase, fear and anger.

iii) Debt is usually involved and in particular overborrowing, driven by greed. Geared (or leveraged) investments perform spectacularly well in good times, but generate calamitous losses when the bubble bursts.

iv)   Inevitably during the episode business morality comes under strain.
        The exploitation of the unsuspecting (gullible?) investor may range
        from liberal interpretation of rules and regulations to outright theft
        and fraud.
v)   The downside, when it finally arrives, is severe and long-lasting.
vi)   Finally, and unfortunately, investors' memories are short. The next
        generation of investor is fated to repeat the mistakes of history.

Figure 8.13 Speculation Marches On

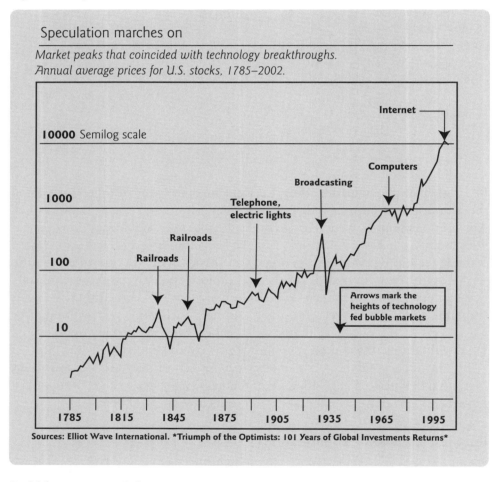

Bubbles: Key Insights

Unfortunately, the history of bubbles does not provide a reliable guide to
pinpointing when the bubble might burst.

More mundane, but nevertheless telling, insights do emerge:

i)   There is a difference between value and price.

As discussed earlier the value of an investment is the present value of the stream of future earning which that investment will generate.

The price of an investment is the result of the interaction of buyers and sellers in the marketplace. When buyers outnumber sellers, the price will rise, perhaps well above the intrinsic value of the investment. The opposite will occur when sellers outnumber buyers.

During episodes of financial mania, price will diverge widely from value. However, an ongoing focus on value offers the investor the best possibility of staying on solid ground.

ii)   Investment is about risk and return. The higher the expected return, the higher will be the risk. Geared (or leveraged) investment is inherently much more risky than an ungeared exposure to the same asset.

SUMMARY

- In determining the value of an asset, the focus of the investor is on future cash flows and their sensitivity to inflation.
- Investors are concerned with developments in the underlying economy, and in particular with growth and inflation.
- Economic activity tends to be cyclical, marked by successive and recurring phases of expansion and contraction. This cyclical activity is reflected in the financial markets.
- Growth and inflation are central to the relationship between the real economy and the financial markets.
- Inflation drives interest rates; interest rates drive bond yields. Growth drives profits. Equity valuations are derived from the interplay between corporate profits and bond yields.
- Every cycle is different. Nevertheless, examination of cyclical economic patterns yields insights for investment management
  - the typical cycle lasts just over 4 years in the US;
  - the equity market acts as an anticipator of economic events;
  - the bond market is extremely sensitive to economic activity.
- There are two key points of time for investors in each cycle: the bond market trough and the equity market peak.
- Periods of speculative fever tend to have common characteristics, notably overborrowing, low standards of business morality and the excesses of human behaviour – greed and euphoria, fear and anger.
- There is a difference between value and price.

Chapter nine

Pension Fund Investment

This chapter introduces pension schemes and the legal and regulatory framework within which they operate. The role and responsibilities of pension fund trustees are outlined, particularly with regard to the fund's investments. The particular risks attaching to pension fund investment are described and investment objectives outlined. The central role of the trustees in determining investment strategy is discussed.

Learning Objectives

After reading this chapter you will be able to:
- Define the principal types of pension funds and the legal and regulatory framework within which they operate in Ireland
- Outline the role and responsibilities of pension fund trustees, particularly with regard to investment
- Describe the long-term and short-term time horizons which influence a fund's investment objectives
- List the various types of risk that are important to pension funds
- Recognise the factors that determine investment strategy and drive the selection of the fund's asset mix, benchmark and added value objective and accompanying exposure to benchmark and active risk
- Appreciate the central role of the trustees in the determination of investment strategy.

PENSION SCHEMES: AN INTRODUCTION

A pension scheme is an arrangement whereby an individual (the employee) and the employer may set aside monies dedicated to providing the employee with an income in retirement.

Monies set aside are paid into a pension fund and in turn are invested. Therefore, the pension fund is comprised both of the monies paid in and the returns – capital and income – generated on them.

It is out of these resources that pensions are paid to scheme members in retirement.

PENSION SCHEME TYPES

There are two broad categories of pension scheme.

i)   *Occupational Pension Schemes*
     Typically, in these schemes both employer and employee make contributions into the pension fund. In some 'non-contributory' schemes only the employer makes contributions.

ii) *Individual Pension Schemes*
     An employee in non-pensionable employment, or a self-employed individual with a source of taxable income from a trade or profession, may establish an individual pension scheme through a retirement annuity policy issued by a life assurance company.
     The relatively recent introduction in 2003 of Personal Retirement Savings Accounts (PRSAs) permits individuals to save for their retirements throughout their careers and to maintain these savings as they move through different employments and between employments.

Defined Benefit and Defined Contribution Schemes

Occupational schemes differ depending upon how the retirement benefits are determined and how the scheme's assets are invested and administered. They may be Defined Benefit Schemes, Defined Contribution Schemes or, occasionally, a combination of these.
     Individual pension schemes are invariably Defined Contribution Schemes.

Defined Benefit ('Final Salary') Schemes

A defined benefit scheme promises the employee a pension in retirement. Generally, the pension is determined as a percentage of final salary for each year the individual member has been in service with the employer. The employer (or 'sponsor') and employee each pay contributions into a common pooled fund. The individual member does not have a specific, identifiable fund; assets of all members are commingled in the common pooled fund.
     A key feature of a defined benefit scheme is that the scheme's commitment to pay the defined percentage of final salary as pension and other benefits is underwritten by the employer. The employer undertakes to ensure that the scheme has sufficient assets to pay the promised benefits. Therefore, in defined benefit schemes, investment risk is borne by the employer.

Defined Contribution ('Money Purchase') Schemes

Under defined contribution schemes the contributions to be paid by the employee scheme member and the employer are defined, rather than the actual retirement benefits. The contributions and the investment returns they generate are accumulated to retirement age and the monies thus accumulated will be applied in purchasing the pension: hence the term 'money purchase schemes'.

In defined contribution schemes each member has a separately identifiable fund. The key feature of the defined contribution scheme is that the retirement benefit depends on the value of the individual's specific fund on retirement and on the investment conditions prevailing at that time (which determine the amount of pension or annuity that the member's fund will purchase). There is no employer guarantee. Therefore, in defined contributions schemes, it is the member who bears the investment risk.

THE REGULATORY FRAMEWORK
Occupational Pension Schemes

The Trust Structure

Occupational pension schemes are normally organised as trusts. A trust is a legal structure or vehicle that places responsibility for the management of a certain property (e.g., a pension scheme) in the hands of a third party – the board of trustees.

The trust is a legal entity in its own right and it is separate and distinct from the sponsoring company (the employer). The trust protects the beneficiaries of the scheme by requiring the trustees to act in their interest.

Legal Framework

The objectives and responsibilities of a pension trust are defined by:

i)   its trust deed, in effect the constitution of the pension scheme, which sets out the rules and responsibilities of the trust;
ii)   trust law, much of it long-standing case law;
iii) specific legislation:
  • Trustee Act 1893
  • Trustee (Authorised Investments) Act 1958
  • Pensions Act 1990, incorporating regulations under the EU Pension Directive
  • Pensions Amendment Act 1996
  • Pensions Amendment Act 2002
  • Various family law, tax and social-welfare legislation.

The Responsibilities of Trustees

General Legal Responsibilities

In discharging their responsibilities to the beneficiaries of the scheme, trustees must:

- act in good faith;
- exercise their own discretion, having made all necessary enquiries and investigations and taken advice as appropriate;
- act in the best interest of the beneficiaries.

In addition, Section 59 of the Pensions Act 1990 imposes the following general duties on pension scheme trustees:

- To ensure that the contributions payable by employer and members are received.
- To provide for the proper investment of the resources of the scheme in accordance with the rules of the scheme.
- Where appropriate to make arrangements for the payment of the benefits as provided for under the rules of the scheme as they become due.
- To ensure that proper membership and financial records are kept.

Investment Responsibilities

The overall responsibility of trustees in relation to investment matters is set out in Section 59(b) of the Pensions Act of 1990: 'to provide for the proper investment of the resources of the scheme in accordance with the rules of the scheme'.

Clearly, the legislation is not over-prescriptive when it comes to matters of investment. The 'proper investment of the resources of the scheme' is not defined.

Trustees, therefore, rely on general trust law for guidance:

i)   Trustees are subject to a duty of care. They must invest with the care which an ordinary prudent person would take in investing for the benefit of other people for whom he or she felt normally bound to provide.

Firstly, the duty of care implies a requirement to invest prudently, i.e., in a diversified manner. Secondly, the duty of care points to a requirement to obtain expert advice. The power to delegate the investment function is implied. However, responsibility cannot be delegated and remains with the trustees, who are obliged to take reasonable steps to satisfy themselves that the appointed fund manager or managers have the necessary knowledge and expertise. The trustees must continue to monitor the management of the investment function.

ii)   The trustees must have regard to the fact that the purpose of the scheme is to provide retirement benefits for the employees. As such, the best interest of all should be taken to mean the best financial interest.

iii) The trustees must recognise also a duty to the sponsoring employer who, as a beneficiary of investment performance, has a legitimate interest in the efficient management of the scheme.

Investment Regulations: The EU Pensions Directive

Regulations under the Pensions Act 1990 have been made to implement the EU Pensions Directive (often referred to as the IORPs Directive) into Irish law.

The regulations reinforce the prudent person principle by requiring trustees to:

- invest the assets of the scheme in a manner calculated to ensure the security, quality, liquidity and profitability of the portfolio as a whole.
- invest the assets of the scheme predominantly on regulated markets.
- properly diversify the assets of the scheme to avoid excessive reliance on any particular asset, issue or group of undertakings.
- only invest in derivative instruments in so far as they –
  (a) contribute to a reduction of investment risks
  (b) or, facilitate efficient portfolio management.
- borrow monies only on a temporary basis for liquidity purposes.

The Regulations also require trustees of large schemes, i.e. with 100 or more members, to prepare a Statement of Investment Policy Principles (SIP) as follows:

(a) a written statement of the principles must be prepared and maintained.
(b) the statement must be reviewed at least every three years and
(c) be revised following any change of investment policy which is inconsistent with the statement.

The SIP must include:

- the investment objectives of the trustees
- the investment risk measurement methods
- the risk management processes to be used, and
- the strategic asset allocation with respect to the nature and duration of pension liabilities.

The Liabilities of Trustees

Any act or neglect on the part of a trustee which is not authorised or excused by the terms of the trust deed, or by law, is a 'breach of trust'.

A trustee will be required to make good, from his or her own personal assets, any shortfall in trust resources arising from a breach of trust for which he or she is deemed responsible.

It is possible for trustees to limit the extent of their liability and to obtain certain indemnities both at law and under the terms of the trust. Also trustees may protect their personal positions further by effecting Trustee Indemnity Insurance Policies.

Section 3 of the Pensions Act 1990 states that where a trustee, in his capacity as trustee, contravenes a provision of the Act or a regulation thereunder, he shall be guilty of an offence. Additionally, where in any report, certificate or other document required by the act a person makes a false or misleading statement, he shall be guilty of an offence. A person guilty of an offence shall be liable on summary conviction to a fine and/or imprisonment.

Individual Pension Schemes

Personal Pensions and PRSAs are essentially contracts between the individual and the pension or PRSA provider. The investment arrangements are defined explicitly in the policy documents or contracts that govern these schemes.

While there may be a choice as to the type of investment available, this choice may be exercised only within the terms outlined in the contract.

THE PENSION FUND'S REQUIREMENTS

The pension fund's requirements extend over a complex and dynamic framework of assets, liabilities and cash flows. The fund's assets generate investment returns that are uncertain and volatile. Liabilities extend into the long-term future and are subject, obviously, to inflation and also to the shifting longevity of beneficiaries. Cash flows are volatile, subject to an ever-changing mix of employer and employee contributions, pension payments and investment returns. Management of the fund is involved with potentially very large sums of money over very prolonged time horizons.

The table below attempts to illustrate the various factors that drive fund requirements:

Figure 9.1 Pension Fund Requirements, The Funding Standard

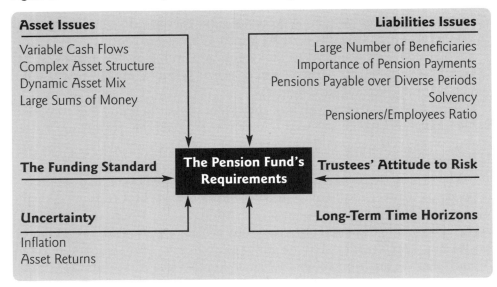

The Funding Standard

Pension fund investment, because of the nature of the fund's promise to pay pensions, is necessarily concerned with the long term. However, the scheme must also be concerned with providing security for beneficiaries on an ongoing basis.

The Pensions Act of 1990 introduced a Funding Standard, which ensures that members of defined benefit schemes can have confidence in the ongoing solvency of the scheme.

Under the Act the fund's trustees must submit to the Pensions Board an actuarial funding certificate, certifying whether or not the fund meets the Funding Standard.

A scheme shall be deemed to satisfy the Funding Standard if, in the opinion of the scheme actuary, the resources of the scheme at the effective date of the actuarial funding certificate would have been sufficient, if the scheme had been wound up at that date, to provide for the liabilities of the scheme and the estimated expenses of winding up the scheme. Liabilities will include pensions in payment, additional benefits due by way of additional voluntary contributions or rights transferred from another scheme, and benefits in respect of reckonable service.

A new actuarial funding certificate must be prepared within three years of the immediately preceding certificate. In addition, each annual report of the scheme must include a statement by the actuary that the Funding Standard continues to be met.

The Funding Standard requirement thus injects a short-term solvency dimension into the long-term nature of pension fund liabilities. The investment objective of the scheme must embrace both these long-term and short-term requirements.

Where a scheme fails to meet the Funding Standard, a funding proposal must be submitted to the Pensions Board. In certain circumstances the end date of the funding proposal may be extended beyond the date of the next Actuarial Funding Certificate, to a maximum period of ten years.

Pension Fund Investment Risk

In Chapter 6 investment risk is defined measured, analysed and discussed.

Because of the critical importance of pensions to the lives of pensioners the pension fund must survive and prevail in the long run. The pension fund will focus in particular on avoiding permanent loss of capital and on its ability to meet essential payments.

However, even within a single pension fund, perceptions of risk may differ.

- On the one hand, the employee may be primarily concerned that the pension fund is soundly invested and will be in a strong position to pay pensions in perhaps twenty or thirty years' time.
- The sponsoring company's finance director, on the other hand, while acknowledging the long-term imperative to pay pensions, may have the additional perspective that strong shorter-term performance will reduce funding costs.
- The fund trustees will attempt to ensure that the investment returns generated by the fund's portfolio will satisfy both these perspectives, whilst maintaining a surplus of assets over liabilities so that the requirements of the Funding Standard are met.

In managing the risks surrounding the pension fund the trustees will pay particular attention to the following.

Liability Risk

This is the risk that the value of the fund's assets over time fails to keep pace with the value of its liabilities.

Historically the conventional wisdom was that equities were the asset best placed to meet pension fund liabilities, because of the linkage that exists between, on the one hand, growth in the economy, growth in profits and growth in share prices and, on the other, growth in the economy, growth in wages and growth in pensions.

However, as discussed in more detail in Chapter 10 below, this conventional wisdom has been questioned in recent years. The present value of the fund's liabilities is determined by a discount factor which keys off bond yields. Therefore, it is argued, bonds are a more appropriate match for liabilities.

Certainly, the difficult investment environment of the early years of the new century has sharpened trustee awareness of the requirement for fund assets to keep pace with fund liabilities.

Downside Volatility

The implosion of the technology bubble ignited the severe equity bear market of 2000 to 2003. Investors received a stark reminder of the downside volatility of equity markets. Pension fund trustees, in particular, discovered that the downside volatility inherent in the high equity exposures of their funds at the market peak in 2000 was unacceptable.

The requirement to avoid unacceptable exposure to downside volatility is underlined by the need to comply with the relatively short-term requirements of the Funding Standard.

Benchmark Risk

In determining their fund's overall investment strategy trustees will often specify a 'benchmark asset mix'. This refers to an ideal portfolio mix which, if maintained over the life of the fund, will deliver the required risk and return characteristics.

Benchmark risk is the risk that the selected benchmark asset mix exposes the fund to fluctuations in asset values that differ over time from fluctuations in the value of liabilities.

Active Risk

The fund's investment manager may be mandated by the trustees to generate 'added value', i.e., returns in excess of benchmark returns. The search for 'added value' or excess return involves taking incremental risk over the risk embedded in the benchmark asset mix.

Active risk refers to the incremental risk entered into by the investment manager, on behalf of the fund, in the search for added value.

As discussed in Chapter 6, volatility is widely employed as the key measure of risk in portfolio construction. However, volatility as a measure of risk has limitations, as is illustrated in that chapter.

Therefore in assessing the overall riskiness of the fund's investment portfolio the quantitative measure of risk – volatility – is augmented by an array of qualitative measures to develop a comprehensive overview of portfolio risk and portfolio diversification.

Among the portfolio characteristics to be monitored are:

- the spread and coverage of the portfolio across asset types and across sectors;
- the concentration of the portfolio by sector and by stock;
- the portfolio's exposures to individual securities;
- the quality of the individual stocks in the portfolio;
- the volatility of the individual holdings;
- the style biases within the portfolio
  - to highly rated (growth) securities;
  - to low-rated (value) securities.

INVESTMENT OBJECTIVES

Having considered the overall legal framework within which the pension scheme operates, together with the fund's particular liabilities and characteristics and their own attitude to risk, the trustees may then proceed to define the fund's investment objectives.

Typically the trustees will have long-term and medium-term objectives for investment returns.

Long-Term Objectives

The trustees will normally express the fund's long-term return objective in terms of a required real return over the rate of inflation. As discussed earlier, pensions are linked to salaries before retirement, which in turn reflect inflation during the employee's working life. An inflation-linked objective is therefore appropriate to the fund's liabilities.

The particular real rate of return chosen will normally be that used by the actuary in the periodic valuation of the fund, e.g. typically 3% to 5% above an assumed long-term rate of inflation.

Importantly, particularly in the light of the difficulties generated by the weakness in equity markets during 2000/2003, the long-term objective is subject to the consideration of downside volatility discussed above.

Medium-Term Objectives

The medium-term objective's main function is to enable the trustees to monitor and control the investment management of the fund's portfolio.

Medium-term objectives may be of two kinds:

i)   *Peer-Group Objectives*
     The investment returns of the pension fund are measured and com-
     pared over different periods with the returns of other Irish pension
     funds, as measured and collated by an independent performance
     measurement specialist, such as Combined Performance Measurement
     Service (CPMS).
         The trustees may decide that the objective of the fund is:
     • to match that of the median or average fund in the survey;
     • or, more demandingly, to outperform the average return by some
       stated margin (e.g. 1% per annum) over some stated period of
       years (say 3 to 5 years);
     • or to rank within the top quartile (i.e., the top 25%) of funds in
       the survey over 3 to 5 years.
     The return objective is thus defined as to return relative to a 'peer
     group' benchmark. Where a 'peer group' benchmark is selected, the
     fund's strategic or benchmark asset mix, by definition, is the average
     asset mix of the universe of pension funds surveyed.

ii) *Customised Objectives*
     Alternatively, the trustees may develop a strategic long-term asset
     allocation, or asset mix, for the fund which is specifically appropriate
     to its requirements and particular financial profile.
         This customised asset mix will be applied in generating a cus-
     tomised performance benchmark by applying market returns for each
     asset class to their respective allocations in the benchmark asset mix.
         The trustees will then define the fund's investment objective, either:
     • to match the return of the benchmark asset mix;
     • or to 'add value' by generating a higher return than the benchmark.
       This latter objective will require the fund to take on incremental
       risk, i.e., risk in excess of the risk embedded in the benchmark.

INVESTMENT STRATEGY

Defining Investment Strategy

It is the trustees' responsibility to identify their investment objectives and to
define the investment strategy of the fund. In particular they must weigh up and:

MATCH

The requirements of the fund –
• its long-term liabilities to pay pensions
• its short-term solvency requirement
• its tolerance for risk

AGAINST

The characteristics of the investment assets –

- their long-term returns
- their volatilities
- their ability to cope with inflation.

Investment strategy must then be crystallised into a strategic or benchmark asset mix. Trustees may take some comfort from the view that the search is not for an ideal asset mix, but for an asset mix that will be appropriate under a wide variety of circumstances.

Indeed, even if an 'ideal' asset mix could be identified the trustees might still reject it – if, for example, they felt that they would perform poorly while other funds did well. The search therefore is for an asset mix that reflects the fund's individual requirements and the trustees' tolerance for risk.

In the table below, an attempt is made to align pension fund requirements with desirable asset characteristics and with asset types.

Figure 9.2 Pension Fund Requirement / Asset Characteristics

Pension Fund Requirement	Asset Characteristics	Asset
i) Inflation Protection	Ability to cope well with inflation	Equities Property, Index-Linked
ii) Growth over Inflation	Ability to generate real growth	Equities, Property, Index-Linked
iii) Currency Match	Euro-denominated	All Euro assets
iv) Income Stream	Relatively low-yielding	Equities, Index-Linked Cash
	Relatively high-yielding	Property Bonds
v) Marketability	High liquidity	Bonds, Equities, Index-Linked Cash

Pension Fund Requirement	Asset Characteristics	Asset
vi) Matching Term	Long-term assets	Bonds, Equities, Property, Index-Linked
	Short-term assets	Cash, Bonds Index-Linked

Because of its long-term nature and requirement to pay pensions that are linked to inflation, it is arguable that the most desirable asset characteristics for a pension fund are the ability to cope with inflation and the ability to provide returns above inflation. Historically, equities have been the asset best equipped to deliver these characteristics, and it is for this reason that equities have emerged as the dominant asset in pension fund portfolios.

Equities, however, do not offer a perfect or ideal solution. Inevitably, high returns from equity markets come at a high cost in risk or volatility terms. Equities are a high-volatility asset. Trustees must balance the high returns from equities against this volatility.

Diversification reduces volatility or risk, as Markowitz showed. By using his 'efficient frontier' – portfolio optimisation – a range of risk/return trade-offs may be examined and a portfolio structure appropriate to the trustee's risk appetite identified.

Equities suffer from other disadvantages:

- They are generally a low-income asset.
- Non-euro (overseas) equities do not provide a currency match for euro liabilities.
- Marketability may be restricted, especially in smaller company shares.

Although examination of the historical evidence shows that equities tend to outperform the other asset classes, there is no guarantee that this outperformance will persist into the future.

Prudence therefore requires that pension funds blend into their portfolios the desirable characteristics of the other investment assets. This provides the essential diversification of assets that is key to the control of risk.

Asset Liability Modelling

Asset Liability Modelling is a formal, quantitative approach to the determination of appropriate investment strategy and benchmark asset mix. As discussed above, the search is not for an ideal asset mix but for one that will be suitable under a variety of circumstances. The chosen asset mix must also encompass the valid, but conflicting, objectives of trustees. For example, the requirement to generate returns that in the long term meet or exceed the actuarial hurdle rate must be balanced against the objective to ensure solvency (i.e. to ensure that the value of assets exceeds the value of liabilities). The role of the Asset Liability Model is to help trustees to identify an efficient asset allocation strategy, which is appropriate to their objectives and risk tolerances.

The technique is an extension of the normal process of actuarial valuation. Where the actuarial valuation assumes fixed parameters, e.g., for growth in liabilities, for investment returns, etc., the Asset Liability Model projects varying courses of inflation, asset returns and related factors into the future. Thousands of such simulations are run, probabilities are attached to certain out-turns and implied funding levels are identified. The implications of different investment strategies are thus highlighted for trustees, helping them to identify the strategy and asset mix most appropriate to their circumstances.

As always with quantitative techniques, there are important caveats. Modelling processes depend heavily on the underlying assumptions and make extensive use of historic time series. The assumptions may be unreliable and historic returns and asset correlations may be of limited use.

The Asset Liability Model may best be seen, therefore, as a tool to help trustees to meet their risk/return objectives, augmenting the more qualitative approach discussed below.

Asset Liability Grid

An Asset/Liability Modelling exercise is a powerful tool in informing the trustees' decision on asset allocation. Note, however, that there are important reservations around the modelling approach. The model generates results that are consistent with the assumptions and parameters fed into it. There is little consensus about these, or even about model design. Nevertheless, where trustees are comfortable with the model and parameters chosen, the Asset/Liability Model is a powerful tool in its ability to illustrate the range of options available to trustees.

A more intuitive, broader-brush approach may be adopted by incorporating the key elements into a check list: see Figure 9.3.

Figure 9.3 Asset/Liability Grid

	Bonds	Emphasise Balanced	Equities
1. Liability Profile			
pension type:			
• fixed	X		
• indexed		X	X
• final salary			X
active/retired ratio:			
• high			X
• low	X	X	
term:			
• long			X
• short	X	X	
2. Fund Solvency			
• strong		X	X
• weak	X	X	
3. Corporate Sponsor			
• strong		X	X
• weak	X	X	
4. Appetite for short-term volatility			
• high			X
• low	X		

The grid is helpful in scoping out the broad asset mix that may be appropriate for a pension fund.

Defined benefit schemes at either extreme of these characteristics will see a reasonably clear solution. The grid shows that a fund where pensions are indexed, the active/retired membership ratio is high, with a long-term perspective, with strong solvency, a substantial corporate sponsor and a high appetite for short-term volatility, will opt for a high equity exposure.

Conversely, where pensions are fixed, where the active/retired membership ratio is low, with a short-term perspective, where both the fund solvency and corporate sponsor are weak and where appetite for short term volatility is low, the trustees will be drawn to a solution which incorporates a high bond content and low equity exposure.

Between these extremes the identification of the appropriate mix becomes an iterative process. In a sense the trustees must attempt to segment the liabilities into broad layers and match these against broad equity and bond characteristics.

A defined contribution scheme without the benefit of a corporate sponsor may, all things being equal, have a lower appetite for equities than a defined benefit scheme with otherwise similar characteristics.

Benchmarks and Added Value

Whether an informal matching process or a formal asset liability modelling exercise is carried out, it is the responsibility of the trustees to identify a benchmark asset mix. This mix is the central asset allocation strategy that is most appropriate to the pension fund's requirements and liabilities.

Having selected the benchmark asset mix the trustees must go on to decide whether the fund's return objective should be to match the return on the benchmark – a 'passive' investment strategy – or to exceed benchmark return by taking on a higher degree of risk – an 'active' investment strategy.

When both the benchmark asset mix and the investment objective have been identified, risk for the fund crystallises into two distinct elements:

i)   *Benchmark Risk*
      The risk that the selected benchmark asset mix exposes the fund to fluctuations in asset values, which differ over time from fluctuations in the value of liabilities.

      Most of the risk to which the fund will be exposed is made up of benchmark risk. This underlines the importance of the decision made by trustees in selecting the appropriate benchmark asset mix.

ii)   *Active Risk*
      The active risk that the fund, because of poor investment decision making, performs poorly against the selected benchmark. Active risk is the increased risk over benchmark risk taken by trustees in an effort to generate added value – incremental return over benchmark return.

The trustees may employ a range of techniques to control active risk:

* tracking error
* risk budget
* control ranges for asset exposures.

Active risk normally accounts for only a relatively minor proportion of total risk.

DETERMINING INVESTMENT STRATEGY

Our examination of investment strategy highlights the central role played by the trustees:

- The key driver of strategy is the trustees' analysis of the particular requirements of the fund and, critically, of its attitude to risk.
- In defining investment strategy, two considerations are critical:
  - diversification controls risk
  - the higher the expected return, the higher the risk.
- Investment strategy is crystallised in Benchmark Asset Mix, an asset mix which will be appropriate over a wide variety of circumstances. Benchmark Asset Mix may be determined by matching fund requirements to asset characteristics or by employing an Asset Liability Model.
- An added-value objective may be set by actively seeking higher than benchmark return. Alternatively the trustees may decide to passively lock into benchmark return.
- Risk at that point then crystallises into two distinct elements: benchmark risk and portfolio risk. Benchmark risk will account for the bulk of risk.

THE INVESTMENT MANDATE

Designing the Investment Mandate

A key duty of the trustees is the design of the Investment Mandate under which the investment manager will carry out the responsibilities delegated to him/her by the trustees for the day-to-day management of the fund assets.

The Investment Mandate, in effect, sets out the 'riding instructions' issued by the trustees to the investment manager. It will typically include:

- investment objective, specifying value added target, if any.
- the selected benchmark
- investment manager's discretion
  - the risk limits (i.e. risk budget)
  - the exposures
  - the instruments
- control procedure
  - risk limits
  - tracking error
  - exposure limits and constraints
- reporting and performance-measurement standards.

The Investment Mandate has three purposes:

- It interprets for the manager the trustees' requirements and objectives.
- It defines for the manager, quantitatively, the expectations of the trustees in respect of risk and return.
- It explicitly establishes the operational parameters within which the manager will operate.

Mandate Design: The Critical Question

The critical question to be addressed by trustees in mandate design is whether or not they wish to generate 'Added Value', i.e., excess return over benchmark return. Inevitably the search for added value involves 'active risk', i.e., incremental risk over benchmark risk.

A passive investment strategy sets out to replicate benchmark returns, i.e., to generate benchmark returns whilst tightly constraining risk to benchmark risk.

An active investment strategy sets out to generate added value, excess return over benchmark return, while accepting some measure of active risk, incremental risk over benchmark risk.

Investment Constraints

In managing the inevitable trade-off between 'added value' and 'active risk' or incremental return (over benchmark return) and incremental risk (over benchmark risk) the trustees will clearly require to control the investment manager's risk exposures. This will be set out in the Investment Mandate either by way of:

- *Control Parameters or Ranges*
  These specify maximum and minimum exposures to the various asset types, e.g., equity exposure might be permitted to range from 50% to 70% of total assets while within the overall equity exposure, Irish equity content might range from 10% to 20%.

- *Tracking Error*
  This quantifies the limit of incremental risk over benchmark risk allowed to the investment manager. For example, the investment manager might be permitted a tracking error of 3%, signifying that the funds return may deviate from benchmark return by +/– 3%. If the benchmark generates a return of 10%, the fund's expected return will be in the range 7% to 13%.

- *Risk Budget*
  The Risk Budget restates Tracking Error as an absolute quantum of incremental risk permitted to the investment manager in the search for

added value. In the example above, Tracking Error of ± 3% is restated as a Risk Budget of 300 basis points. The investment manager then allocates the Risk Budget over the various assets types. This permits the investment manager to closely track some markets where, perhaps, potential for added value is low, thus releasing Risk Budget for markets where potential for added value is high.

In addition to the quantitative constraints on risk discussed above, the trustees may place additional constraints on the investment manager's discretion. These might include:
- limits on the proportion of the fund that may be invested in a single stock or in the combined issues of a single entity;
- limits on the proportion of an issue that may be owned by the fund;
- limits on exposures to derivatives;
- limits on exposures to overseas currencies and investments;
- limits on borrowings.

The Investment Mandate will also set out the trustees' requirements for high standards of corporate governance both by the investment manager itself, e.g., in avoiding conflicts of interest, and in the investment manager's discharge of its duties as the representative of the trustees as shareholders in investee companies, e.g., in the exercise of voting rights on company resolutions, in the appointment and remuneration of directors, and generally in protecting the interests of the fund as shareholder.

SUMMARY

- Under Defined Benefit Schemes, contributions are paid into a common pooled fund. Promised benefits are underwritten by the employer, who thus takes the investment risk.
- Under Defined Contribution schemes each member has a separately identifiable fund. There is no employer guarantee. The member takes the investment risk.
- Pension funds are governed by their trust deeds, trust law and specific legislation which requires funds to meet a Funding Standard.
- The trustees are responsible for 'the proper investment of the resources of the scheme'.
- The key risk for a pension fund is that the value of its assets over time might fail to keep pace with the value of its liabilities.
- The pension fund will have investment return objectives ➡

- in the short term, of meeting the requirements of the Funding Standard;
- in the medium term, of generating returns which match or exceed customised or peer-group benchmarks;
- in the long term, of generating a real rate of return over inflation.

- In determining the appropriate asset mix the trustees may informally, or formally using Asset/Liability Modelling, match the fund's requirements against the characteristics of the investment assets.
- Investment strategy is crystallised into a benchmark asset mix. Benchmark risk is the risk that the benchmark selected will not reflect the value of liabilities over time.
- The trustees may decide to generate added value over benchmark return. This exposes the fund to active risk.
- Active risk is incremental risk over benchmark risk taken on by the fund in the search for added value, incremental return over benchmark return.

Chapter ten

Fund Management

This chapter examines the fund management industry, its scope, recent development, role and organisational structure. The key elements of investment management firms are introduced – philosophy, process, people and performance – and investment styles and skill sets are explored. The industry's investment decision-making processes and risk-control framework are outlined.

Learning Objectives

After reading this chapter you will be able to:
- **Outline the scope, recent development, role and organisation of the Irish fund management industry and discuss the challenges facing it**
- **Define and assess the key elements of fund management firms – philosophy, process, people and performance**
- **Distinguish between the various investment styles adopted by investment managers and the skill sets required to support them**
- **Recognise the essential difference between passive and active fund management**
- **Understand the different philosophies and focuses of value and growth managers**
- **Outline the steps in investment decision making, from analysis of client requirements to selecting individual stocks**
- **Review the risk-control framework normally put in place by industry participants.**

THE FUND MANAGEMENT INDUSTRY

Total assets managed by the world's largest 500 fund managers grew to an estimated $48,800 billion in 2004, as increase of 13% on 2003. The Pensions and Investment/Watson Wyatt survey also revealed that assets of the top twenty managers totalled $18,200 billion, representing 37% of total assets.

Key players in the industry range at one extreme from the investment management activities of major global financial conglomerates such as UBS and Allianz Group, through the dominant managers of passive portfolios, Barclays Global Investors and State Street Global Advisors, and the large privately owned specialist fund managers such as Fidelity Investments and Capital Group, to relatively small independent specialist asset management firms at the other end of the spectrum.

The Pensions and Investment/Watson Wyatt survey showed that while the smaller, niche managers are growing their assets at the expense of larger managers, nevertheless the industry remains quite concentrated, with the 50 largest managers accounting for 60% of total assets. Firms ranked in size from 251 to 500 managed only 6% of total assets.

The industry's clients include sovereign governments, pension funds, the family trusts of the wealthy, charities, corporates and private individuals. Monies managed on behalf of private individuals range from extremely large sums managed in dedicated portfolios for the mega-wealthy to quite modest amounts accumulated in a pooled fashion through collectivised investment (or savings) vehicles – mutual funds, unit trusts and life assurance policies.

The Irish fund management industry in December 2004 managed over €202bn of assets, of which €85bn was on behalf of Irish clients and €117bn was on behalf of international clients. *Source: Irish Association of Investment Managers.*

The Irish industry is dominated by two managers, Pioneer Investment Management – a subsidiary of the Italian bank, Unicredito – and BIAM (Bank of Ireland Asset Management), the fund management arm of Bank of Ireland Group. BIAM is differentiated from its domestic competitors by its success over a long period in the 1980s and 1990s in winning substantial international business.

Other key domestic players in the Irish market include Irish Life Investment Managers, AIBIM and KBC Asset Management. Other managers include the investment management arms of life assurance and general insurance companies and a number of smaller independent fund managers and hedge-fund managers.

The distribution of total assets at 31 December 2004 was as follows:

Table 10.1 Assets Under Management: 31 December 2004

	%		%
Equities	56	Ireland	26
Fixed Income	30	Euro ex Ireland	42
Property	6	Non Euro	32
Cash	7		
Other	1		
	100		100

The distribution of Irish Residents assets at 31 December 2004 is shown below:

Table 10.2 Assets of Irish Residents: 31 December 2004

	%
Pensions	60
Charities/Religious	2
Life Funds	25
Private Clients	1
Tracker Bonds	1
Other *	11
	100

* primarily General Insurance, Corporates and Building Societies

Source: Irish Association of Investment Managers.

The Irish industry enjoyed an enormously favourable operating environment for much of the 1980s and 1990s. Assets under management, the basis upon which fees are charged, benefited from strong investment returns, particularly in Ireland, during these two decades. The economic boom of the Celtic Tiger years, apart altogether from its impact on asset valuations, benefited the industry in two ways. Numbers in employment, and therefore in pension schemes, increased steadily and high levels of wealth creation expanded the opportunity to market investment products and services.

In recent years the operating environment has become substantially more challenging. Firstly, there has been a significant shift of client funds from active management to lower-margin, passive management. Secondly, an ongoing switch from balanced mandates to specialist mandates has presented an opportunity to the major international players to win the business of Irish pension fund clients. Finally, the relatively poor market conditions which have prevailed since the peak of the technology bubble in 2000 have curtailed the underlying growth in assets under management.

Development

The modern investment management industry developed in response to the crisis presented by the high-inflation 1970s, when investment returns were extremely poor and the industry's clients deeply dissatisfied. The industry was obliged to embrace higher standards of professionalism, sophistication and importantly, risk management and control. Change was accelerated by the implementation of ERISA 1974 (The Employment Retirement Income Security Act 1974) in the US. ERISA refined the duties of pension fund trustees, obliging them to act not just as 'prudent men' but as 'prudent experts'. Trustees, in turn, required greater expertise of their investment managers.

In the 1980s and subsequently, the industry developed a wider and more sophisticated product range designed to deliver differentiated investment solutions appropriate to client requirements and within required risk tolerances.

The exceptional investment returns generated by markets during the disinflationary period from 1982 to 1999 boosted assets under management and these were further augmented by large inflows of new money as demographic factors shifted in the industry's favour, notably as the post-war 'baby boom' generation entered the savings phase of its lifespan.

Role and Organisation Structure

The role of the investment manager is to accept, safeguard, protect and invest client assets and all rights attaching thereto, to generate required returns on the assets within appropriate risk parameters, to account and report on its activities and actions, and to repay monies to the client as required.

Organisational structures vary from investment manager to investment manager, depending on the historical development of the business, its size and organisation culture. Common functions will include:

Function	Activities
Fund Management	Investment Decision Making: – strategic – tactical Portfolio Construction Transactions Treasury – deposits – foreign exchange
Research	Fundamental Economic and Company Research Stock Screening
Marketing	Marketing Strategy Business and Product Development Client Liaison

Function	Activities
Investment Accounting	Settlements Safekeeping and Custody Client Accounting Valuation and Reporting Tax Reclaims
Performance Measurement	Measurement of Risk and Return
Business Management	Strategic and Operational Management
Financial Accounting	Corporate Budgeting and Accounting Internal Audit
Compliance	Regulatory Reporting Development and Monitoring of Internal Compliance
Information Systems	Systems Development and Maintenance

Each of these activities is important in its own right. However, from the client's perspective the key differentiator in selecting an investment manager is that manager's ability to generate superior investment returns, i.e., the fund management function.

In assessing the investment organisation's fund management capability the client will focus particularly on:

i)   **Investment Philosophy**
     For active investment managers, investment philosophy identifies where value is available in markets and demonstrates how this insight may be applied in generating superior investment returns.
     For passive investment managers, investment philosophy is defined in the belief that the pursuit of added value is futile and that, therefore, the focus of investment management should be on the replication of market outturns.

ii) **Investment Process**
     Investment process refers to the methodology whereby the investment firm's philosophy is implemented in a consistent, disciplined and systematic manner in the construction of portfolios that are designed to deliver repeatable added value.

iii)   **People and Resources**
        The fund management activity should be staffed and led by high-quality, experienced and committed investment professionals who have the support of an effective technology platform, e.g. information systems, databases, screening tools, etc.

iv)   **Performance**
        Investment performance should support the investment manager's claims for the effectiveness of its philosophy, process, people and resources. Historical performance should be examined to test and understand:

  - Its consistency
    - with the manager's philosophy
    - with the manager's investment style.
  - Its recurring nature
    - was added value generated in a consistent smooth manner or was it attributable to a small number of 'lumpy' periods of out-performance?
  - Its riskiness
    - how much risk was taken in generating the returns (i.e., what tracking error?)
    - what information ratio was achieved? (i.e. the ratio of added value to tracking error).

Historical performance is not necessarily a good guide to future outcomes.

The key question is whether the outperformance achieved in the past is repeatable. Is there present in the philosophy, process, people and resources an investment engine that will consistently generate superior returns in the future?

Investment Style

An investment manager's style is defined by the investment philosophy and process that determine the manager's approach to stock selection and portfolio construction.

Active and Passive Investment

The Efficient Market Theory argues that:

  - markets are efficient;
  - markets do a good job in reflecting information in prices;
  - adding value over market returns is not easy;
  - forecasting market out-turns is difficult.

Subscribers to this theory believe that assets are fairly priced by the market and that the search for added value is futile. Investors, therefore, should adopt a passive approach to investing by seeking only to replicate market returns.

The passive investor therefore sets out to replicate market or benchmark outturns, i.e., to construct portfolios that track, as closely as is practicable, the risk and return outcomes of the market or benchmark.

The key skills employed by the passive investment manager include:

- in-depth understanding of benchmarks and of market indices;
- portfolio construction skill to replicate the benchmark and minimise tracking error;
- efficient management of cash flows;
- timely and accurate implementation of corporate events
  - mergers and acquisitions
  - secondary and scrip issues
  - share buy-backs;
- effective management of transaction costs.

Active investors, however, reject Market Efficiency, believing that pricing anomalies exist in the market and that, with skill and expertise, value may be generated above market returns. Of course, the active investor acknowledges that added value (additional return over market or benchmark return) cannot be accessed without incurring active or incremental risk (additional risk over market or benchmark risk). The actively managed portfolio will have higher volatility than the market or benchmark, i.e., the tracking error of the active portfolio will be higher than that of the passive portfolio. The ratio of added value to tracking error is known as the information ratio.

The key skills employed by the active manager include:

- effective data management and information collection;
- screening skill to permit a focus on key data;
- research skills;
- portfolio construction skills;
- efficient transaction management;
- risk management.

Active management requires the creation of an investment management infrastructure, people and systems to build a database, design screens, research opportunities, construct portfolios and trade in markets. By comparison with passive investing active management is a high-cost activity. Active investment management fees, therefore, are higher than passive fees.

Successful active management has the potential to generate returns that more than compensate for the extra fees involved.

Active returns are uncertain both in absolute terms and relative to the market or benchmark. Passive returns also are unpredictable in absolute terms, but they are predictable relative to the market or benchmark.

The development of passive investment has thrown the burden of proof firmly onto the active manager. On the one hand, the active manager must persuade the client that the manager possesses a particular insight that offers the potential for repeatable added value at a cost, both in terms of fees and incremental risk, that is acceptable to the client.

On the other hand, the client in employing an active manager makes two critical judgments:

i)   that markets are inefficient;
ii)   that the client has the ability to identify a manager who will successfully add value in the future.

Market efficiency, and thus passive investment, relies on the active investor. If everybody believed that all publicly available information is already reflected in market prices, then nobody would do any fundamental research and the market would be denied the information it relies on to create efficiency.

The passive and active investment styles may be combined in a 'Core/Satellite' approach to investment. The larger 'core' portfolio is managed passively, designed to deliver returns which closely replicate benchmark outturns, i.e., it is managed with low tracking error against the benchmark. The smaller 'satellite' portfolio is actively managed, designed to generate added value over benchmark returns. The active satellite may be permitted to exhibit a relatively wide divergence from benchmark returns, i.e., to be managed with high tracking error.

The relatively low tracking error of the 'core' portfolio when combined with the relatively high tracking error of the 'satellite' portfolio results in the overall tracking error of the total portfolio being maintained within prescribed limits.

A key attraction of the Core/Satellite approach is that a successful active manager may be able to exploit this wide discretion to generate substantial added value.

Balanced and Specialist Investment

A balanced investment manager manages a total fund or a cross-section thereof. The balanced manager makes decisions across the full range of asset and decision levels, determining asset mix, currency mix, country mix and sector and stock allocations.

The specialist investment manager focuses on a particular decision-making level, e.g., emerging market equities, or US equities. The specialist manager therefore typically manages only a portion of the total fund.

As discussed above, the recent trend in Ireland has been towards specialist managers and away from balanced managers, partly driven by a shift from peer-group to customised benchmarks.

The move to specialist mandates involves the client more intensively in the investment process. Whereas with balanced mandates the investment manager appointed determines the portfolio mix at each decision level (e.g., asset mix, country allocation, etc.), with specialist managers the client must first decide the proportion of the total fund to be allocated to each specialist mandate.

Top-Down and Bottom-Up Investment

The top-down investment manager employs his global macro-economic and cyclical overview to inform decision making in sequence at the asset allocation, currency, country, sector and stock selection decision levels.

For example, a top-down investment manager might conclude, given his overall global macro-economic view:

- that equities are the asset of choice;
- that within global equities, preference is for US equities because, perhaps, the US economy is most advanced on the path to recovery;
- within US equities, because of the particular stage of the US economic cycle, that retailers are an attractive sector;
- and within retailers, preference might be for Wal-Mart.

In direct contrast, the bottom-up manager focuses, in the first instance, on stock selection. The stock selection process in turn drives sector, country, currency and asset allocations, i.e., they are an outcome of the stock selection process.

In effect, the top-down manager is drilling downwards from his global macro-economic overview to stock selection. The bottom-up manager, though, believes that his fundamental analysis gives him a more tangible sense of value at the stock level. Stock selection drives the other decisions.

In practice, both approaches are normally implemented in a risk-controlled manner to ensure that portfolios are appropriately diversified and in compliance with mandated risk tolerances. Both top-down and bottom-up managers might conclude, from their different perspectives, that only bank stocks and oil stocks are attractive.

However, prudent portfolio construction would not permit portfolios to be comprised only of bank and oil stocks. Appropriate diversification would be built in to ensure that the portfolio exhibited and maintained the required tracking error against its benchmark.

Growth and Value Investment

The growth and value styles of investment refer to approaches to active equity investment.

The growth manager is growth-oriented and focuses on companies with relatively high growth in projected earnings. The growth manager believes that market valuations do not fully reflect the expected growth in earnings per share of growth companies. When the growth companies deliver this growth, their share prices will be adjusted upwards and will outperform the general market. In essence, the growth manager believes that growth companies are underpriced by the markets. In his/her analysis of candidate companies for inclusion in portfolios, the growth manager focuses on growth in earnings, dividends, cash flows, book values and sales.

The focus of the value manager is on stocks that are lowly rated relative to the market as a whole, i.e., where the price earnings ratio and price-to-book ratio are lower and the dividend yield is higher than the market average. The value manager believes that over time stock-market valuations have a 'reversion to mean' tendency, i.e., that over time highly rated stocks are pulled down to average ratings, while low-valued stocks are pulled up to average ratings. In terms of valuation metrics, the focus of the active manager is on price earnings ratios, price-to-cash-flow ratios, dividend yields and price-to-book ratios relative to the market average. Value investment rests on the belief that where stock prices fall below what might be regarded as their long-term mean or normal valuation, catalysts will emerge, whether it be shareholder pressure for change, management change or strategic change (such as disposal of non-core activities), which will drive the stocks back to normal values. The research effort of the value manager is thus devoted to the identification of these catalysts within companies.

Figure 10.1 Value Investing

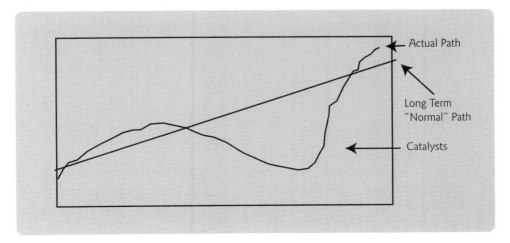

Again, as with the top-down and bottom-up approaches, the construction of growth and value portfolios is typically implemented within a risk-controlled framework. Portfolios are unlikely to be comprised solely of value or growth stocks, but rather will exhibit a bias to the managers' styles.

INVESTMENT DECISION MAKING

Overview

The following chart presents an overview of the investment decision-making process.

Figure 10.2 Overview of the Investment Decision-Making Process

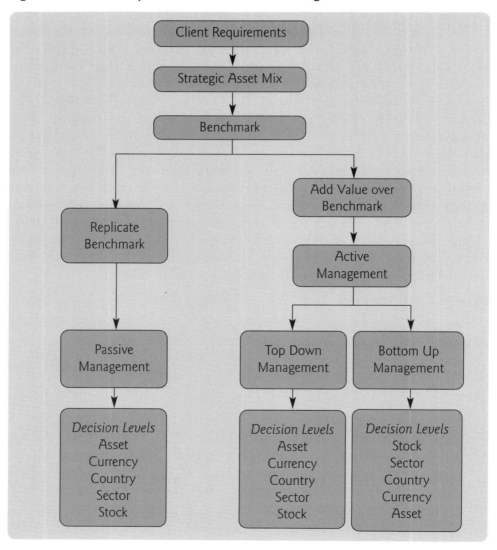

Analysis of Client Requirements

The first step in investment decision making is the analysis of client requirements. In particular the client's time horizons, short- and long-term return objectives, need for income, need for liquidity, and exposure to tax and regulatory issues are identified. A key ingredient in the analysis is the client's attitude to risk.

The process, while recognising that there is no single ideal asset, attempts to match the requirements of the client against the characteristics of the different asset classes. In Chapter 9 an Asset Liability Grid was illustrated to support the process for matching a pension fund's requirements against asset characteristics. The following table adapts this idea for clients generally:

Figure 10.3 Client Requirements / Asset Characteristics Grid

	Equities	Property	Bonds	Cash
• Liabilities				
Fixed			x	
Inflation Linked	x	x		
• Time Horizons				
Long	x	x		
Short			x	x
• Income Requirement				
High		x	x	
Low	x			x
• Liquidity Requirement				
High	x		x	x
Low		x		
• Attitude to Risk				
Aggressive	x	x		
Cautious			x	x

The clear understanding of the client's requirements, and their reflection in an asset mix designed to meet them, are the essential first step in investment decision making. Because of the uncertainties attaching to the future – future inflation rates, future market conditions, prospective investment returns – this cannot be a precise exercise, and subjective judgments must be made over the precise weight of the different asset types in the overall mix, e.g., whether the equity content should be 40%, 45% or 50%.

Examples of typical mixes for various categories of client are available from the asset distributions of Irish unit–linked, insurance-managed funds during early 2005:

Table 10.3 Representative Managed Fund Asset Mixes: March 2005

	Cautious	Balanced	Aggressive
Bonds	30	16	6
Equities	14	73	88
Property	11	8	3
Cash	45	3	3
	100	100	100

However, these mixes are currently the subject of some controversy, because of the impact of the equity bear market of 2000/2003. Some observers are concerned that the equity content of the balanced and aggressive mixes above overstates the risk appetite of the typical investor in these categories.

Strategic Asset Mix and Benchmark

As discussed in Chapter 9, the Investment Mandate agreed between the client and the investment manager is a key document, which interprets client requirements, quantifies client expectations and establishes the operational parameters within which the manager will operate.

The Investment Mandate will define the long-term strategic asset mix best designed to deliver client expectations. This strategic asset mix sets out the normal, or central, asset mix and it is embedded in the client's benchmark.

The benchmark asset mix is the ideal portfolio mix which, if maintained over the life of the fund, will deliver the risk and return outcomes required by the client.

Replicating Benchmark Out-turns: Passive Management

When the client requirement is to replicate benchmark out-turns passive management offers a relatively low-cost solution. The benchmark, as discussed in Chapter 9, may be either a customised or peer-group benchmark. In approaching the various decision levels the passive manager must decide as follows, depending on the Investment Mandate:

Table 10.4 Passive Management: Decision-Making Alternatives

Asset Level	Bonds v Equities v Property v Cash	Peer Group or Customised
Currency Level	US v Euro v Stg£ v Yen	Peer Group or Customised
Country Level	US v Europe v UK v Japan	Peer Group or Customised or Indexed
Sector Level	Bonds: Short v Medium v Long Dated	Indexed
	Equities: Consumer v Financial v Resources	Indexed
	Property: Office v Retail v Industrial	Indexed
Stock Level	Stock Selection	Indexed

At the Asset level, the mix decision is determined by the benchmark. A customised benchmark specifies the precise asset mix to be maintained. A peer-group benchmark requires the manager to replicate in the asset mix the consensus or average asset mix of the specified peer group.

At the Currency Level a similar approach is followed, although here there is the complication that the peer-group currency mix may not be readily available and therefore may need to be estimated. The currency mix to be maintained will be specified in the customised benchmark.

At the Country Level, a third possibility presents itself. Besides matching the peer-group or customised benchmark's country mixes, there is the option of matching the country mix within an appropriate index, e.g., the MSCI World Index for the equity content.

The sectoral mix of the peer group's investment portfolio is normally not available. The customised benchmark normally refers to the sectoral mixes of some appropriate indices that the passive manager will then replicate in the client portfolio. Typically, therefore, whether the benchmark follows the customised or peer-group model an indexed mix is applied at the sectoral level.

Finally, at the stock level the passive manager will normally be expected to replicate an appropriate or pre-specified index or indices. However, because of the unique nature of property investment there cannot be an available index at the stock selection level. Selection of individual properties, therefore, is always an active process.

Generating Added Value: Active Management

The role of the active manager is to generate added value over and above benchmark returns. The active manager makes active decisions at each of the decision levels. These active decisions move the portfolio away from the mixes embedded in the benchmark.

Therefore the portfolio, once it has deviated from benchmark mix, no longer replicates benchmark risk and return outcomes. Added value is the excess of the portfolio return over benchmark return. Incremental risk measures the difference between portfolio risk and benchmark risk. The information ratio, which measures the effectiveness of the manager, is the ratio of added value to incremental risk.

The degree of deviation from benchmark mix permitted to the investment manager will be set out in the client's investment mandate and will be quantified by tracking error, the extent to which the volatility of the portfolio is permitted to deviate from benchmark volatility.

The extent to which the investment manager will exercise the discretion allowed will be determined by the strength of the manager's convictions in his investment insights. The client, having permitted the manager to take higher risk in the search for higher return, is entitled to expect that the manager will, except in unusual conditions, normally exercise that discretion.

Active Management: The Top-Down Approach

As discussed above, the investment decision making of the top-down active manager is informed by his global macro-economic overview. This global overview drives decision making, in sequence, at the asset, currency, country, sector and stock levels.

The methodology followed by individual investment firms is outlined in their investment process and will vary from firm to firm. No firm has a monopoly of wisdom. Unique insights are rare.

A brief discussion of some of the approaches used at each decision level is set out below.

Top-Down Decision Making: The Asset Level

Cyclical Approach

The economic and investment cycles are examined and the relative attractions of the different asset classes identified.

Risk Premiums Approach

The relative attractions of the different assets are determined by comparing prevailing risk premiums to historical patterns.

Scenario Analysis

Risk and return projections are prepared for each asset. These projections are then optimised to produce the required mix.

Top-Down Decision Making: The Currency Level

Among many factors examined in determining the attractions of currencies are:

- relative levels of consumer prices in the different currency blocs;
- relative interest-rate differentials;
- relative projected asset returns;
- capital flows;
- trade flows;
- currency price momentum;
- long-term currency trends.

A key decision, to be embedded in the benchmark, is the required level of exposure to the client's domestic currency. This may be heavily influenced by the currency in which the client's liabilities are denominated. Other factors influencing this decision include the liquidity, depth and breadth of the domestic equity market. On the one hand US investors, whose domestic equity market exhibits these characteristics, traditionally have invested relatively minor proportions of their assets outside the US. Irish investors, on the other hand, because of the relatively small domestic equity market, have for many years invested a relatively large part of their equity portfolios overseas. Irish institutional investors since the beginning of 1999 have reduced their exposure to Irish equities, availing themselves of the opportunity presented by the introduction of the euro to further diversify their portfolios by purchasing euro-denominated equities without incurring currency risk.

Currency markets can be volatile. Currency decision making is complex. In approaching the currency-mix decision the investor should emphasise

- clarity of strategic approach;
- consistency of implementation;
- strict control and risk management.

Top-Down Decision Making: The Country Level

Since the advent of the euro there is a trend amongst Irish managers to treat Europe on a euro- (e.g., France, Germany) or non-euro basis (e.g., the United Kingdom, Switzerland), rather than on a country basis.

In assessing the relative attractions of a region or country the investment manager will review:

• relative long-term economic prospects;
• relative short-term cyclical prospects
• relative investment cycles;
• relative valuations
  – by comparison with the different regions or countries;
  – by comparison with the domestic historical pattern.

The country selection decision is complicated not only by the difficulties of forecasting economic and market outcomes, but also by political and cultural differences among the various countries. Technical complications also arise on account of differences in accounting standards and variations in index composition.

Top-Down Decision Making: The Sector Level

Bonds

Bonds may be categorised by issuer (e.g. government or corporate), maturity (e.g. long-dated, medium-dated, short-dated) and by credit rating (e.g., high quality, high yield).

The relative attractions of the different categories of bond may be assessed by examining:

• anticipated cyclical patterns in economies;
• anticipated trends in inflation;
• anticipated trends in interest rates;
• anticipated trends in the yield curve, i.e., the term structure of interest rates;
• the relative attractions of bonds within individual maturity categories;
• anticipated shifts in credit ratings and credit-rating differentials.

Equities

Sector selection for equities may take place at the global, regional or country levels. Up to quite recently sector selection was country-based. The investment manager would compare the attractions of Irish banks against Irish construction companies and against Irish food companies. More recently sector selection is increasingly being approached on a European or global basis.

Methodologies employed in assessing the relative attractions of the different equity sectors include:

- fundamental analysis of the sectors' relative long-term prospects;
- projections of relative sector profitability;
- comparisons of relative valuation;
- examination of relative price momentum.

Property

Commercial property investment sectors may be categorised as office, retail and industrial. Residential property, particularly in recent years, has become a widely used investment vehicle in Ireland, esepcially for individual investors.

The examination of the relative attractions of the different sectors includes review of the following factors:

- long-term demographic and employment trends;
- short-term cyclical economic developments;
- relative sectoral valuations;
- supply and demand background within each individual sectoral category.

Top-Down Decision Making: The Stock Level

Investment portfolios, whether directly invested or invested via pooled vehicles, are comprised of individual securities. The implementation of all investment decisions requires action at the stock selection level. Every investor, therefore, has an interest in stock selection and, unsurprisingly, a myriad of approaches to decision making at the stock selection level have been developed. A general introduction to stock selection is outlined below.

Bonds

Having considered the influences on the sectoral selection decision discussed above, the top-down investor in determining the attractiveness of a particular bond will:

- compare one bond against another on the basis of credit rating, yield and sensitivity to projected changes in interest rates and the yield curve;
- compare one bond against the market as a whole on the basis of sensitivity to projected changes in interest rates and the yield curve.

Bond selection in practice ranges from the straightforward comparison of yield spreads (the difference between the yield on one bond and the yield on another) to complex quantitative modelling techniques.

Equities

All investment management firms place particular emphasis on their equity stock selection process. A wide array of different methodologies have been developed, generally based on one or more of the following approaches:

Fundamental Analysis

Fundamental analysis focuses in the first instance on the investee company itself:

- its operations
  - facilities, buildings and plant
  - products, brands, market shares
  - workforce
  - clients and customers
  - competitors
  - sensitivity to cyclical economic development.
- its management
  - development and implementation of strategy
  - operational ability
  - commitment to shareholders.
- its finances
  - generation of sales, profits and earnings growth
  - cash generation
  - dividend-paying capability
  - balance-sheet strength.
- its growth potential
  - prospects for future growth in sales, profits, earnings and dividends.

Secondly, the fundamental investor reviews the company's valuation as measured by its price earnings ratio, price to cash-flow ratio, dividend yield and other measures, often by reference to peer-group and market comparisons, to determine the extent to which the company fundamentals are reflected in the share price.

Quantitative Analysis

Whereas the fundamental approach is heavily human-driven, quantitative analysis is computer-based. Financial, accounting and valuation data is collected on the universe of companies followed by the investment manager. Quantitative screens are then applied to this data to identify attractive stocks. The screens applied will vary according to the investment philosophy of the investment manager. Value managers will develop valuation-based screens, e.g., screens based on price earnings ratios, dividend yield, price-to-book ratios and others. Growth managers will develop screens based on measures of growth, e.g., short- and long-term measures of growth in sales, earnings, dividends and asset value.

Technical Analysis

Adherents of technical analysis will analyse and interpret charts of historical price data to forecast future price movements and thus identify attractive stocks. The technical analysis approach to investment rests on the belief that all available data is already reflected in the share price, so that no further fundamental analysis is required.

Property

Individual properties, unlike quoted equities and bonds, are neither continuously traded nor divisible. Large sums of money may be required for investment in an individual property, particularly for a high-quality, well-located commercial property.

For many investors, investment in property is possible only if financed to a large degree by borrowings. Banks are usually prepared to lend money secured against property. However, it is important for the investor to bear in mind that a 'geared property' (i.e., a property with associated borrowings) takes on different characteristics from that property in its ungeared state. The income attractions of property investment are diluted as the rent is offset against interest on borrowings, while the capital stream of return becomes more volatile.

Many investors, including large pension funds, carry out their property investment through pooled vehicles such as property unit trusts, limited partnerships and property syndicates.

Key considerations in property stock selection for those investors who make direct investments include:

- location
- rental yield (current rental yield and equivalent yield)
- rental growth
- risk.

Cash Deposits

In selecting a home for cash at a deposit-taking institution, the investor will take into consideration:

- the interest rate available
- the creditworthiness of the institution.

For investment managers, cash deposits are normally a temporary home for monies awaiting investment in long-term assets. At a certain cyclical point, however, cash can play an important role in investment strategy. It cushions the client portfolio from the impact of falling prices in the long-term assets and provides the wherewithal to purchase assets at lower prices after the fall.

The basic principle of diversification may be applied to cash balances. Cash is normally spread over different deposit-taking institutions and different maturities. Liquidity is a key attraction of cash balances. Investment managers normally maintain ongoing access to cash to permit them to avail of investment opportunities as they arise.

Active Management: The Bottom-Up Approach

As discussed above, the bottom-up manager focuses in the first instance on the stock selection decision level. Decisions taken at the stock selection level determine outcomes at the sector, country, currency and asset levels. In making stock selection decisions the bottom-up manager will be subject to similar considerations and influences as those outlined above for the top-down manager.

The underlying belief of the bottom-up manager is that the prospects for, and valuations of, individual companies can be assessed and predicted with a greater degree of assurance than macro-economic outcomes and their implications for countries, sectors and stocks.

Risk Control

The precise risk-control framework operated by an investment management company will vary from firm to firm, depending on the firm's development, its culture, ownership and organisational structures.

Elements of the risk-control framework will typically include:

i)   **External Audit**
     The External Auditor, besides making his report to shareholders as required by company law, will also report to the firm's board on the effectiveness of the firm's risk-management and risk-control systems.

ii) **Internal Audit**
     The internal audit function challenges, tests and reports, usually to board level, on the firm-wide risk-management and internal control systems.

iii) **Compliance**

The compliance function is charged with ensuring that the firm is in strict adherence to regulatory and mandated requirements and to its own internal rule-book. The compliance function ensures that appropriate and fully documented processes and procedures are in place.

iv) **Operational Risk**

The operational risk-management function develops processes and procedures for control and management of operational risk, e.g., technological or systems failures, human error or disaster recovery.

v) **Investment Risk**

Typically there are three elements to control of investment risk.

a) *Portfolio Review*

Portfolio Review subjects all client portfolios to regular monitoring and review. Portfolio Review ensures that portfolios as constructed are aligned with the guidelines and limits as detailed in the relevant client mandate, for example:

- tracking error
- sectoral and stock exposure limits
- portfolio distribution
- portfolio concentration.

A procedure for identifying and rectifying, within prescribed deadlines, breaches of mandate will be outlined and implemented.

b) *Portfolio Construction*

The first line of defence against investment risk is, of course, at the fund manager level. Typically the fund manager will have the support of technological systems that will assist in ensuring that portfolios are constructed in line with mandated guidelines and limits.

c) *Performance Measurement*

The performance measurement function provides detailed analysis of each client portfolio's risk and return characteristics. Portfolios are subjected to attribution analysis, peer comparisons and style analysis. Reports are prepared for the fund management team, for Portfolio Review and, usually, for the chief investment officer or investment committee.

SUMMARY

- The implementation of ERISA 1974 raised the hurdle of investment expertise for pension fund trustees, and in turn, for investment managers.
- The role of the investment manager is to accept, safeguard, protect and invest client monies and to generate the required returns within appropriate risk parameters.
- The key elements to be addressed in assessing the capability of the investment manager are philosophy, process, people (and resources) and performance.
- Investment style refers to the philosophy and process which inform the investment manager's approach to stock selection and portfolio construction.
- Passive managers set out to replicate benchmark returns. Active managers attempt to add value over benchmark returns.
- In employing an active manager the client makes two judgments
  - that markets are inefficient;
  - that the client can identify successful active managers.
- The passive and active approaches may be combined in a Core/Satellite approach.
- The top-down manager uses his global macro-economic view to inform decision making, first at the asset level and thereafter, in turn, at the currency, country, sector and stock selection levels. The bottom-up manager focuses on the stock selection level. In practice, portfolios are constructed in a risk-controlled fashion.
- Growth managers focus on measures of growth, in earnings per share, cash flows, asset values. Value managers are focused on measures of valuation.
- Understanding client requirements is the first step in the investment process and from this flow strategic asset mix, benchmark selection and added-value objectives.
- At each decision level – asset, currency, country, sector, stock – the active manager may make decisions which move the portfolio away from the benchmark.
- Added value is the excess return of the portfolio over benchmark return. Active or Incremental risk is the difference between portfolio risk and benchmark risk. The information ratio, the ratio of added value to incremental risk, measures the effectiveness of the investment manager.
- The risk-control framework, typically, will include external audit, internal audit, the compliance function, operational risk management and investment risk management.

Chapter eleven

Performance Measurement and Style Analysis

This chapter deals with the measurement of investment returns. The calculation methodologies most commonly used are described and their suitability for comparing returns across managers discussed. Risk-adjusted return methodologies are also covered. The attribution of performance over the various sources of return is briefly outlined. The CFA Institute's Global Investment Performance Standards for the calculation and presentation of investment returns are described. The chapter concludes by discussing Style Analysis and Manager Selection.

Learning Objectives

After reading this chapter you will be able to:
- Describe the important methods of calculating returns, the time-weighted and the money-weighted rates of return, and their uses
- Explain the importance of dealing appropriately with cash inflows and outflows to and from the portfolio
- List the key principles involved in comparing returns of different managers
- Describe the measures of risk-adjusted returns
- Explain the methodology underlying performance attribution
- Describe the vision, objectives, scope and fundamentals of GIPS
- Analyse an investment manager's style, using both quantitative and qualitative approaches.
- Know the key questions to be asked in manager selection.

PERFORMANCE MEASUREMENT: KEY PRINCIPLES

Whether the investment portfolio has been directly invested by the investor or entrusted by the investor to an investment manager, the calculation of investment returns and the attribution and comparison of investment performance are critical elements in portfolio monitoring and control.

The key principles of performance measurement are outlined below:

Total Returns

Measurement is of total returns, comprising both capital growth and income return.

Time-Weighted Rate of Return

The time-weighted rate of return is the compounded rate of growth of the initial portfolio market value during the evaluation period.

The overall evaluation period is divided into subperiods. A new subperiod is established whenever a cash inflow or cash outflow arises. The time-weighted rate of return for the period as a whole is calculated by compounding the returns of the subperiods.

The methodology assumes that all income arising is reinvested in the portfolio during the evaluation period. All cash inflows and outflows are assumed to occur on the first day of each subperiod.

Assume that a portfolio at market value of €1m on 1 January 2005 experienced flows and market valuation changes as follows:

Table 11.1 Portfolio Valuations and Flows €000

Cash Flow	Opening Fund	Income Arising	Portfolio Valuation @ MV	Closing Fund
	1.1.05 1,000	Jan'05 5	31.1.05 1,050	31.1.05 1,055
1.2.05 100	1.2.05 1,155	Feb'05 4	28.2.05 1,100	28.2.05 1,104
1.3.05 200	1.3.05 1,304	Mar'05 10	31.3.05 1,400	31.3.05 1,410

i)   Cash inflows of €100,000 on 1 February 2005 and €200,000 on 1 March 2005 determine the beginning of new subperiods.

ii) The invested portfolio is valued at close of business on the day preceding cash inflows (or outflows).

iii) Income is assumed to arise gross of tax. Income arising of €5,000, €4,000 and €10,000 is assumed for the three subperiods.

iv) Income arising is added to the closing portfolio valuation at the end of each subperiod to give closing valuations for the fund at the end of each subperiod.

Subperiod returns are calculated as follows:

Table 11.2 Time-Weighted Returns: Subperiod Returns

$$\text{Return} = \frac{\text{Closing Fund} - \text{Opening Fund}}{\text{Opening Fund}}$$

Subperiod 1 (January):

$$\frac{1,055,000 - 1,000,000}{1,000,000}$$

$$= .055$$
$$= 5.5\%$$

Subperiod 2 (February):

$$\frac{1,104,000 - 1,155,000}{1,155,000}$$

$$= -.044$$
$$= -4.4\%$$

Subperiod 3 (March):

$$\frac{1,410,000 - 1,304,000}{1,304,000}$$

$$= .081$$
$$= 8.1\%$$

Subperiod returns are combined to give the time-weighted return for the total period as follows:

Table 11.3 Time-Weighted Returns: Full-Period Return

$$RT = [(1 + Rp1)(1 + Rp2)(1 + Rp3)] - 1$$

where: RT is the time-weighted return for the full evaluation period
        Rp1 is the return for subperiod 1.
        Rp2 is the return for subperiod 2.
        Rp3 is the return for subperiod 3.

$$= [(1 + .055)(1 - .044)(1 + .081)] - 1$$
$$= 1.090 - 1$$
$$= 0.090$$
$$= 9.0\%$$

Because the time-weighted rate of return excludes the impact of cash inflows and outflows it is a good measure of the performance of the investment manager, and it permits the performance of one manager to be compared to that of another, given the conditions for fair comparisons are complied with.

The methodology does require, of course, that portfolio valuations be prepared whenever inflows or outflows take place. With modern technological systems this is no longer an onerous requirement. Indeed most large-investment managers have the capability of producing daily time-weighted returns.

Money-Weighted Rate of Return

The money-weighted rate of return is an internal rate of return over the full evaluation period. It accounts for the impact of cash inflows and outflows which are assumed to arise midway through the period, i.e., the calculation assumes the investment manager had (or had not) use of cash flows for half of the evaluation period.

Using the details of the previous example, the money-weighted rate of return emerges as follows:

Table 11.4 Money-Weighted Return: Full Period

$$\frac{\text{Closing Fund} - \text{Opening Fund} \pm \text{Net Cash Inflows}}{\text{Opening Fund} \pm \frac{1}{2}(\text{Net Cash Inflows})}$$

$$= \frac{1,410,000 - 1,000,000 - 300,000}{1,000,000 + 150,000}$$

$$= .096$$
$$= 9.6\%$$

and compares to our earlier calculation of the time-weighted return of 9.0%. Note that where there are no cash inflows or outflows, the time-weighted and money-weighted returns will be the same, e.g. subperiod 1 above.

Table 11.5 Money-Weighted Return: Sub period 1

$$\text{Money-Weighted Return} = \frac{1,055,000 - 1,000,000 - 0}{1,000,000}$$

$$= 0.055$$
$$= 5.5\%$$

But where the inflows or outflows are large in relation to the opening valuation, significant differences will emerge, e.g., subperiod 3 above:

Table 11.6 Money-Weighted Return: Sub period 3

$$\text{Money-Weighted Return} = \frac{1,410,000 - 1,104,000 - 200,000}{1,104,000 + 100,000}$$

$$= 0.88$$
$$= 8.8\%$$

compared to our earlier calculation of a time-weighted return for this sub-period of 8.1%.

The money-weighted rate of return does provide the client with useful information on the growth of the fund.

However, it is affected by the timing and amounts of cash inflows and outflows, which are beyond the control of the investment manager. It is therefore not a good measure of the performance of the investment manager, neither is it useful in making comparisons of different managers' performances.

The time-weighted rate of return has been adopted as the industry standard for performance measurement purposes.

Like-for-Like Comparisons

Where the returns of different funds are being compared it is important that comparisons are on a like-for-like basis, i.e., that the funds share certain key characteristics:

Investment Mandate

The investment mandate – the investment manager's riding instructions – sets out the objectives of the fund and the scope and discretion allowed the investment manager in delivering those objectives. Comparisons of the investment returns generated by different managers should be informed by the discretion allowed to them in the mandates. Obviously, the risk tolerance allowed the manager is critical in assessing returns. Risk is dealt with separately below.

Asset Class and Currency

Clearly, out-turns of funds that are invested in different asset classes or denominated in different currencies are not comparable.

Treatment of Income

It is important, particularly when measuring and comparing the returns of unit trusts and mutual funds, to ensure that treatment of income is comparable. Most funds roll income arising into the unit price. Some funds, however, distribute income to unitholders.

Treatment of Costs

Treatment of costs may vary between different types of fund. The returns of segregated funds, for example, are normally shown gross, i.e., before costs, while the returns of unit funds are normally shown net, i.e., after costs.

Tax Treatment

Tax treatment varies widely, depending on the type of investor and the type of fund. Common treatment of tax is essential in making comparisons.

Risk

The investment mandate defines the risk tolerance permitted to the investment manager in the search for investment returns. Comparisons of the manager's investment returns must be assessed in the light of the risks taken to generate them.

Volatility, as discussed in Chapter 6, is the standard measure of risk.

Among the measures commonly used in measurement of risk and return are:

i)   **The Sharpe Ratio**
      The Sharpe Ratio is a measure of the excess return over the risk-free rate of the portfolio relative to the total volatility (standard deviation) of the portfolio:

$$\frac{\text{Portfolio Return} - \text{Risk-Free Rate}}{\text{Standard Deviation of the Portfolio}}$$

ii)   **The Treynor Ratio**
      The Treynor Ratio, like the Sharpe Ratio, is a measure of excess return per unit of risk. Excess return is again defined as the difference between the portfolio's return and the risk-free rate.

      The risk measure, however, is the relative systematic risk as measured by the portfolio's beta. The portfolio's beta is regarded as an appropriate measure of risk because, with a well-diversified portfolio, the unsystematic risk is close to zero. The Treynor Ratio is calculated as follows:

$$\frac{\text{Portfolio Return} - \text{Risk-Free Rate}}{\text{Portfolio Beta}}$$

iii) **The Information Ratio**

The Information Ratio measures excess return over benchmark return against incremental risk over benchmark risk (i.e. tracking error):

$$\frac{\text{Portfolio Return} - \text{Benchmark Return}}{\text{Tracking Error}}$$

The Information Ratio recognises that excess return cannot be generated without accepting incremental risk. It measures the success of the investment manager in translating incremental risk into excess return.

All three ratios may be used to rank the returns of different investment managers.

Performance Attribution

Attribution of investment performance – the analysis and identification of sources of investment return – is an essential tool of investment management, with applications at the fund manager level for both passive and active managers; at the risk-control level; and in client reporting.

Investment management firms employ sophisticated statistical tools, such as multi-factor models, for performance attribution purposes. These may be proprietary or commercially available. These models attribute performance over the various investment decision levels discussed in Chapter 10 – asset allocation, currency, country, sector and stock selection – as well as over market timing and over the factors that determine stock selection.

The following example is advanced to illustrate the principle of performance attribution in a simple fashion.

Assume that an active investment manager has constructed a portfolio that deviates from benchmark both at the asset allocation and stock selection levels. Portfolio weightings and returns compared to benchmark are set out below:

Table 11.7 Investment Out-turn

| | Benchmark | | Portfolio | |
	Weight	Return	Weight	Return
Equities	70	10	60	12
Bonds	30	5	40	4
Return		8.5%		8.8%

At the Asset Allocation level, the portfolio's exposure to equities at 60% is 10% less than Benchmark exposure. The equity benchmark returned 10%. This underexposure of 10% cost 1% of return. Bond exposure in the Portfolio at 40% was 10% above Benchmark. The bond benchmark returned 5%. The overexposure to Bonds added 0.5% to return. Overall, however, the Asset Allocation decision cost –0.5% of return.

At the Stock Selection level, the Portfolio returned 12% against the Benchmark's 10% on its 60% equity exposure, for a contribution of 1.2% to performance. The Portfolio returned 4% against the Benchmark's 5% on its 40% exposure to bonds, which cost –0.4%. Overall, the Stock Selection decision added +0.8% to return.

At the total fund level, therefore, outperformance of +0.3% is made up of a negative contribution from Asset Allocation of –0.5% and a positive contribution from Stock Selection of +0.8%.

This information is extremely valuable for the investment management firm. Whilst a single period's out-turn, say for a quarter or even one year, might not prompt major changes in approach, persistence of this trend might alert the fund manager to the need to sharpen or add resources to asset allocation decision making. Again, persistence of the trend might encourage the risk-control function to initiate a process with the fund manager which might result in asset exposures being brought closer to benchmark. At the client reporting level, the performance attribution analysis provides useful information for updating the client on developments in the portfolio.

Table 11.8

Global Investment Performance Standards (GIPS)

The CFA Institute (formerly known as the Association for Investment Management and Research) has championed, sponsored and funded Global Investment Performance Standards, a single standard for presenting investment performance. To date some 25 countries, including Ireland, have adopted the GIPS Standards.   ➡

The Benchmark return of 8.5% is made up as follows:

Equity Contribution	70% × 10%	7.0%
Bond Contribution	30% × 5%	1.5%
		8.5%

The Portfolio return of 8.8% is made up as follows:

Equity Contribution	60% × 12%	7.2%
Bond Contribution	40% × 4%	1.6%
		8.8%

This results in outperformance of 0.3% for the period by the investment manager. Next, the sources of this outperformance are identified:

Sources of Performance

Asset Allocation

Equities (60% − 70%) × 10%	−1.0%
Bonds (40% − 30%) × 5%	+0.5%
	−0.5%

Stock Selection

Equities (12% − 10%) × 60%	+1.2%
Bonds (4% − 5%) × 40%	−0.4%
	+0.8%
Outperformance	0.3%

Vision Statement

A global investment performance standard leads to readily accepted presentations of investment performance that:

i)   present performance results that are readily comparable among investment management firms without regard to geographical location;

ii)   facilitate a dialogue between investment managers and their clients
        about the critical issues of how the investment management firm
        achieved performance results and determines future investment
        strategies.

Objectives

i)   To obtain worldwide acceptance of a standard for the calculation and
        presentation of investment performance in a fair, comparable format
        that provides full disclosure.
ii)   To ensure accurate and consistent investment performance data for
        reporting, record keeping, marketing and presentations.
iii)   To promote fair, global competition among investment management
        firms for all markets, without creating barriers to entry for new invest-
        ment management firms.
iv)   To foster the notion of industry 'self-regulation' on a global basis.

Fundamentals of Compliance: Key Requirements

Definition of the Firm

- The standards must be applied on a firm-wide basis.
- Total firm assets must be the aggregate of the market value of all discretionary and non-discretionary assets under management within the defined firm.

Document Policies and Procedures

- Firms must document, in writing, the policies and procedures they use in
  establishing and maintaining compliance with all the applicable requirements
  of the GIPS standards.

Firms' Fundamental Responsibilities

- Firms must make every reasonable effort to provide a compliant presentation to all prospective clients.

Input Data

- Portfolio valuations must be based on market values.
- For periods between 1 January 2001 and 1 January 2010 portfolios must
  be valued at least monthly. For periods beginning 1 January 2010 firms
  must value portfolios on the date of all large external cash flows.
- Accrual accounting must be used for fixed-income securities and all other
  assets that accrue interest income. Market values of fixed-interest securities
  must include accrued income.

Calculation Methodology

- Total returns must be used.
- Time-weighted rates of return that adjust for external cash flows must be used. Periodic returns must be geometrically linked.
- Composite returns must be calculated by asset weighting the individual portfolio returns using beginning-of-period value and external cash flows.
- A composite is an aggregation of individual portfolios representing a similar investment mandate, objective or strategy.
- All returns must be calculated after deduction of the actual trading expenses incurred during the period.

Composite Construction

- All actual, fee-paying, discretionary portfolios must be included in at least one composite.
- Terminated portfolios must be included in the historical returns of the appropriate composite up to the last full measurement period that the portfolio was under management.
- Carve-out segments excluding cash are not permitted to be used to represent a discretionary portfolio.
- Firms are not permitted to link simulated or model portfolios with actual performance.

Disclosures

- Firms must disclose the minimum asset level, if any, below which portfolios are not included in a composite.
- Firms must disclose the currency used to express performance.
- Returns must be disclosed as gross-of-fees or net-of-fees.
- Firms must disclose relevant details of the treatment of withholding taxes.
- Firms must disclose the fee basis appropriate to the presentation.

Presentation and Reporting

- The following items must be reported for each composite presented:
  - i) at least 5 years of performance that meets the requirements of the GIPS standards; after presenting 5 years of performance the firm must present additional annual performance up to 10 years;
  - ii) annual returns for all years;
  - iii) the number of portfolios and the amount of assets in the composite;
  - iv) a measure of dispersion of individual portfolio returns for each annual period.

- Returns of portfolios and composites for periods of less than 1 year are not permitted to be annualised.
- Performance track records of a past firm or affiliation must be linked to, or used to represent, the historical record of a new firm or new affiliation if:

  i) Substantially all the investment decision makers are employed by the new firm.
  ii) The staff and decision-making process remain intact and independent within the new firm.
  iii) The new firm has records that document and support the reported performance.

- The new firm must disclose that the performance results from the past firm are linked to the performance record of the new firm.

Besides the requirements and mandatory disclosures detailed in the GIPS standards, guidelines and recommendations for reporting are also provided. These GIPS standards, which were revised in 2005 for implementation from 1 January 2006, promote the highest performance measurement and presentation practices and they eliminate the need for separate local standards.

Verification

Detailed verification procedures are also set out in the GIPS standards. Verification is the review of an investment management firm's performance measurement processes and procedures by an independent, third-party verifier.

Verification Tests

These involve:

- whether the firm has complied with all the composite construction requirements of the GIPS standards on a firm-wide basis;
- whether the firm's processes and procedures are designed to calculate and present performance results in compliance with the GIPS standards.

A single verification report is issued in respect of the whole firm; verification cannot be carried out for a single composite. Without such a report from the verifier, the firm cannot state that its claim of compliance with the GIPS standards has been verified.

Sample Presentations

Samples of GIPS-compliant presentations are shown at the end of this chapter.

STYLE ANALYSIS: GROWTH AND VALUE INVESTMENT

Introduction

As discussed in Chapter 7, an equity investment manager's style is defined by the investment philosophy and process that determine the manager's approach to stock selection and portfolio construction.

The predominant styles adopted by active equity investment managers are growth and value. Both growth and value may be further categorised into large capitalisation and small capitalisation.

Style analysis is designed:

- to help the investor understand the investment manager's approach to equity investment;
- to confirm that the investment manager has the capability to deliver, over a reasonable period of time, results which are in line with the investment style adopted;
- to confirm that the characteristics of the portfolios constructed are aligned with the style adopted.

The growth manager is focused on growth, and in particular on growth in earnings per share, and seeks stocks which will have relatively high earnings growth within the universe of stocks followed.

The value manager is focused on valuation, and in particular on stocks which are relatively low-valued within the universe of stocks followed.

The Price/Book Ratio (i.e., Market Price/Net Asset Value per share) is typically used to categorise stocks into growth or value. Growth stocks are those stocks within the stock universe that exhibit a higher Price/Book ratio than the average of the universe. Value stocks have a lower Price/Book ratio than the average.

The growth manager believes that growth in earnings per share will normally increase the Book Value per share. Assuming no change in the Price/Book ratio, the share price will grow if earnings grow.

The value manager believes that over time the Price/Book ratio of low-rated stocks will return to some normal level, i.e., will revert to mean. Therefore even with no change in book value per share, the share prices will rise.

The major risk faced by the value manager, therefore, is that the Price/Book ratio does not increase. The growth manager faces two risks:

- that earnings growth does not occur as expected;
- and that the Price/Book ratio declines, preventing the earnings growth from being reflected in the share price.

Style Analysis: Qualitative Inputs

Analysis of the inputs of both growth and value managers focuses on the key elements of successful investment management firms discussed in Chapter 10. A qualitative examination is carried out of the investment manager's:

- philosophy
- process
- people.

Emphasis is placed in particular on:

- the key, or ideally the unique, insight which the manager brings to stock selection;
- the repeatability and consistency of the investment process in generating superior investment returns;
- the stability and expertise of the investment team;
- the competitive advantages and potential weaknesses of the investment management firm.

In particular, this process of due diligence of the capabilities of the investment manager is designed to determine the conviction which drives the manager's philosophical growth or value approach, the discipline and rigour of the investment process, and the knowledge, expertise and commitment of the investment team.

Style Analysis: Quantitative Outputs

The output of the equity investment manager – the completed portfolio – is examined quantitatively with specific measurements for value and growth portfolios.

Value Portfolios

Analysis of the value portfolio is relatively straightforward. Focus is on the valuation of the portfolio relative to the appropriate market index.
   Key measures examined include:

- Portfolio Price Earnings Ratio (PER) relative to Index PER
- Portfolio Dividend Yield (DY) relative to Index DY
- Portfolio Price-to-Book Ratio (P/B) relative to Index P/B.

A value portfolio will stand on valuations which are below market valuations. Therefore, the portfolio PER will be lower than the index PER.

The portfolio DY will be higher than the index DY, and the portfolio P/B will be lower than the index P/B.

Growth Portfolios

The measurement of the characteristics of the growth portfolio are significantly more complex and require a considerable data bank, because focus is on fundamental profit and earnings growth data.

Key measures include:

Historical Growth

Earnings per share	–	relative to index
Dividend per share	–	relative to index
Book value per share	–	relative to index
Cash flow per share	–	relative to index

Prospective Growth

Earnings per share

Short-term	–	relative to index
Long-term	–	relative to index

Shorter-term measures of earnings momentum may also be examined, e.g., incidence of rising and falling estimates of earnings per share (based on 'sell side' stockbroking analysts' estimates) and incidence of positive and negative surprises in earnings-per-share outcomes against estimates.

Performance

The ultimate measure of the investment manager's ability to construct successful value or growth portfolios is, of course, investment performance. Portfolio outturns for risk and return are measured against index outcomes and, where available, against relevant style indices, e.g., value or growth indices.

MANAGER SELECTION: KEY QUESTIONS

The investor, or the trustees of a pension fund, in embarking upon a process designed to select a manager who is to be entrusted with the management of their investments, will consider the key elements of successful investment firms as discussed in Chapter 10, and the issues involved in performance analysis and attribution and style analysis as discussed earlier in this chapter.

In addition, the investor might usefully revert to first principles. The first step in investment is in the investor's own mind. Requirements and objectives must be clearly outlined and communicated to prospective investment managers. Secondly, no matter how detailed or sophisticated the manager-selection process, eventually the manager-selection decision is reduced to the investor or trustees making the judgment that Manager A is better equipped to meet the fund's requirements and objectives than Manager B. A useful, practical step in informing this judgment is a site visit to the investment manager's offices, where ideally a meeting with the investment team might also be arranged.

Key Questions

Philosophy

What is the key insight that enables the investment manager to add value over market returns?

Process

Describe how the investment process implements philosophy in a consistent and repeatable fashion. Is there a process that applies to the house as a whole or is it individual to a particular manager, team, fund or product?

Outline the investment firm's risk-control framework.

Outline the following with respect to process:

... valuation metrics
... stock characteristics
... portfolio construction.

People

Is there a dominant individual (a 'star manager'), or is there a team-based approach? What discretion does the manager/team have? Describe the team members':

... background and experience
... responsibilities
... reward and incentivisation.

SUMMARY

- The time-weighted rate of return is the compounded rate of growth of the initial portfolio market value during the evaluation period.
- Because the time-weighted rate of return excludes the impact of cash inflows and outflows, it is a good measure of the performance of the investment manager and it enables the performance of one manager to be compared to that of another. The time-weighted rate of return is the industry standard.
- The money-weighted rate of return accounts for the impact of cash inflows and outflows. It provides useful information on the growth of the fund. It is not suitable for making comparisons.
- Comparisons should be made on a like-for-like basis.
- Measures of risk-adjusted return include the Sharpe Ratio, the Treynor Ratio and the Information Ratio.
- Performance attribution over the sources of return has wide application across the investment firm.
- The CFA Institute has developed standards for the calculation, disclosure and presentation of investment performance. These have been adopted in 25 countries, including Ireland.
- Style Analysis employs both qualitative and quantitative techniques. The investment manager's inputs – philosophy, process, people and resources – are examined qualitatively. Quantitative analysis of the portfolio and its constituent stocks employs an array of ratios which vary according to the manager's growth or value style.

APPENDIX — SAMPLE GIPS-COMPLIANT PRESENTATIONS

Example 1:

Sample 1 Investment Firm
Balance Composite
1 January 1995 through 31 December 2004

Year	Gross-of-Fees Return (%)	Net-of-Fees Return (%)	Benchmark Return (%)	Number of Portfolios	Internal Dispersion (%)	Total Composite Assets (CAD Million)	Total Firm Assets (CAD Million)
1995	16.0	15.0	14.1	26	4.5	165	236
1996	2.2	1.3	1.8	32	2.0	235	346
1997	22.4	21.5	24.1	38	5.7	344	529
1998	7.1	6.2	6.0	45	2.8	445	695
1999	8.5	7.5	8.0	48	3.1	520	839
2000	−8.0	−8.9	−8.4	49	2.8	505	1014
2001	−5.9	−6.8	−6.2	52	2.9	499	995
2002	2.4	1.6	2.2	58	3.1	525	1125
2003	6.7	5.9	6.8	55	3.5	549	1225
2004	9.4	8.6	9.1	59	2.5	575	1290

Sample 1 Investment Firm has prepared and presented this report in compliance with the Global Investment Performance Standards (GIPS®).

Notes:
1.   Sample 1 Investment Firm is a balanced portfolio investment manager that invests solely in Canadian securities. Sample 1 Investment Firm is defined as an independent investment management firm that is not affiliated with any parent organisation. For the periods from 2000 through 2004, Sample 1 Investment Firm has been verified by Verification Services Inc. A copy of the verification report is available upon request. Additional information regarding the firm's policies and procedures for calculating and reporting performance results is available upon request.
2.   The composite includes all nontaxable balanced portfolios with an asset allocation of 30% S&P TSX and 70% Scotia Canadian Bond Index Fund, which allow up to a 10% deviation in asset allocation.
3.   The benchmark: 30% S&P TSX; 70% Scotia Canadian Bond Index Fund rebalanced monthly.
4.   Valuations are computed and performance reported in Canadian dollars.
5.   Gross-of-fees performance returns are presented before management and custodial fees but after all trading expenses. Returns are presented net of nonreclaimable withholding taxes. Net-of-fees performance returns are calculated by deducting the highest fee of 0.25% from the quarterly gross

composite return. The management fee schedule is as follows: 1.00% on first CAD25M; 0.60% thereafter.

6. This composite was created in February 1995. A complete list and description of firm composites is available upon request.

7. For the periods 1995 and 1996, Sample 1 Investment Firm was not in compliance with the GIPS standards because portfolios were valued annually.

8. Internal dispersion is calculated using the equal-weighted standard deviation of all portfolios that were included in the composite for the entire year.

EXAMPLE 2:

Sample 2 Asset Management Company
Equities World BM MSCI Active Mandates Direct

	Reporting Currency CHF				Creation Date 01 July 1999	
Period	Total Return (%)	MSCI World (ri) in CHF Benchmark Return(%)	Number of Portfolios	Composite Dispersion (Range)	Total Composite Assets (millions)	Percentage of Firm Assets (%)
2004	18.0	19.6	6	0.2	84.3	<0.1
2003	−35.3	−33.0	8	0.7	126.6	0.1
2002	−16.0	−14.5	8	1.5	233.0	0.2
2001	−13.5	11.8	7	1.3	202.1	0.2
2000	60.2	46.1	<5	N/A	143.7	0.2
1999	21.3	17.5	<5	N/A	62.8	<0.1
1998	22.5	26.3	<5	N/A	16.1	<0.1

Compliance Statement
Sample 2 Asset Management Company has prepared and presented this report in compliance with the Global Investment Performance Standards (GIPS®).

Definition of the Firm
Sample 2 Asset Management Company is an independent investment management firm established in 1997. Sample 2 Asset Management Company manages a variety of equity, fixed income, and balanced assets for primarily Swiss and European clients. Additional information regarding the firm's policies and procedures for calculating and reporting performance returns is available upon request.

Benchmark
Sources of foreign exchange rates may be different between the composite and the benchmark.

Fees
Performance figures are presented gross of management fees, custodial fees, and withholding taxes but net of all trading expenses.

List of Composites
A complete listing and description of all composites is available on request.

Verification
Sample 2 Asset Management Company has been verified by an independent verifier on an annual basis from 1998 through 2003.

Fee Schedule
The standard fixed management fee for accounts with assets under management of up to CHF50 million is 0.35% per annum.

Minimum Account Size
The minimum portfolio size for inclusion in Equities World BM MSCI composite is CHF1 million.

Chapter twelve

Derivatives

Chapter 12 analyses derivative contracts, which are now an intrinsic part of the financial fabric. Derivatives first emerged in a significant way in agricultural commodities markets in Chicago in the mid-nineteenth century. Although financial derivatives made their appearance quite early in the history of stock markets, they have really come to prominence only from the early 1980s. Today financial derivatives play a central role in all developed financial markets. This chapter focuses on describing basic futures and options contracts and analysing how they can be used either to manage risk, or to speculate on the price movements of underlying securities.

Learning Objectives

After reading this chapter you will:
- Be familiar with the characteristics of a basic futures contract
- Be familiar with the characteristics of a call option and a put option
- Understand how futures and options contracts can be used to alter the risk/reward profile of investment exposures
- Understand the principles underlying option valuation
- Be aware of the existence of over-the-counter derivative markets.

Financial derivatives are essentially instruments that call for money to change hands at some future date, with the amount to be determined by one or more reference items, such as interest rates, stock prices or currency values. The main economic function of derivative contracts is to provide a means of hedging. Companies such as Ryanair and Irish Continental Group may use derivative contracts to protect themselves against the fluctuating price of oil. A company such as Waterford Wedgwood, which generates the bulk of its revenues in dollars, may use derivative contracts to hedge itself against the fluctuating €/$ exchange rate. Over the past decade financial institutions have developed innovative retail products such as tracker bonds, which are generally backed by derivative contracts, in order to enable millions of small investors to benefit from the risk-reduction benefits offered by derivative contracts.

Derivatives were primarily invented to reduce risk and not to fuel speculative activity. They developed in order to enable buyers and sellers of commodities to avoid the uncertainty associated with price fluctuations. Physical commodities and financial instruments are typically traded in cash markets. A cash contract calls for immediate delivery and is used by those who need a commodity now or who have cash to invest. There are two types of cash market: spot markets and forward markets. Spot markets are for immediate delivery and forward markets are for deferred delivery. The forward price is the price of an item for forward delivery. Forward contracts are centuries old, whereas the story of futures contracts begins in the Chicago futures exchanges of the mid-nineteenth century.

At that time Chicago had become the biggest agricultural trading centre in the US. Forward contracts in agricultural commodities such as wheat and other grains quickly developed. The American Civil War gave a huge boost to the volumes traded on the Chicago exchanges. At the time of the American Civil War the horse was the key mode of transport, so that any planned military campaign required a large supply of oats to feed the horses. Therefore, if this is spring and the generals are planning a big offensive in the autumn, the quartermaster knows that there will be a large requirement for oats in the autumn. By purchasing September futures contracts today, the quartermaster can secure a supply of the required quantity of oats at the current price of the relevant contract. On the other side of the bargain, a farmer will have entered into a futures contract to deliver oats in September at the same fixed price. In this example both parties have hedged their exposure to fluctuations in the price of oats. Both parties have averted the risk of prices going against them. Of course both parties have also given up the potential for windfall profit, but that is a price they are willing to pay.

Taking a more modern example, an airline such as Ryanair knows that summer is its busiest season. In January it could enter into a forward contract with Shell Oil to purchase jet fuel to be delivered in June. The price of the transaction would be agreed between the parties in January and, come June, Shell would deliver oil to Ryanair in exchange for cash. In this case the parties must negotiate the terms of the forward contract with one another. A futures contract is exactly the same as a forward contract, except that the futures contract will be standardised in terms of quality of commodity, expiry date, etc. and as a result it can normally be traded on a futures exchange.

Going back to the mid-nineteenth century, it was not long before organised futures exchanges developed in Chicago, where forward contracts became standardised in terms of contract size, delivery dates, and the condition of the items that could be delivered. Therefore, only the price and number of contracts were left for futures traders to negotiate. In effect, futures contracts are organised and standardised forward contracts. From around the 1970s the potential offered by futures contracts on financial instruments began to be recognised, and since then there has been an explosion in the range of financial derivative contracts available and in the volumes traded.

FINANCIAL FUTURES

A financial future is a contractual notional commitment to buy or sell a standard quantity of a financial instrument at some point in the future, at a price determined today. The risk profile of a futures contract is identical to the risk profile of an equivalent quantity of the relevant underlying security. The profit or loss on a futures contract is determined by the movement in the price of the underlying security. Today, standardised futures contracts are traded in large volumes on a wide variety of stock-market indices and government bonds over a range of maturities. Futures contracts are also available on all the key currency-exchange rates. Indeed, there are also futures contracts on specific sectors of the equity market and on some individual securities.

Expiry

On the expiry date of any futures contract one of the following must occur:

i)   The seller of the contract must deliver the appropriate physical amount of the underlying commodity or security (so many bushels of wheat or barrels of oil, so much of a government bond). The buyer of the contract must take delivery and pay the appropriate settlement amount as determined by the price of the futures contract.

ii)   For most financial futures contracts, physical delivery does not take place. Instead the difference between the futures contract strike price and the price of the underlying asset at the futures expiry date is used to calculate the profit (loss) of the buyer/seller of the contract. A cash settlement amount is thus calculated and one party pays the other.

Role of the Clearing House

Futures contracts that are traded on exchanges are normally settled through a Clearing House. The Clearing House guarantees the fulfilment of each contract and becomes the formal counterparty for both buyer and seller. The key functions of a Clearing House are twofold:

i)   It establishes the credibility of the market and participants in the market have only one counterparty (the Clearing House) to vet regarding counterparty risk.

ii)   It improves the liquidity of the contracts traded in the relevant market.

In order to ensure that the market operates smoothly the Clearing House normally sets out the margin requirements of each contract that must be paid to it by participants. Normally, the margin required will be a relatively small percentage of the face value of the contract and will have two components:

i)   **Initial Margin:** this must be paid to the Clearing House on the day the futures contract is entered into. It will usually be calculated with reference to the likely maximum daily loss associated with the contract.

ii)   **Variation Margin:** each day the profit (loss) of the futures position is calculated. If it moves to a loss the Clearing House receives the cash, and if there is a profit the Clearing House credits the holder's account. For each contract the Clearing House has two open positions: one with the buyer of the contract and the other with the seller of the contract.

Figure 12.1 **Gain/Loss from Buying a Futures Contract**

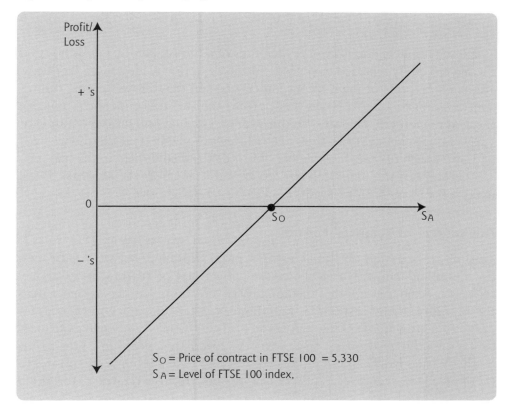

S_O = Price of contract in FTSE 100 = 5,330
S_A = Level of FTSE 100 index,

The margining system should therefore act to limit the likelihood of participants being unable to meet their obligations.

Figure 12.1 illustrates the profit/loss profile associated with the purchase of a futures contract.

The line S_A plots the prices of the underlying commodity, security or index. The point S_0 represents the price paid for the futures contract.

Let's assume that I am bullish regarding the UK equity market and I decide to use the futures contract on the FTSE100 index to gain exposure to UK shares. It's late March and the the FTSE100 is trading at 5,310. I buy (go long of) the FTSE June contract at a price of 5,330. I am paying a small premium to today's index level (price) because I will not have to put up cash (except for a small margin requirement) until June. The potential profit (loss) profile that I am exposed to is illustrated in Figure 12.1.

An FTSE100 futures contract relates to a value of stock equal to the futures index multiplied by £10. So if I buy one futures contract at 5,330 (S_0 on chart) it equates to 5,330 * £10 = £53,330 worth of shares. If the index rises to 6,000 I will make a profit of 6,000 – 5,330 = 670 * £10 = £6,700 (ignoring transaction costs and taxes). This is the same profit I would make if I had invested £53,300 in the FTSE100 index (for example, through investing it in a fund that tracks the index).

Likewise, if the index falls to 5,000 I will make a loss of 5,000 – 5,330 = –330 * £10 = –£3,300.

This example highlights the key features of a futures contract, which is that the buyer is fully exposed to both the upside and downside caused by fluctuations in the price of the relevant underlying security. The seller of a futures contract is exposed to a profit (loss) profile that would be identical to going short of the underlying index. In this example, selling one futures contract at 5,330 would expose me to the same risk/reward profile as if I had borrowed £53,300 worth of the constituents of the index and sold them in the market.

Therefore, if the index falls to 5,000 and I am short the contract, I will make a profit of: 5,330 – 5,000 = +330 * £10 = +£3,300.

Advantages of Financial Futures

Trading volumes in financial futures have exploded over the past two decades in tandem with a huge increase in the range of instruments available. Now, it is often the case that the liquidity of a futures contract is greater than the liquidity of the respective underlying market. Futures contracts are a cash-efficient way of taking a position and can be used to hedge exposures to the underlying securities and/or to take speculative positions. Effectively, market participants can use futures contracts to take a leveraged exposure to the underlying securities. Traders can also use futures contracts to take a short position to the underlying security. Finally, transactions costs are often lower in the futures markets as compared with the relevant markets in the underlying securities.

Pricing of Futures Contracts

The pricing of futures contracts can be viewed as being based on the alternative of borrowing funds to invest in a market. The futures price should be such that there is no arbitrage profit from buying stock (with borrowed money) and simultaneously selling futures contracts. Staying with the FTSE100 index of the top 100 UK-quoted companies we can readily estimate the fair price of a futures contract on the index.

Assume that it is end-March and the FTSE100 is trading at 5,000. I wish to purchase a futures contract expiring at end-June, i.e., in exactly three months. I could borrow funds at a 5% annual rate of interest and invest in a FTSE100 Index fund that has an expected annual dividend yield of 2% over the next three months. The difference between my borrowing rate of 5% and divided yield of 2% represents a 'cost-of-carry' of 3%. Ignoring margin requirements and transactions costs, I can calculate the price of a futures contract where I will be indifferent as to which alternative I use as:

Fair Futures Price (FP) = Spot Index Level *multiplied by* (Interest Cost *less* Dividend Yield) *multiplied by* Time (expressed as a fraction of a year)

$$FP = 5,000 * (.05 - .02) * 0.25 = 25$$

Therefore the fair value premium is 25, so that the fair price of the FTSE100 June futures contract will be 5,025. Arbitrageurs will ensure that futures contracts will normally trade at or very close to the 'Fair Price' as calculated here. Transactions costs, uncertainty regarding the exact expected dividend yield on the market, etc. mean that the 'no-arbitrage fair price' will be a range rather than an exact premium. However, this range will normally be very narrow, although it can at times be significant. At expiry the price of any futures contract must converge on the spot price of the relevant index. Hedgers and speculators will naturally endeavour to purchase futures contracts when they are below fair value (and of course sell contracts when they are above fair value). This is known as basis trading and if the position is held to maturity an additional small profit will accrue.

THE NO-ARBITRAGE PRINCIPLE

The example above illustrates the key underlying principle that determines the values (and hence market prices) of all derivative instruments. This states that in efficient markets there should not be a riskless profit to be gained by combining a forward contract position with positions in the relevant related assets. Remember that futures contracts are essentially forward contracts with standardised terms and conditions.

OPTIONS

In this section we are going to discuss options relating to company shares or a group of shares represented by market or sector indices. However, option contracts are available on an enormous range of securities and commodities. Options represent claims on an underlying ordinary share and are created by investors and sold to other investors. The company whose stock underlies these claims has no direct interest in the transactions. There are two basic types of option:

- A call option gives the holder the right to buy (or 'call away') 1,000 shares of a particular company, at a specified price, at any time up to a specified expiration date.
- A put option gives the buyer the right to sell (or 'put away') 1,000 shares of a particular company, at a specified price, at any time up to a specified expiration date.

Investors purchase call options if they expect the price of the underlying share to rise and purchase put options if they expect the price of the underlying share to fall.

Why Options Markets?

i)   Puts and calls expand the range of opportunities available to investors, making available a wider range of risk/return opportunities.
ii)   Options provide leverage.
iii)   Put options, in particular, allow the buyer to hedge underlying positions in stocks.
iv)   Institutional investors that actively sell (or write) options can generate extra income on their portfolios.

Pay-off Profiles of Options

Pay-off Profile of a Call Option

Figure 12.2 illustrates the pay-off profile at expiry of the buyer and seller, respectively, of a call option.

Figure 12.2 Profit and Loss Profiles of Buyer and Seller of a Call Option in ABC plc

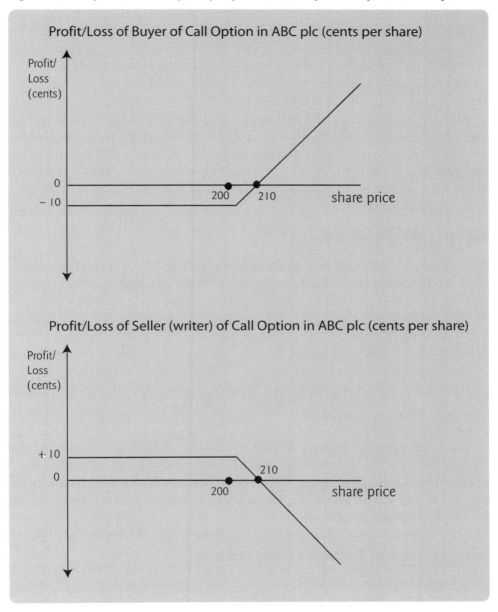

Profit/Loss of Buyer of Call Option in ABC plc (cents per share)

Profit/Loss of Seller (writer) of Call Option in ABC plc (cents per share)

In the example the call option details are:

Option premium:	10 cents per share
Strike price:	€2.00

If the share price rises above €2.00, the call option is said to be 'in the money'. However, the share price needs to rise above €2.10 (strike price plus premium) before the buyer moves into profit. The buyer can benefit from all the potential upside in the stock, whilst at the same time his potential loss is limited to the premium paid (10 cents per share in this example).

The risk/reward profile of the seller (or writer) of the call option is the mirror image of the buyer's profile.

Effectively, the writer of a call option is going short of the stock. As the share price rises ever higher, the seller is exposed to ever-greater losses. In this example the seller of the call option will suffer a loss once the share price moves above €2.10 (strike price plus premium received). In the case of the seller his potential profit is capped at the premium received, but his potential losses are unlimited.

Pay-off Profile of a Put Option

The buyer of a put option benefits when the price of the underlying share falls. In the example illustrated in Figure 12.3 the put option details are:

Option premium: 12 cents per share
Strike price: €2.00

If the share price falls below €2.00 the buyer of the option is in the money, but starts making a profit only when the share price goes below €1.88 (strike price minus premium).

The exact reverse is the case for the seller (writer) of the put option. As the price falls below the 'break-even' level of €1.88, the seller is exposed to ever-greater losses. If the company were to go bankrupt, the seller would suffer the full loss of €1.88 per share. The seller's maximum profit is the premium received of 12 cents per share.

Some Investment Strategies Using Options

There are many situations where options may be used to efficiently implement a desired investment strategy. Often the desired risk/reward profile may be achieved only through the employment of derivative contracts. Because of the small initial cash outlay required and the potentially large pay-off, purchasing options will often appeal to those who wish to speculate on share price movements. For the sellers (or writers) of options, a policy of continuously writing options may be adopted to earn a small additional income for an equity portfolio. Studies have shown that the odds favour the sellers of

Figure 12.3 Profit and Loss Profiles of a Buyer and Seller of a Put Option in ABC plc

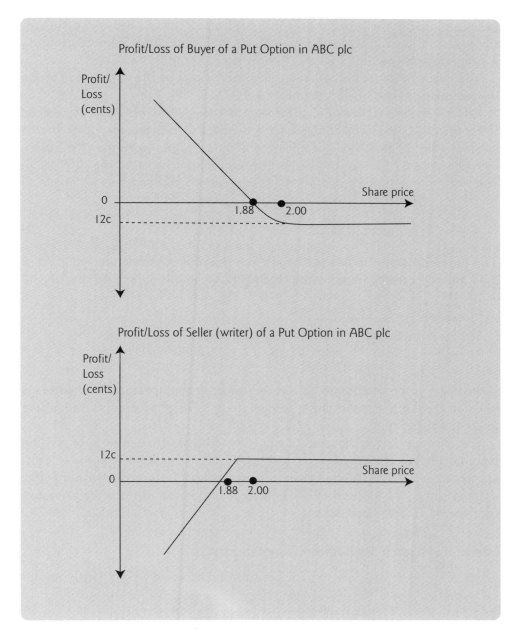

options in a somewhat similar fashion to where the odds over time favour the bookies rather than the punters.

Above we illustrated the profit/loss profiles of the buyers/sellers of a call option and a put option, ignoring any position that the participants may

Figure 12.4 Pay-off Profile for a Covered Call Position

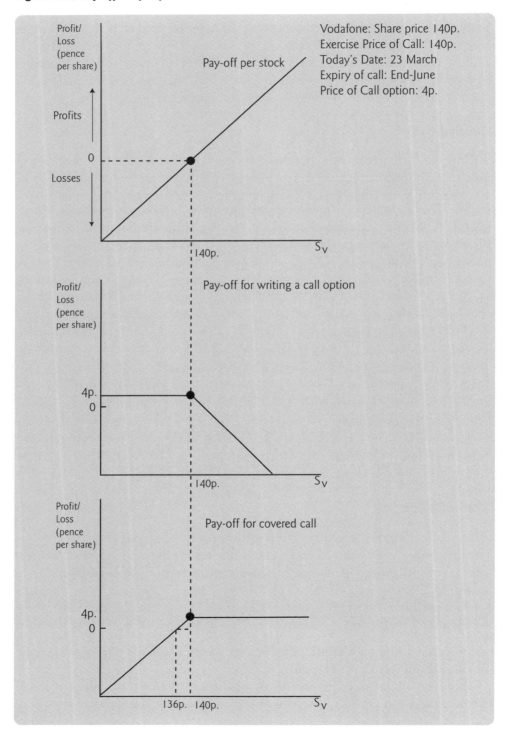

have had in the underlying security. A key attraction of option contracts is that used in combination with other positions, either in the underlying security or in other derivative contracts, they can be used to hedge underlying investment exposures. A hedge is a combination of an option and its underlying security designed such that the option protects the stock against loss or the stock protects the option against loss. We are going to analyse two such strategies, namely, Covered Calls and Protective Puts.

Covered Calls

A Covered Call involves the purchase of ordinary shares and the simultaneous sale of call options on that share. Figure 12.4 illustrates what is happening to the risk profile of an investor engaging in this strategy in Vodafone shares.

The top two diagrams illustrate the pay-off profiles for the share purchase and the sale of the option respectively, and the third diagram illustrates the pay-off profile for the combined position. Starting with the purchase of Vodafone shares at 140p we have the familiar symmetrical profit/loss profile – if the share price moves higher the investor moves into profit, and if the share price moves lower the investor suffers losses. The second diagram illustrates the pay-off profile of the sale of a call option – referred to as taking a naked call option position. In this case the investor does not own any shares in Vodafone and the maximum profit is the option premium of 4p. Potential losses are large and grow as the Vodafone share price rises. The final diagram illustrates the pay-off profile for the combined position. Compared with ownership of the stock the investor's downside has changed a little in that the break-even share price is now 136p (purchase price of the shares less the premium received). The potential upside is very different as it is limited to just 4p per share – the option premium received. The reward for limiting the upside is the premium received for the option.

Protective Puts

This strategy involves buying a put option on a share that is already owned (or the share may be purchased at the same time). Figure 12.5 illustrates the pay-off profile for this strategy, taking information on Vodafone as an example.

As always, the pay-off for ownership of stock is a straight line, with profits or losses dependent on the share price in a symmetrical fashion. The pay-off for the put on its own is an asymmetrical line in two segments, and the second diagram in Figure 12.5 clearly illustrates how the option strategy truncates the distribution of returns. Above the exercise price of 140p the pay-off line is horizontal and reflects the fact that loss is limited to the 3p cost of the put. The position moves into profit as the share price falls below

Figure 12.5 Pay-off Profile for a Protective Put Position

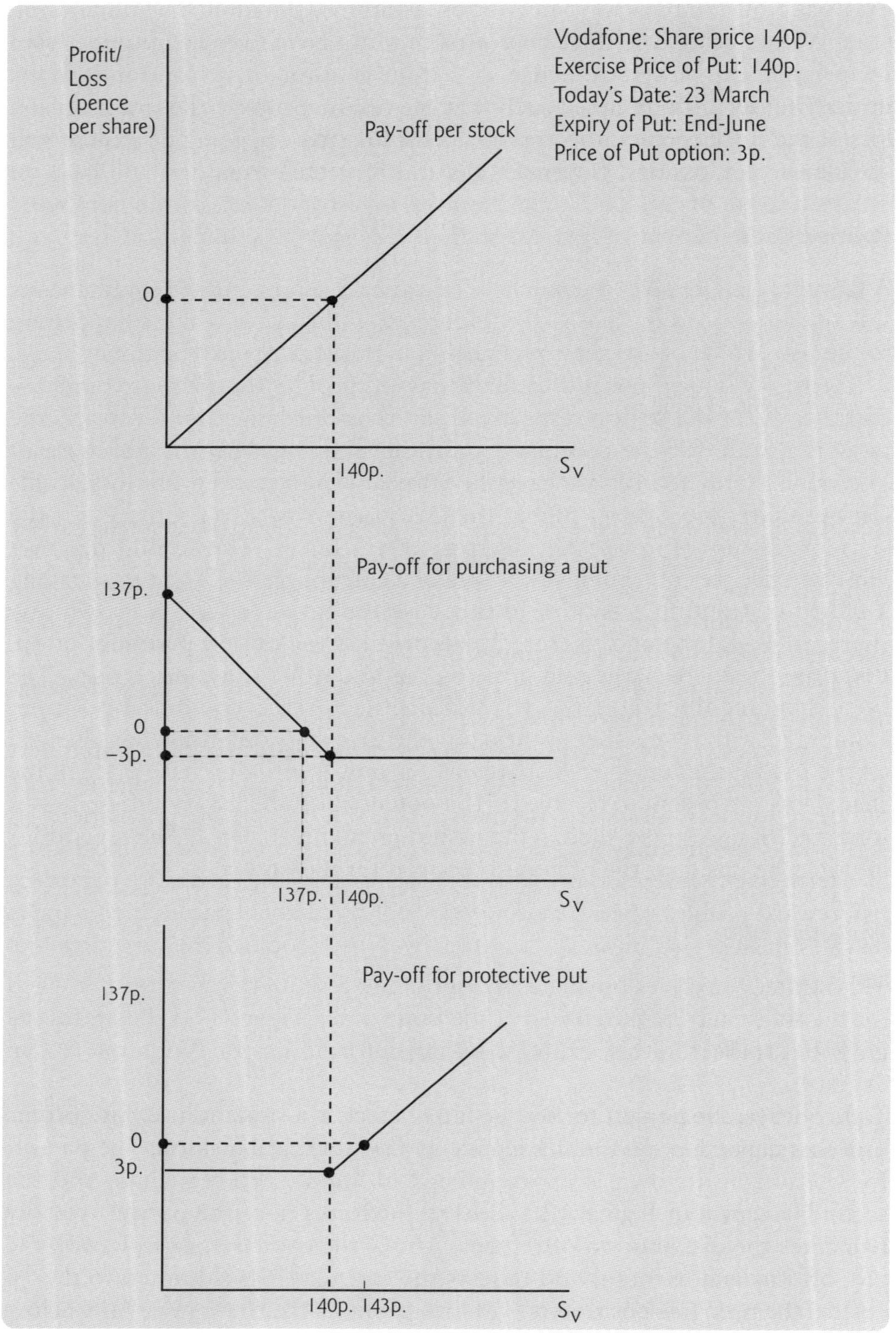

the exercise price less the premium, which is 137p in this example. The third diagram plots the pay-off profile for the combined position. The break-even point occurs at 143p – the exercise price plus the option premium. Above 143p ownership of the stock ensures that the investor participates fully in the upside. Below 140p the stock position moves into loss but the put position offsets the losses penny for penny. If the share price falls to 139p there will obviously be a loss of a penny per share, whilst the put option will have an intrinsic value of 1p. The impact on the investor's P&L of the combined position for a number of selected share prices may be summarised as:

Share Price of:	139p	137p	130p	150p
Stock Position	−1p	−3p	−10p	+10p
Option Value	+1p	+3p	+10p	0
Option Premium	−3p	−3p	−3p	−3p
Net Position	−3p	−3p	−3p	+7p

Above the break-even point of 143p, ownership of the stock ensures that the protective put strategy (simultaneous purchase of stock and put option) fully participates in the gains as the share price rises. Clearly, the key attraction of a protective put strategy is that it provides a relatively simple and easily executed method to limit the downside of investing in shares.

It is beyond the scope of this text to provide more detail on the wide range of strategies that can be created using derivative contracts.

The protective put strategy and the covered call strategy illustrated here highlight how the combination of a position in an underlying security with option contracts alters an investor's risk/reward profile. A variety of derivative securities may also be combined to create an almost limitless array of alternative risk/reward profiles. It is this variety and flexibility regarding risk/reward profiles offered by derivative contracts that enables the financial services industry to innovate so extensively to provide new products and services.

EVERYDAY USE OF DERIVATIVES

Today derivative contracts play a big role across a vast range of industries. The participants in these markets fall into two broad categories:

i) **Hedgers** will normally hold risky positions in the underlying securities or markets, and will use options or futures to offset or limit some of this risk. By taking a position opposite to one already held in the physical market, hedgers plan to reduce the risk of adverse price fluctuations. Essentially, a hedger is prepared to forgo some profit potential in exchange for having someone else assume part of the risk. Hedging therefore reduces the risk of loss, at the cost of reducing the return possibilities compared with the unhedged position.

ii) **Speculators** will buy or sell futures or options contracts with the sole object of profit and will be attracted by the leverage offered by options and the ability to go short of the underlying securities. Unlike hedgers, speculators do not normally transact in the physical commodity or financial security underlying the futures contract. Speculators are essential to the functioning of derivatives markets, absorbing the excess demand or supply generated by hedgers and assuming the risk of price fluctuations that hedgers wish to avoid. Speculators add to the overall liquidity of the market and their trading activity should reduce the variability of prices over time.

An individual or an institution may of course take out some positions in a hedging capacity, but at the same time may take speculative positions in a different segment of their business. Derivatives are most widely used in the financial sectors of banking and insurance and indeed trading in derivative contracts forms a separate business unit in many financial institutions. The explosive growth in both the variety of derivative contracts traded, and the value of transactions, are due to both the hedging options offered and the speculative opportunities.

In some quarters derivative contracts have a bad name, due to several very high-profile financial scandals and disasters. John Rusnack racked up losses from trading currency contracts totalling close to $800m before his superiors in AIB's Allfirst subsidiary discovered the fraud. Rusnack is now in jail and AIB is pursuing legal action against some of Allstate's counterparties such as Citigroup and Bank of America. AIB has recovered from the debacle, but it acted as a catalyst for the merger of its wholly owned Allfirst subsidiary into M&T Bank. AIB now has a 22.5% interest in the merged entity. AIB was sufficiently strong to emerge relatively unscathed from the Rusnack affair, although its credibility has been somewhat tarnished. Baring's Bank was not so lucky when rogue trader Nick Leeson was allowed to run amok in Singapore. The derivative contracts that he entered into were so large that they led to the collapse of the long-established and respected bank.

Another high-profile collapse was Long Term Capital Management in 1998. This was an enormous hedge fund whose founding partners included Robert Merton and Myron Scholes, Nobel laureates in economics, who between them all but invented modern finance through their theory on pricing options. At its peak LTCM commanded funds of $130 billion and a derivatives portfolio with a notional value of $1.25 trillion. A financial crisis precipitated by the failure of Russia to honour its debts led to the near-collapse of the Fund, which was saved only by a rescue package organised by the banks as the US Federal Reserve worried that it could damage the entire financial system.

Irrespective of these failures it is generally accepted that the development of derivatives markets radically improves the risk-sharing capacity and innovative ability of the financial system.

Valuing Options

In thinking about the value (or price) of an option, it is useful to analyse it in terms of two factors. This discussion will cover a call option, but the principles are also the same for a put option. Firstly, if a call option is 'in the money' (share price is above the strike price), the option has an immediate value that is the difference between the two prices (share price *minus* strike price). In other words, the buyer of the call option could exercise the option and immediately sell the stock on the market at a profit. This is referred to as the **intrinsic** value of the option and is the difference between the current market price of the underlying share and the strike price. If the market price of the share is at or below the strike price, the intrinsic value of the option is **nil**.

Even if the intrinsic value of a call option is nil, it can still have a positive value. This is because there is a second source of value, commonly referred to as **'time value'**. In general, the longer the time to the option expiry date, the greater will be the time value of the option. This time value is influenced by the interest rate over the relevant period and the volatility of the underlying share. The higher (more risky) the volatility, the higher will be the time value of the option. Also, given that ownership of the underlying asset is deferred until the expiry date, higher interest rates will be reflected in a higher premium. However, in a low-interest-rate environment the time value of an option is primarily determined by the volatility of the underlying security.

Assume that the current share price of CRH is €21 and that a 3-month call option is available at an exercise price of €20. This option is 'in-the-money' because the share price is greater than the exercise price.

$$\text{Intrinsic value of call option} = €21 - €20 = €1$$

Puts work in reverse. A 3-month put option with a strike price of €20, with the shares trading at €21, has an intrinsic value of nil.

$$\text{Intrinsic value of put option} = €20 - €21 = -€1$$

However, a put option (or a call option) cannot have a negative value. Therefore, the formula for estimating the intrinsic values of calls and puts may be written as:

$$\text{Intrinsic value of a call} = \text{Maximum } (S_0 - E), 0$$
$$\text{Intrinsic value of a put} = \text{Maximum } (E - S_0), 0$$
$$\text{where:} \quad S_0 = \text{price of underlying security}$$
$$E = \text{exercise price}$$

In plain English, the formula states that the intrinsic value of a call option is equal to the share price less the exercise price, as long as the result is positive. If the result is negative, then the intrinsic value is zero. For a put option the intrinsic value is the exercise price less the share price, again as long as this value is positive. Otherwise the intrinsic value of the put option is zero. On the expiry date the intrinsic value of the option will equate to the price or value of that option. Prior to the expiry date the price of the option will equal the intrinsic value plus the time value of the option. As we saw above, the call option in CRH with an exercise price of €20 has an intrinsic value of €1 if the shares are trading at €21. The price of this option in the market will be €1 if today is the expiry date. However, if the option has a significant amount of time to run to expiry, it will be worth more than €1. It should be intuitively clear that if we have two call options that are identical in every respect except with regard to time to expiry, the option with more time to expiry will be more valuable.

Estimating the Time Value of Options

This is much more difficult than estimating the intrinsic value. The three variables that determine time value are:

- the time remaining to the expiration of the option
- the interest rate
- the volatility (as measured by standard deviation) of the underlying security.

The Black–Scholes (B/S) Model is a widely used model, developed by Fischer Black and Myron Scholes for the valuation of call options. The model itself is mathematically complex and beyond the scope of this text. However, the model can be easily accessed and is widely used to estimate the fair value of call options. The B/S Model uses the following five variables to value the call option of a non-dividend paying share:

- the price of the underlying security
- the exercise price of the option
- the time remaining to the expiration of the option
- the interest rate
- the volatility of the underlying share.

As discussed earlier, the first two variables determine the intrinsic value of the option, i.e., whether it is 'in-the-money' or 'out-of-the-money'. If the option is 'out-of-the-money', the option has only time value. Time remaining to expiration (measured as a fraction of a year) is relevant because value generally increases with maturity. The interest rate affects option values because of the opportunity cost involved. Buying a call option is an alternative to purchasing shares using borrowed funds, on which interest must be paid. The higher interest costs are, the more interest is saved by buying options, and therefore higher interest rates add to the value of call options.

The first four variables are all observable in the market, and it is only the last one, the stock's volatility, that has to be estimated. Volatility is normally estimated from historical price data. The greater the volatility, the higher the price of a call option, because of the increased potential for the share price to move up. Strictly speaking, the B/S Model applies to non-dividend-paying stocks. The payment of a dividend will cause the price of a share to fall and will lead to a reduction in the price of call options on that share (and a rise in the price of put options). Taking into account shares that pay dividends, the relationship between the price of call options and the factors that determine such prices is summarised below:

Effects of Variables on Prices of Call Options

Variable	Impact on Value of Call Option
Share Price	Positive
Exercise Price	Negative
Time to Expiration	Positive
Volatility of Underlying Share	Positive
Interest Rates	Positive
Cash Dividends	Negative

So if the share price rises, it will have a positive impact on the price of a call option. A higher exercise price will mean a lower price for the call option etc. It is clear from this table that at any point in time the only variable that will cause differences in the estimate of the fair value of a call option is the volatility of the underlying security. Whilst such estimates rely heavily on historical data, most market participants take into account potential events that may impact on a share's volatility. Therefore, the announcement of an unexpected item of news concerning a company can lead to an almost instantaneous change in the price of options as market participants 'price in' higher expected volatility in the relevant share price.

Market participants often use the B/S Model to estimate the level of volatility in the marketplace implied by the price of traded options. The market prices of traded options are plugged into the Model, together with the other variables with the exception of volatility. If the Model shows that implied volatility is high (compared with a benchmark level which may be some historical average), then it suggests that option prices are high compared with historical norms. An institution that holds a large equity portfolio may use this information to increase its sales of options to take advantage of the higher premium available. A private investor who is considering the purchase of put options to hedge their investments in the equity market may decide to hold off until implied volatility declines.

Pricing Put Options

The B/S Model applies initially to call options, but the existence of the principle of Put–Call Parity means that it can also be used to price put options. The Put–Call Parity expresses the relationship between the prices of puts and calls on the same stock that must hold if arbitrage is to be ruled out. It can be expressed as:

Price of a Put = Exercise Price/e^{rt} – Share Price + Price Call Option

where: e = the base of natural logarithms
             r = riskless rate of interest
             t = time to expiry of the option expressed as a fraction of a year.

If this relationship does not hold between a put and a call, then arbitrageurs will be able to make risk-free profits. In efficient markets such a situation cannot persist, and therefore the put-call parity means that the B/S Model can be used to price both calls and puts.

FUTURES AND OPTIONS EXCHANGES

Futures contracts are essentially forward contracts with standardised terms and conditions. It is worth enumerating the similarities and what differentiates them.

In general, both forward and futures contracts:

i)   Obligate the buyer to buy and the seller to sell a certain quantity of an asset at a price determined today at a specified future date.
ii)   Can be settled through cash settlement based on the value of the relevant contract at the expiry date.

iii) Have prices determined by the No-Arbitrage Principle, so that at the initiation of the contract it has zero value.

The differences include:

i) Forward contracts are private contracts negotiated between the relevant parties and usually are not tradable. Futures contracts trade on organised exchanges.

ii) Forward contracts are customised contracts satisfying the needs of the parties involved and this is an attraction over futures contracts, which are highly standardised.

iii) Counterparty risk is a factor to be taken into account with forward contracts. For futures contracts the clearing house is the single counterparty for all transactions.

iv) Futures contracts are marked to market every day and variation margin has to be paid to (received from) the clearing house. As they are not traded, forward contracts are not marked to market each day.

v) Futures exchanges are normally regulated by the respective financial regulators.

A similar situation exists regarding options contracts. Contracts that are entered into privately are customised to the needs of the parties concerned. Such contracts will usually not be traded and there will normally be a cash settlement between the parties on the expiry date. Options traded on exchanges are standardised, but the valuation principles are exactly the same for both. Standardised futures and options contracts now trade in large volumes on various exchanges such as Euronext.liffe. Information on these contracts is readily available in the financial pages. Exhibit 12.1 shows the information provided in the *Financial Times* on equity options on a daily basis.

This lists call and put options in FTSE100 stocks. For example, it can be seen that on 15 November 2005 BP shares were trading at 634p. Calls exercisable at end-December with a strike price of 600p traded at a premium of 41.5p. The call option with a strike price of 650p traded at a premium of 11.50p. The December 600 put option had a premium of 4.75p and the December 650 put option had a premium of 24.25p.

Accessing the respective websites of the various futures and options exchanges will reveal extensive information regarding the contracts traded, latest traded prices, open positions, etc. The advantages of exchange-traded standardised contracts are numerous and include:

• Counterparty risk resides with the respective exchange's clearing house for both buyers and sellers of derivative contracts.

Exhibit 12.1 Equity Options

EQUITY OPTIONS

Option	Nov	Dec	Jan	Nov	Dec	Jan
	Calls			Puts		
AstraZeneca 2500	82.0	123.5	155.0	2.0	36.0	57.5
(*2578.0) 2600	13.0	62.5	95.5	34.0	75.5	98.5
Aviva 650	33.0	40.0	46.5	-	5.0	9.0
(*682.5) 700	0.5	10.5	17.5	18.0	25.5	30.0
Barclays 600	7.50	18.75	26.25	3.25	13.25	18.50
(*603.00) 650	-	4.50	8.00	46.75	49.25	50.75
BP 600	34.50	41.50	48.25	-	4.75	9.00
(*634.00) 650	1.25	11.50	18.00	17.00	24.25	29.25
BAT 1300	32.0	52.0	69.5	2.0	18.5	27.5
(*1329.0) 1350	4.0	24.0	42.0	24.0	40.0	51.0
BSkyB 460	32.5	37.5	42.5	-	3.5	6.5
(*492.0) 500	1.5	10.5	16.0	9.5	16.5	21.0
BT Group 200	4.25	8.00	8.50	0.75	3.75	7.00
(*203.50) 220	-	1.25	-	16.50	17.00	20.50
Diageo 800	36.5	43.5	52.0	-	5.0	8.5
(*836.0) 850	2.5	12.0	21.0	15.0	24.0	28.0
GlaxoSmKl 1500	22.5	46.0	62.0	7.5	26.5	37.5
(*1513.0) 1600	-	9.0	20.0	86.0	90.5	98.0
HSBC 75p 900	27.5	31.0	36.5	-	6.0	10.5
(*926.5) 950	-	4.5	10.5	23.0	32.5	35.5
LloydsTSB 460	9.50	16.25	21.50	1.00	5.75	8.75
(*468.50) 500	-	2.50	5.50	31.25	32.50	33.50
Marks & S 420	25.25	25.25	30.50	-	-	6.50
(*445.00) 460	-	5.25	8.75	19.75	23.25	25.25
Pearson 650	7.0	17.5	26.0	4.5	12.5	18.0
(*652.0) 700	-	2.0	7.0	48.0	48.0	50.5
Prudential 500	11.75	11.75	25.50	1.50	1.50	11.50
(*510.00) 550	-	-	5.50	39.75	39.75	42.25
Rio Tinto 2300	56.0	108.0	146.0	10.0	54.0	82.0
(*2344.0) 2400	9.5	58.0	94.0	63.0	106.0	132.5
Royal Bk Scot 1600	72.5	87.5	102.5	-	10.0	18.5
(*1671.0) 1700	33.0	41.0	31.5	48.0	57.5
Royal Dutch Shell 'B' 1800	48.25	48.25	99.00	2.00	2.00	38.75
(*1845.00) 1900	1.00	1.00	48.50	55.00	55.00	86.75
Sainsbury 280	14.50	13.75	18.25	0.25	3.00	5.25
(*291.75) 300	0.75	3.25	7.25	8.50	13.00	15.00
Vodafone 120	9.75	10.00	10.25	0.25	1.50	2.00
(*129.25) 130	3.25	3.25	3.75	2.75	5.25	5.75

Option	Dec	Mar	Jun	Dec	Mar	Jun
3i Group 800	24.0	47.5	64.5	19.5	35.5	47.0
(*805.0) 850	6.5	26.0	41.5	53.5	65.0	75.0
Alice & Leics 850	35.0	58.5	65.0	7.5	21.5	42.0
(*874.0) 900	9.5	30.5	38.0	32.0	44.5	69.5

Option	Dec	Mar	Jun	Dec	Mar	Jun
	Calls			Puts		
Amvescap 360	30.5	43.5	49.5	4.0	13.5	20.0
(*385.0) 390	11.5	25.5	32.5	15.5	25.5	33.5
Anglo Amer 1800	66.5	122.0	155.0	48.0	103.5	128.5
(*1812.0) 1900	25.0	75.5	106.0	106.5	158.5	181.0
ARM 120	5.50	10.75	13.75	3.75	7.50	9.75
(*121.50) 130	1.75	6.25	9.00	10.00	13.00	15.00
BAA 600	34.0	47.0	55.5	3.0	10.0	17.5
(*628.5) 650	4.5	18.0	28.5	24.0	31.5	41.5
BAE Systems 330	14.75	25.00	29.00	5.50	12.00	17.75
(*337.75) 360	2.75	11.25	15.50	23.50	28.25	34.50
BG Group 500	44.50	60.25	71.50	5.25	16.25	24.00
(*537.00) 550	14.75	31.50	44.50	25.75	37.75	45.75
BHP Billiton 800	63.5	90.5	108.0	10.5	34.0	46.5
(*850.0) 850	31.5	60.5	80.5	28.5	54.5	67.5
BOC Group 1100	55.5	74.0	95.5	17.5	40.5	51.0
(*1134.0) 1150	28.0	49.0	68.5	40.0	66.0	74.5
Boots Group 600	22.0	40.0	51.0	11.5	24.0	36.0
(*609.0) 650	4.0	18.0	28.5	43.5	52.5	65.5
Br Airways 300	22.75	34.75	42.75	5.25	13.50	19.00
(*317.50) 330	6.75	18.00	26.50	18.50	26.75	32.50
Cable & Wire 110	10.00	13.75	16.75	1.50	5.00	6.75
(*119.50) 120	3.50	8.00	11.00	5.25	9.25	11.25
Cadbury Sch 550	27.5	43.0	52.0	8.0	17.0	24.00
(*567.0) 600	6.0	20.5	27.5	37.0	46.5	55.5
Capita 360	32.0	39.0	43.5	1.0	4.0	8.0
(*390.0) 390	9.0	18.5	24.0	8.0	13.5	19.0
Carnival 3100	124.0	203.5	260.0	52.0	116.5	152.0
(*3175.0) 3200	68.5	150.5	205.5	98.0	163.0	196.5
Centrica 240	9.0	16.5	19.5	0.7	12.5	17.5
(*241.0) 260	3.0	8.0	11.0	20.5	24.0	29.5
Colt Tel 50	9.00	11.50	13.50	0.75	2.50	4.00
(*58.00) 60	2.50	5.75	7.75	4.25	6.75	7.75
Compass 200	13.00	19.75	22.50	5.50	14.50	17.00
(*206.50) 220	4.25	12.00	14.75	17.00	27.25	29.75
Corus 45	4.75	6.75	7.50	1.00	2.75	3.75
(*48.50) 50	1.75	4.00	5.00	3.00	5.00	6.25
DSG Intl 140	11.25	14.50	17.25	1.25	4.50	6.25
(*149.50) 160	1.25	4.75	7.50	11.25	15.00	16.50
EMAP 850	28.0	48.5	64.0	14.0	27.5	36.5
(*866.0) 900	6.0	23.0	39.5	45.0	55.0	63.5
EMI 200	19.50	26.50	31.00	2.50	8.75	11.75
(*216.00) 220	7.25	14.75	19.50	10.25	17.00	20.25
Gallaher 850	55.5	76.0	83.5	3.5	23.0	32.5
(*899.0) 900	19.5	44.0	54.5	18.5	45.5	55.5

Option	Dec	Mar	Jun	Dec	Mar	Jun
	Calls			Puts		
GUS 850	28.0	46.0	66.0	18.5	38.5	45.5
(*857.5) 900	8.5	24.0	43.0	49.0	66.0	73.5
Hanson 550	47.0	62.0	69.0	4.5	15.0	25.0
(*590.0) 600	15.0	33.0	40.5	22.5	34.5	47.5
HBOS 900	23.0	44.0	51.5	16.0	41.0	49.0
(*901.5) 950	5.5	21.5	28.5	50.5	71.5	78.0
Hilton 330	25.00	33.75	40.25	4.50	12.50	18.00
(*349.25) 360	7.25	16.75	23.75	16.50	26.50	31.75
ICI 300	23.25	31.00	36.00	3.50	10.50	14.25
(*318.50) 330	6.75	14.75	20.50	16.75	25.00	28.75
Impl Tobacco 1600	101.0	121.0	142.0	8.5	41.0	58.0
(*1686.0) 1700	34.0	60.5	87.0	41.5	88.5	103.5
IntCont Hotels 778	34.0	58.0	58.0	17.5	35.5	35.5
(*791.5) 830	12.0	32.5	32.5	47.5	62.5	62.5
Intl Power 240	11.50	20.00	25.25	6.75	13.00	18.25
(*243.50) 260	4.00	11.25	16.50	19.25	24.50	29.25
Invensys 14	2.25	3.25	3.75	0.50	1.25	2.00
(*15.75) 15	1.50	2.75	3.25	0.75	1.75	2.25
ITV 100	10.50	13.50	15.25	1.00	2.75	4.50
(*109.00) 110	4.25	7.75	9.75	4.50	7.00	9.00
Kingfisher 200	18.50	26.00	27.75	2.00	7.00	12.00
(*215.50) 220	6.25	14.75	17.00	10.00	15.75	22.00
Land Secur 1500	40.0	74.5	102.5	44.0	68.5	82.0
(*1503.0) 1600	9.0	35.5	58.0	116.5	131.0	140.5
Legal & Gen 110	3.50	7.00	8.00	2.00	4.25	6.75
(*111.00) 120	0.50	2.75	3.75	9.00	10.00	13.00
LogicaCMG 141	11.5	18.0	21.0	3.0	8.0	11.5
(*148.5) 158	3.5	9.5	12.5	11.5	16.5	20.0
Lon Stk Exchg 550	53.0	63.5	71.0	5.0	13.0	16.5
(*598.0) 600	18.5	32.0	39.5	22.0	31.5	34.5
Man Group 1600	101.5	155.5	197.5	28.5	68.0	94.0
(*1680.0) 1700	44.5	103.0	142.5	74.0	115.0	138.0
Mitchlls&Butlrs 360	13.5	22.0	30.5	11.0	21.5	25.5
(*362.5) 390	3.0	10.0	17.5	33.0	40.5	43.0
Morrison (Wm) 160	15.25	20.25	22.75	1.00	4.00	7.00
(*173.75) 180	2.75	8.25	11.00	8.50	12.00	15.50
Natl Grid 499	35.50	44.75	44.75	4.00	12.25	12.25
(*532.00) 549	5.75	18.25	18.25	28.25	35.75	35.75
Next 1300	59.0	97.0	119.5	21.5	48.0	71.0
(*1345.0) 1350	29.5	69.5	91.5	43.5	69.0	93.0
Northern Rock 800	33.5	54.0	64.0	10.0	23.5	39.5
(*819.0) 850	8.5	28.5	38.0	36.0	48.5	65.5
O2 180	16.25	20.50	24.75	-	3.00	6.00
(*195.50) 200	6.50	8.25	13.75	4.75	11.00	14.75
P & O 420	33.00	41.25	51.50	5.75	14.25	21.25
(*446.50) 460	9.75	20.50	31.00	24.00	32.25	40.00

Option	Dec	Mar	Jun	Dec	Mar	Jun
	Calls			Puts		
Reckitt Bnckisr 1700	110.5	149.0	177.0	10.5	42.5	60.5
(*1793.0) 1800	44.5	86.5	118.5	44.5	82.0	101.5
Reed Elsevier 500	51.5	61.0	66.5	0.5	5.0	11.5
(*549.0) 550	11.0	25.0	32.5	10.0	19.5	29.0
Rentokil Init 140	17.75	21.50	23.00	0.50	3.00	5.50
(*156.75) 160	3.50	8.75	10.75	6.25	10.50	14.25
Reuters 360	33.25	44.75	51.25	3.25	13.50	19.25
(*388.75) 390	13.00	26.75	34.00	13.00	25.50	31.75
Rolls-Royce 360	17.75	30.00	35.75	6.00	16.00	20.75
(*370.25) 390	4.25	15.25	20.25	22.75	31.00	36.00
Royal/Sun Al 100	7.75	10.75	11.5	1.25	4.25	5.75
(*106.00) 110	2.25	5.50	6.75	5.75	9.50	11.00
SAB Miller 1050	30.5	61.0	80.5	27.0	47.5	57.5
(*1056.0) 1100	11.0	36.0	56.0	58.5	74.0	83.5
Sage 220	10.00	16.25	20.75	4.75	9.75	13.50
(*224.25) 240	2.00	6.75	11.25	17.25	20.50	24.00
Scot Power 550	29.0	40.5	48.0	6.0	15.5	22.0
(*576.5) 600	6.5	16.5	22.5	33.0	42.0	46.5
Scot & Newcastle 460	25.5	39.0	43.0	6.5	15.5	24.0
(*477.5) 500	7.0	19.5	24.5	26.5	36.0	47.0
Scot & Sthn Energy 1000	37.0	58.5	74.5	13.5	32.5	44.0
(*1020.0) 1050	12.0	43.0	49.0	39.0	58.5	69.0
Shire Pharm 700	38.0	67.5	84.5	20.0	43.0	55.0
(*715.0) 750	16.5	43.0	60.5	48.5	69.0	80.5
Sm & Nephew 460	45.0	59.5	68.0	3.5	12.5	19.5
(*500.0) 500	17.5	34.0	44.0	15.5	27.5	35.0
Std Chartd 1200	64.0	95.5	115.5	18.5	52.5	67.5
(*1240.0) 1250	35.0	68.0	88.5	39.0	76.0	91.5
Tesco 300	14.00	22.75	26.25	3.00	8.50	13.50
(*309.75) 330	1.50	7.75	11.50	21.00	24.25	29.25
Tomkins 260	17.50	24.75	28.00	1.75	6.25	11.50
(*274.50) 280	5.25	12.50	16.25	9.50	14.25	20.75
Unilever 550	22.75	36.50	44.50	6.00	14.25	20.25
(*571.00) 600	2.75	11.75	19.25	36.50	41.00	50.75
Utd Utilities 600	48.5	54.0	61.5	2.0	12.5	27.5
(*644.0) 650	13.0	23.0	33.0	16.5	34.0	53.0
Whitbread 929	37.5	37.5	37.5	18.5	18.5	18.5
(*945.0) 978	17.0	17.0	17.0	44.5	44.5	44.5
WPP Group 550	31.0	47.5	58.0	5.5	16.0	23.0
(*573.0) 600	5.5	19.5	30.5	30.0	38.0	45.0

Option	Dec			Dec		
Ald Domecq xe 650	42.0	-	-	-	-	
(*691.0) 700	2.5	-	-	-	10.5	-

* Underlying security price. Premiums shown are based on settlement prices. **Source:** Euronext.liffe November 15 Total contracts, Equity & Index options: 192,568 Calls: 70,200 Puts: 95,169

- The existence of the clearing house also ensures anonymity for participants.
- Standardised contracts ensure that interest in each market is concentrated into a relatively small number of contracts. This improves liquidity in each contract, as volumes traded are limited to the available contracts. This can create a virtuous circle where high volumes in a contract generate low bid/offer spreads and high liquidity, which in turn generates even more activity.
- Transparency is a key feature of these markets. Traded prices and open interest are available virtually on a real-time basis. As well as providing

timely information to market participants on specific contracts, the information available can also reveal important information concerning the associated underlying securities/markets.

- Regulation: the transparency of derivative exchanges is very appealing to the respective regulatory authorities. Also, the existence of a clearing house allows regulators to easily monitor the adequacy of the capital that is committed to the various markets.

Over-the-Counter (OTC) Derivative Markets

The diversity of derivative contracts that are traded on exchanges, and the enormous volumes traded, do not represent the full picture of derivative activity. There is an extensive market in derivative contracts that are not traded on regulated exchanges. These are contracts where the buyer and seller come together directly and agree the terms of the contract between themselves. Therefore, such contracts can be tailored to meet the specific requirements of the parties involved. The explosion in the so-called OTC market has been driven by a number of factors:

- Most contracts that are traded on exchanges have expiry dates of less than one year. Demand for longer-dated contracts has grown exponentially and can be fulfilled only on the OTC market.
- OTC markets enable participants to tailor contracts to their specific requirements.

With regard to pricing and valuation, the same principles apply to OTC derivatives as to those traded on exchanges. Counterparty risk, however, is a key aspect of OTC markets and one that all participants must carefully manage. From the perspective of market regulators the counterparty risk of each individual entity is not of any particular concern. However, regulators are concerned about the systematic risk posed by the explosion in the scale and diversity of OTC derivative contracts. Respected market participants and observers have been pointing out the potential dangers posed by these markets.

- The volumes of outstanding positions are impossible to quantify, but are now sufficiently large to pose a risk to the entire financial system if there was a wide-scale crisis.
- The variety of contracts is extensive and could be creating unknown risks to the financial system.
- Because these contracts do not trade on regulated exchanges they may fall outside the scope of financial regulators.

Despite these risks, the benefits offered from the ongoing development of the OTC markets in derivatives will ensure continued growth in variety of contracts and the volumes outstanding. Such contracts facilitate the spreading of risks amongst a wide variety of players across the entire economic and financial system, and greatly enhance the innovative capacity of the financial sector. The explosive growth in derivative markets of all types in recent decades is testament to the valuable benefits that they deliver, either directly or indirectly, to business, government and the consumer. They are likely to continue to grow in importance over the long term.

SUMMARY

- Financial derivatives are essentially instruments that call for money to change hands at some future date, with the amount to be determined by one or more reference items, such as interest rates, stock prices or currency values.
- Derivatives were primarily invented to reduce risk and not to fuel speculative activity.
- The risk profile of a futures contract is identical to the risk profile of an equivalent quantity of the relevant underlying security.
- On the expiry date of most financial futures contracts the difference between the futures contract strike price and the price of the underlying asset at the futures expiry date is used to calculate the profit (loss) of the buyer/seller of the contract. A cash settlement amount is thus calculated and one party pays the other.
- Futures contracts that are traded on exchanges are normally settled through a Clearing House. The Clearing House guarantees the fulfilment of each contract and becomes the formal counterparty for both buyer and seller.
- Initial Margin must be paid to the Clearing House by both the buyer and seller of a futures contract on the day the futures contract is entered into.
- Each day the profit (loss) of the futures position is calculated. If it moves to a loss the Clearing House receives the cash, and if there is a profit the Clearing House credits the holder's account.
- The No-Arbitrage Principle states that in efficient markets there should not be a riskless profit to be gained by combining a forward contract position with positions in the relevant underlying assets.
- A call option gives the holder the right to buy (or 'call away') 1,000 shares of a particular company, at a specified price, at any time up to a specified expiration date.   ➡

- A put option gives the buyer the right to sell (or 'put away') 1,000 shares of a particular company, at a specified price, at any time up to a specified expiration date.
- Puts and calls expand the range of opportunities available to investors, making available a wider range of risk/return opportunities.
- Options provide leverage.
- Put options, in particular, allow the buyer to hedge underlying positions in stocks.
- Institutional investors that actively sell (or write) options can generate extra income on their portfolios.
- Hedgers will normally hold risky positions in the underlying securities or markets, and will use options or futures to offset or limit some of this risk.
- Speculators will buy or sell futures or options contracts with the sole object of profit and will be attracted by the leverage offered by options and the ability to go short of the underlying securities.
- The intrinsic value of an option is the difference between the current market price of the underlying share and the strike price. More precisely, the intrinsic value of a call option is equal to the share price less the exercise price, as long as the result is positive. For a put option the intrinsic value is the exercise price less the share price, again as long as this value is positive.
- The three variables that determine time value are the time remaining to the expiration of the option; the interest rate and the volatility (as measured by standard deviation) of the underlying security.
- The advantages of exchange-traded standardised contracts include counterparty risk limited to the clearing house; standardised contracts improve liquidity in each contract, as volumes traded are limited to the available contracts; transparency is a key feature of these markets.
- Over-the-Counter (OTC) derivatives are contracts where the buyer and seller come together directly and agree the terms of the contract between themselves.
- OTC contracts have gained in popularity because most contracts that are traded on exchanges have expiry dates of less than one year, and demand for longer-dated contracts has grown exponentially.
- OTC markets enable participants to tailor contracts to their specific requirements.

QUESTIONS

1. **Which of the following statements is FALSE?**

   A. Futures contracts originated in the agricultural trading markets in Chicago in the mid-eighteenth century.
   B. The activities of speculators benefit the marketplace by increasing the liquidity of the contracts traded.
   C. Too much speculative activity can generate additional volatility in the prices of underlying assets.
   D. An American-style option can be exercised only at the expiry date and not before.

2. **If you had €100,000 invested in CRH shares, which of the following option strategies would be most appropriate to hedge your investment?**

   A. Buy call options.
   B. Buy put options.
   C. Write/Sell call options.
   D. Write/Sell put options.

3. **Which of the following is the correct definition of a traded call option in ABC company shares?**

   A. The right to buy shares in ABC at a fixed price with a fixed expiry date.
   B. The right to sell shares in ABC at a fixed price with a fixed expiry date.
   C. The right to buy or sell shares in ABC.
   D. The right to buy shares in ABC at a fixed price with a variable expiry date.

4. **The _____ is the price paid by the option buyer to the writer of either a call or a put option.**

   A. exercise price
   B. option premium
   C. current stock price plus liquidity premium
   D. call (Put) risk premium

➡

5. **A call option contains the following information, EXCEPT:**

   A. expiration date of call contract
   B. number of shares that can be bought
   C. current market price of a stock
   D. exercise price at which investor can buy the stock

6. **Regarding call options, which of the following statement(s) is/are TRUE?**

   A. Trading in call options is a zero-sum game, that is, the gain for a call buyer is the same as the gain for a call writer, ignoring expenses.
   B. The break-even price for a call buyer is the sum of the option premium and exercise price plus expenses such as commissions.
   C. A call option could be unprofitable for both the buyer and writer, ignoring expenses.
   D. The pay-off of the call option is the same as the net profit of the call option.

   1. A & B only
   2. All the above
   3. A, B & C only
   4. B, C & D only

7. **A call option written on a stock that is not owned by the writer is called a _____ :**

   A. naked call
   B. risky call
   C. covered call
   D. volatile call

8. **A call option is said to be _____ if the exercise price is higher than the current stock-market price.**

   A. At the money (ATM)
   B. Out of the money (OTM)
   C. In the money (ITM)
   D. Zero money (ZM)

Chapter thirteen

Investment Arithmetic

This is a catch-all chapter that sets out to bring together the key quantitative yardsticks and financial ratios that are commonly used by investment practitioners. A brief description is provided for each concept together with illustrative examples where appropriate. Many, but not all, of the definitions outlined here appear in other chapters.

ACCOUNTING RATIOS

There are many ratios derived from published company accounts. The more important ones are described here by reference to information relating to a hypothetical company.

Table 13.1 ABC plc: Key Numbers

– Share Information		
	Shares in Issue	1000m
	Share price	200c
	Market Capitalisation	€2000m

– Excerpts from the Profit & Loss Account 2005	€m	Per Share
Sales	2000	200c
Operating Costs	(1650)	
Operating Profit	350	
Depreciation	(75)	7.5c
Interest Charge	(125)	
Pre-tax Profit	150	
Taxation	(30)	
After-tax Profits	120	12.0c
Dividend	(40)	4.0c
Retained Profits	80	

> **– Excerpts from the Balance Sheet at end-December 2005**
>
> | | |
> |---|---|
> | Fixed Assets | 1300m |
> | Net Current Assets | 1400m |
> | Total Assets | 2700m |
> | Less Net Debt | 1500m |
> | Shareholders Funds (Equity) | 1200m |

When analysing quoted companies a useful starting point is information on the company's capital structure, i.e., a list of the securities issued by the company and their market price. ABC has a simple structure with 1,000 million shares in issue and its share price of 200c results in a market capitalisation of €2,000 million (200c * 1,000m).

From the Profit and Loss Account it can be seen that sales in 2005 amounted to €2000 million and, after various expenses, profit after tax (PAT) amounted to €120 million. Sales, depreciation, PAT, and dividends paid are also shown on a per-share basis, which is simply calculated by dividing each figure by the number of shares in issue (ABC has 1,000 million in issue).

For investors the two most important per-share statistics are the PAT per share, which is normally referred to by investment analysts as earnings per share (EPS), and the dividend per share (DPS). These are particularly important because they are the building blocks for three of the most commonly used valuation yardsticks, namely:

- the price earnings ratio (PER)
- the earnings yield
- the dividend yield

Price Earnings Ratio (PER)

ABC's PER is calculated as:

$$\frac{\text{Share Price}}{\text{EPS}} = \frac{200}{12} = 16.7$$

It is important to note that the PER is a ratio. In this example ABC's PER of 16.7 is often referred to as its **historical PER**, given that it is derived from ABC's last published EPS. Investment analysts generally also calculate the **prospective PER,** which is derived from a forecast of a company's EPS for the upcoming accounting period. Therefore if a company's earnings are forecast to grow, the prospective PER will be lower than the historical PER.

Earnings Yield

The earnings yield takes the same two pieces of information as the PER, but it is the inverse of it and is calculated as:

$$\frac{EPS}{\text{Share price}} \times 100 = \frac{12 \times 100}{200} = 6\%$$

Dividend Yield

ABC's dividend yield is calculated as:

$$\frac{\text{Dividend Per Share}}{\text{Share Price}} \times 100 = \frac{4}{200} \times 100 = 2\%$$

The dividend yield and earnings yield are closely related and the relationship between the two is expressed in terms of the pay-out ratio and the retention ratio. The pay-out ratio is defined as the proportion of earnings that are paid out in dividends to shareholders. ABC's pay-out ratio and retention ratio are:

$$\text{Pay-out Ratio} = \frac{\text{Total Dividend}}{\text{PAT}} = \frac{40m}{120m} = 0.33.$$

This ratio tells us that ABC has paid out 33% of profits in dividends to its shareholders;

and

$$\text{Retention Ratio} = \frac{\text{Retained Profits}}{\text{PAT}} = \frac{80m}{120m} = 0.67$$

Therefore, we can see that the following holds:

$$\text{Pay-out ratio} = 1 - \text{Retention ratio}$$

Dividend Cover

Where an investor relies on the dividend yield as a valuation yardstick it will be necessary to establish what level of risk applies to future dividend payments. The dividend cover is a ratio that informs the investor in this respect, and is calculated as:

$$\text{Dividend Cover} = \frac{\text{PAT}}{\text{Cost of Dividend}} = \frac{120m}{40m} = 3$$

The dividend cover is a ratio, and in the case of ABC tells us that its dividend is covered three times by its earnings. This is quite a high cover ratio and indicates that even if ABC's profits were to fall sharply in the future, the company would still have sufficient earnings to afford to maintain its dividend payments to shareholders. A low number for dividend cover would raise questions about the sustainability of dividend payments. For example, a dividend cover of one means that the dividend cost equals all profits after tax for the period in question.

Cash Flow Per Share

Measures of cash flow have become increasingly important in recent years. In the case of ABC its cash flow may be defined as:

$$\text{Cash Flow} = \text{PAT} + \text{Depreciation} = €120m + €75 = €195m$$

and

$$\text{Cash Flow per Share} = \frac{€195m}{1,000m} = 19.5c$$

Analysts have become increasingly reliant on valuation yardsticks that are built on cash flows rather than accounting flows, although both are closely interrelated. These include the following:

Earnings Before Interest, Tax, Depreciation and Amortisation (EBITDA)

This is really a new name for operating profits, but it has the advantage of making explicit what is excluded from this number. In the case of ABC it can be seen that EBITDA equals €350m.

In recent years many analysts have given greater prominence to investment ratios derived from EBITDA for a number of reasons. Firstly, globalisation of investment flows means that fund managers are increasingly investing on a global basis. Differences in accounting conventions create difficulties in interpreting traditional ratios such as price earnings ratios. Secondly, accounting scandals in the early years of the millennium highlighted the benefits of cash-flow-based measures, as they are more difficult to manipulate than accounting-based measures. A number of ratios have become popular based on enterprise value (EV).

Enterprise Value (EV)

This is the value of the total assets controlled by a business and it is usually defined as the sum of debt securities and equity securities issued by a company at their respective market values. The EV of ABC plc is:

$$EV = \text{Market Value of Debt} + \text{Market Value of Equity}$$
$$= \text{€}1{,}500\text{m} + \text{€}2{,}000\text{m} = \text{€}3{,}500\text{m}$$

Earnings Before Interest, Tax, Depreciation and Amortisation (EBITDA) is often expressed as a ratio to EV and for ABC we have:

$$EV/EBITDA = 3{,}500\text{m} /350\text{m} = 10$$

This ratio is akin to the PER. In businesses such as telecommunications, where capital investment is very high leading to high depreciation charges, this ratio is often preferable, given its focus on cash flows rather than accounting earnings, and on the market value of the total assets controlled by the company. Because of its focus on total assets it is useful in making comparisons of companies with different capital structures.

RATIOS BASED ON THE BALANCE SHEET

The ratios and valuation yardsticks set out so far are derived from the profit and loss account. We now turn to information that may be gleaned from the balance sheet. For investors and investment analysts the key information contained in the balance sheet relates to the net asset value or book value of a company, and various ratios that calibrate the strength of a company's balance sheet. Turning to the latter first, for ABC we have:

$$\text{Debt/Equity Ratio} = \frac{\text{Net Debt}}{\text{Shareholders' Funds}} = \frac{\text{€}1500\text{m}}{\text{€}1200\text{m}} * 100 = 125\%$$

$$\text{Debt/Capital Employed} = \frac{\text{Net Debt}}{\text{Capital Employed}} = \frac{\text{€}1500}{\text{€}2700} * 100 = 55.6\%$$

Note: Capital employed is equal to Fixed Assets + Net Current Assets, or Net debt + Shareholders' Funds.

If these ratios are 'too high', then it indicates that the company is in a weak financial position. What constitutes 'too high' depends on the type of industry in question and on the overall economic climate. For example, in a climate of low interest rates and strong economic growth company balance sheets could sustain higher debt ratios than in a period of high interest rates and low growth.

Net Asset Value (NAV), Book Value and Shareholders' Funds

These amount to one and the same, and in ABC's case the number is €1200m. Again, investors like to express this number on a per-share basis to make it easy to compare one company with another and with averages for industry sectors and the overall market. ABC's NAV per share is:

$$\text{NAV per Share} \quad = \quad \frac{\text{Shareholders' Funds}}{\text{Number of Shares in Issue}} \quad = \quad \frac{€1200\text{m}}{1,000\text{m}} \quad = \quad 120\text{c}$$

This is sometimes referred to as the Book Value per Share, and is often related to the current market share price:

$$\text{Price/Book or Price/NAV} \quad = \quad \frac{\text{Share Price}}{\text{NAV per Share}} \quad = \quad \frac{200\text{c}}{120\text{c}} \quad = 1.7$$

This ratio is not relied on to the same degree as those based on cash flows. It is useful in industry sectors such as property, where tangible assets are very important and where market values for those assets can be ascertained. In industries where human capital is the main asset this ratio is virtually useless.

MEASURING INVESTMENT RETURNS

Investment return typically consists of two components:

- income return
- capital return.

Assume that you purchased shares in Company A exactly one year ago and that you have just sold them on the stock market. The details of your transactions are as follows:

Table 13.2

Transaction	Number of Shares	Stock	Purchase or Sale Price	Consideration or Income
Bought on 2/01/2005	1	Company A	100c	100c
Sold on 2/01/2006	1	Company A	120c	120c
Dividend received on 2/01/2006				5c

The percentage capital gain (return) on this investment is:

$$\text{Capital Gain} \quad = \quad \frac{\text{Sale Price} - \text{Purchase Price} * 100}{\text{Purchase Price}}$$

$$= \quad \frac{120c - 100c * 100}{100c} = 20\%$$

and the total percentage return is:

$$\text{Total Return} = \frac{(\text{Sale Price} - \text{Purchase Price}) + \text{Income} * 100}{\text{Purchase Price}}$$

In the case of this transaction the total return is 25%, calculated as follows:

$$\frac{120c - 100c + 5c * 100}{100c} = 25\%$$

This is usually referred to as the Holding Period Return.

Stock-Market Indices

The performance of investment portfolios is normally assessed relative to an appropriate benchmark index. Analysis of historical market returns relies on time series of stock-market indices to provide the raw data on overall market returns. Finally, investment strategists often try to quantify their expectations in terms of forecasting the levels of various stock-market indices. Indeed, during the Christmas and New Year 'silly season' forecasting the coming year's index performance becomes a sport, as celebrities, fund managers and investment analysts are asked for their predictions.

Stock-market indices are now published on a daily basis covering global equity markets and bond markets. Exhibit 13.1 shows information published daily in the *Financial Times* covering equity-market indices.

Construction of a Stock-Market Index

Step one involves deciding which universe of stocks is to be covered by the index. In the case of the Irish market the obvious starting point is all companies publicly quoted and traded on the Irish Stock Exchange. However, the Irish exchange does have more than one market. It has the 'Official List', which includes the majority of quoted companies, but it also has the IEX, which is geared to facilitate smaller companies. Therefore a

Exhibit 13.1 Equity Market Indexes

WORLD EQUITY MARKETS AT A GLANCE

Country	Index	Nov 10	Nov 9	Nov 8	2005 High	2005 Low	Yield	P/E
Argentina	Merval	1573.47	1592.43	1615.59	1731.33 3/10	1276.48 15/4	1.72	11.5
Australia	S&P All Ordinaries	4492.3	4476.3	4501.2	4617.40 29/9	3905.50 4/5	3.67	16.7
	S&P/ASX 200 Res	3273.1	3256.4	3289.4	3499.70 29/9	2407.40 6/1		
	S&P/ASX 200	4543.7	4526.1	4554.5	4671.70 29/9	3947.10 4/5		
Austria	ATX Index	3331.97	3326.41	3346.38	3503.65 3/10	2415.01 13/1	1.51	20.9
Belgium	BEL20	3362.26	3337.33	3336.58	3373.83 4/10	2958.79 14/1	3.16	15.3
	BEL Mid	3245.81	3242.17	3255.47	3338.97 3/1	2645.88 3/1		
Brazil	Bovespa	30300.25	30666.07	30970.60	31856.13 3/10	23909.97 20/1	3.95	9.3
Canada	S&P/TSX Met & Min	361.68	362.20	359.97	368.44 11/10	249.29 5/1	2.15	18.5
	S&P/TSX 60	594.99	601.30	598.73	626.19 27/9	498.36 7/1		
	S&P/TSX Comp	10546.39	10656.54	10616.22	11081.19 3/10	9006.22 7/1		
Chile	IGPA Gen	9418.22	9461.38	9388.43	10179.23 4/10	8620.06 18/1	2.52	17.8
China	Shanghai A	1143.92	1164.81	1166.97	1383.68 8/3	1062.45 17/7	1.35	12.5
	Shanghai B	60.56	61.56	61.38	83.98 9/3	51.34 21/7		
	Shenzhen A	274.79	281.50	282.39	344.05 9/3	244.71 18/7		
	Shenzhen B	195.07	198.04	196.73	276.84 9/3	186.53 28/10		
	FTSE/Xinhua A200	2551.82	2595.19	2599.96	3196.73 8/3	2492.37 8/3		
	FTSE/Xinhua B35	2658.55	2696.94	2676.43	3720.70 8/4	2555.31 28/10		
Colombia	CSE Index	7896.11	7751.67	7646.53	7751.67 9/11	4270.11 6/1	2.31	19.2
Croatia	CROBEX	2053.99	2069.40	2053.52	2156.97 5/10	1566.43 7/1	na	na
Cyprus	CSE General	106.15	105.80	107.30	107.30 8/11	72.23 3/1	2.33	21.3
Czech Republic	PX 50	1410.5	1416.1	1421.6	1478.30 4/10	1050.60 3/1	2.08	23.4
Denmark	OMX Copenhagen 20	363.67	365.70	365.47	377.72 16/9	285.22 24/1	1.67	18.2
Egypt	Hermes Financial	5247.25	5654.30	5213.11	5213.11 8/11	2502.12 3/1	na	na
Estonia	OMX Tallinn	678.80	676.99	677.64	709.52 3/10	451.13 3/1	na	na
Finland	OMX Helsinki General	7680.25	7677.21	7663.72	7930.52 3/10	6094.13 24/1	2.7	15.2
France	CAC 40	4479.50	4480.23	4503.62	4650.24 4/10	3816.14 12/1	2.79	14.2
	SBF 120	3215.63	3218.37	3233.27	3342.04 4/10	2711.68 12/1		
Germany	M-DAX	6937.78	6922.55	6959.03	7165.30 5/1	5409.81 5/1	2.13	13.4
	XETRA Dax	5015.55	5011.38	5006.83	5138.02 4/10	4178.10 28/4		
	TecDAX	576.99	580.72	581.26	596.12 4/10	498.71 28/4		
Greece	Athens Gen	3391.42	3417.73	3415.98	3417.73 9/11	2818.33 5/1	2.76	20.4
	FTSE/ASE 20	1890.50	1902.88	1899.84	1902.88 9/11	1567.29 3/5		
Hong Kong	Hang Seng	14633.33	14597.55	14403.20	15466.06 15/8	13355.23 18/4	3.18	12.8
	HS China Enterprise	4949.79	4920.80	4876.87	5539.39 15/8	4501.61 26/5		
	HSCC Red Chip	1885.19	1876.15	1836.56	2018.49 29/9	1441.33 11/1		
Hungary	Bux	20658.71	20981.45	21159.23	23671.96 10/1	14598.69 10/1	2.51	18.9
India	BSE Sens.	8308.93	8308.78	8317.80	8799.96 4/10	6102.74 5/1	1.8	14.9
	S&P CNX 500	2177.25	2166.60	2173.00	2327.75 4/10	1663.80 24/1		
Indonesia	Jakarta Comp.	1043.70	1052.82	(c)	1192.20 3/8	994.77 29/8	3.69	11.2
Ireland	ISEQ Overall	6743.79	6726.20	6720.55	6891.29 4/10	5798.49 28/4	2.19	13.8

Country	Index	Nov 10	Nov 9	Nov 8	2005 High	2005 Low	Yield	P/E
Spain	Madrid SE	1125.17	1127.41	1125.71	1178.06 4/10	950.93 12/1	2.4	18.8
	IBEX 35	10438.4	10456.3	10440.2	10919.20 4/10	8945.70 12/1		
Sri Lanka	CSE All Share	2446.56	2456.79	2482.36	2625.72 2/11	1509.25 3/1	2.44	16.1
Sweden	OMX Stockholm 30	900.64	900.97	899.28	905.38 3/10	727.56 24/1	2.54	18.3
	OMX Stockholm AS	281.11	280.90	280.30	282.80 3/10	225.82 24/1		
Switzerland	SMI Index	7243.14	7238.48	7257.48	7257.48 8/11	5669.60 12/1	1.56	18
	WeightedPr.	5988.37	5971.06	5849.63	6455.57 3/8	5632.97 28/10	4.31	12.7
Taiwan	Bangkok SET	694.44	695.60	695.85	741.55 28/2	638.31 7/7	3.75	9.9
Turkey	IMKG Nat 100	34709.65	33948.29	33749.43	36924.79 4/10	23265.94 18/4	2.09	14
UK	FTSE 100	5423.5	5439.8	5460.9	5501.50 3/10	4783.60 12/1	3.13	14
	FT30	2252.4	2245.4	2248.5	2254.20 5/1	1966.00 5/1		
	FTSE All-Share	2724.54	2730.39	2740.07	2756.75 3/10	2393.29 28/4		
	FTSE techMARK 100	1302.40	1298.18	1299.34	1302.40 10/11	1082.20 29/4		
	FTSE4Good UK	4739.62	4755.85	4775.68	4813.49 3/10	4245.57 28/4		
US	DJ Industrials	10555.49	10546.21	10539.72	10940.55 4/3	10012.36 20/4	1.72	18.2
	DJ Composite	3521.57	3538.19	3621.28	3642.87 3/10	2402.30 12/9		
	DJ Transport	3999.92	3961.24	4004.37	4004.37 9/11	3382.89 15/4		
	DJ Utilities	387.13	395.86	393.77	437.63 3/10	324.68 7/1		
	S&P 500	1219.83	1220.65	1218.59	1245.04 3/8	1137.50 20/4		
	FTSE NASDAQ 500	5455.83	5466.85	5460.37	5545.26 3/8	4791.50 15/4		
	NASDAQ Cmp	2168.86	2175.81	2172.07	2218.15 28/4	1904.18 28/4		
	NASDAQ 100	1627.35	1630.21	1628.40	1630.21 28/4	1406.85 20/4		
	Russell 2000	654.74	659.81	656.23	688.51 28/4	575.02 28/4		
	NYSE Comp.	7476.80	7500.99	7489.72	7963.82 28/4	6935.31 20/4		
	Wilshire 5000	(u)	12227.01	12204.36	12469.86 28/8	11217.81 20/4		
Venezuela	IBC	20417.03	20420.33	20324.35	20756.45 9/3	18517.89 11/8	9.44	6.6
CROSS-BORDER	DJ Stoxx 50 €	3260.79	3264.41	3271.57	3326.78 21/9	2763.16 11/8		
	DJ Euro Stx 50 €	3361.05	3355.77	3361.75	3464.23 4/10	2924.01 12/1		
	DJ Glb Titans 50 $	(u)	194.50	194.56	198.75 4/3	187.58 20/4		
	FTSE Multinatls $	(u)	967.07	968.27	983.12 16/9	899.62 24/1		
	FTSE Glob 100 $	(u)	903.24	904.96	916.85 29/9	842.48 24/1		
	FTSE4Good Glob $	(u)	4773.67	4782.35	4870.64 9/9	4571.22 28/4		
	FTSE E300 €	1225.43	1225.26	1226.61	1242.04 4/10	1038.64 12/1		
	FTSEurofirst 80 €	4198.38	4194.58	4200.10	4325.23 4/10	3671.96 28/4		
	FTSEurofirst 100 €	4036.31	4039.11	4043.56	4111.12 4/10	3463.84 12/1		
	FTSE Latibex €	1701.0	1721.3	1712.2	1751.50 4/10	968.10 16/5		
	FTSE Gold Min $	(u)	1620.38	1777.55	1951.44 29/9	1342.99 16/5		
	FTSE All World £	(u)	162.82	162.97	163.57 30/9	135.72 20/4		
	FTSE All World $	(u)	191.13	191.17	194.00 30/9	175.00 28/4		
	MSCI ACWI Fr $	1203.05*	1206.97	1206.97	1225.59 9/9	1114.45 18/4		
	MSCI Europe €	(u)	295.78	295.87	299.87 29/9	273.87 27/4		
	MSCI Pacific $	(u)	1225.60	1228.09	1246.00 4/10	1054.22 12/1		
	S&P Glob 1200 $	(u)	2140.62	2152.45	2173.00 29/9	1798.45 18/4		
	S&P Europe 350 €	(u)	1327.30	1328.25	1347.15 9/9	1224.23 28/4		
	S&P Glob 1200 $	(u)	1234.11	1235.63	1248.68 4/10	1044.30 12/1		
	S&P Euro €	(u)	1320.86	1321.79	1360.27 4/10	1142.99 12/1		

decision has to be made on whether to include all stocks, or to have different indices for the various 'sub-markets'. The normal solution is to construct different indices for the various markets. Therefore, in Ireland the ISEQ Overall index does not include IEX-listed companies.

   The stocks included in a stock-market indicator must then be combined in certain proportions to construct the index or average. Therefore, each stock must be assigned some relative weight. Three possible approaches can be used:

i)   Weighting by the company's current market capitalisation
ii)   Weighting by the price of one unit of the company's stock
iii)   Weighting each company equally regardless of its market price.

The vast majority of stock-market indices are constructed using market capitalisations as weights. Once this is decided, it is then necessary to average the individual components. Two methods of averaging are possible: arithmetic or geometric. Virtually all indices are now constructed using arithmetic averaging.

QUESTIONS

I. You are given the following information for the Balance Sheet of ABC plc:

	€ million
Fixed Assets	120
Net Current Assets	100
Total Assets	220
Less Net Debt	70
Shareholders' Funds (Equity)	150

The Debt/Equity Ratio of ABC plc is:

A. 31.8%
B. 46.7%
C. 70.0%
D. 62.1%

2. You are further told that ABC plc has 100 million shares in issue
   and the shares are trading at a current market price of 100c.
   Earnings per share (EPS) for this year are expected to be 13c.

   What are the net asset value (NAV) per share: and the price
   earnings ratio (PER)?

   A. 150c : 12.9
   B. 220c : 7.69
   C. 150c : 7.69
   D. 70c : 13.0%

3. You are given the following information for XYZ plc:

	€ Million
Sales	100
Operating Profit	15
Profit after Tax	10
Dividend	5
Retained Profits	5

   XYZ has 150 million shares in issue and the current market price is
   100c.

   What are XYZ's Earnings Per Share (EPS), and Dividend Per
   Share (DPS)?

   A. 66.7c; 20c
   B. 100c;   10c
   C. 6.7c;   3.3c
   D. 10c;   6.7c

Chapter fourteen

Investment Returns: History and Prospects

This chapter presents extensive data on the historical returns achieved by the various asset categories for the major markets. Investment returns for Irish assets are also examined in detail. The more recent experience of low equity returns since 2000 is contrasted with the era of high returns in the 1980s and 1990s. The chapter concludes with the authors' assessment of some of the key issues that are likely to dominate investment thinking and practice over the medium term.

Learning Objectives

After reading this chapter you will:
- **Be familiar with long-term historical investment returns**
- **Be aware of the unusually high returns delivered by both bonds and equities during the 1980s and 1990s**
- **Be able to identify the problems created for pension funds due to the combination of low equity returns and low long-term government bond yields.**

In Chapter 8 the linkages between the real economy and the financial markets are explored and two common drivers – growth and inflation – identified.

Inflation is important for its effect on interest rates and bond yields. Growth is important for its positive effect on the future cash flows generated by the real assets: equities and property. The price of the real assets, the present value of those future cash flows, is determined by applying a discount factor which keys off bond yields.

The Irish economy and financial markets in recent decades offer a powerful illustration of the influence of growth and inflation.

Table 14.1 The Irish Economy, % p.a.

	Real GNP Growth	Inflation
The Sixties	4.0	5.4
The Seventies	3.5	14.8
The Eighties	2.1	6.0
The Nineties	6.7	2.7

(Source: Dept of Finance)

Table 14.2 Real Returns on Irish Assets, % p.a.

	Bonds	Equities	Cash	Property
1960–1969	(2.1)	11.1	1.4	N/A
1970–1979	(5.2)	0.5	(3.1)	(2.6)
1980–1989	9.5	14.0	4.1	1.5
1990–1999	8.1	11.8	5.4	12.5

(Source: © 2005 E. Dimson, P. Marsh, M. Staunton, IPFPUT, IPO)

In the 1960s real growth in GNP was an impressive 4.0% per annum, as Irish economic development belatedly accelerated after the stagnation of the 1950s. Inflation gradually picked up during the decade, averaging a relatively high 5.4% per annum for the full period. As shown in Table 14.2, Irish equities responded well to the good growth background, generating real returns of 11.1% per annum. Bonds suffered, generating negative returns in real terms because of their inability to cope with rising inflation. Cash deposits generated real returns as deposit rates responded to higher inflation.

The high-inflation 1970s proved an especially traumatic decade for investors as inflation surged following two oil shocks and inappropriate government responses both in Ireland and in our main trading partners. Bonds, cash and property real returns were heavily negative for the full decade. The dynamic characteristic of equities, the ability of companies to respond to a changing environment, enabled equities, despite some dramatic capital declines particularly in 1974, to generate a marginally positive real return of 0.5% per annum over the decade. Growth in GNP in the 1970s, despite the very difficult inflationary background, was respectable at 3.5% per annum and supported equity returns.

Inflation in Ireland peaked in 1981 at 20.4%. The long downward journey in inflation was a key influence in the dramatically good returns generated by all asset classes in the 1980s and 1990s. Equity performance in the 1980s was particularly noteworthy, as it was achieved against a relatively poor growth background. Clearly, in the 1980s the impact of the significantly lower discount factor was the more important influence in determining equity prices.

The 1990s' combination of high growth and low inflation generated high returns across all four asset classes.

Ireland, of course, as a small, open economy is sensitive to international developments. Ireland benefited from two particular global trends of the 1980s and 1990s: disinflation and globalisation. Globalisation was important in that trade liberalisation benefited Ireland's important export business, while liberalisation of capital flows helped Ireland to attract substantial volumes of Foreign Direct Investment. Important domestic factors in Ireland's economic transformation included a sustained improvement in the national finances, wage moderation resulting from Social Partnership, a three-way contract between labour, employers and the State, and a young, productive and growing labour force. Meanwhile, Ireland's participation in the euro in January 1999 resulted in full convergence, give or take some basis points, between Irish and German interest rates. The low-inflation environment discussed earlier, of course, would of itself have resulted in significant reductions in interest rates and bond yields from those prevailing during the 1980s. However, membership of the Euro zone eliminated the premium (for market size, liquidity and risk) which had historically attached to Irish rates.

The transformation of the Irish interest-rate structure during the 1990s was dramatic. At year-end 1992, during the currency crisis of that winter, Irish three-month money-market rates stood at just under 17%, while ten-year bond yields were at 9.5%. By the end of 1999, money-market rates had fallen to 3.33% and bond yields to 5.55%.

The combination of a favourable international background and a transformed domestic economy permitted Irish financial assets to generate returns in the 1990s that compared with the very best of those generated by our major trading partners:

Table 14.3 Real Returns on Bonds, % p.a.

1990–1999	
Ireland	8.1
US	5.7
Germany	5.6
UK	9.3
(Source: © 2005 E. Dimson, P. Marsh, M. Staunton)	

Table 14.4 Real Returns on Equities, % p.a.

1990–1999	
Ireland	11.8
US	14.2
Germany	9.9
UK	11.2
	(Source: © 2005 E. Dimson, P. Marsh, M. Staunton)

The significant outperformance of Irish equities by US equities during the 1990s was a function of the US equity market's greater exposure to the technology bubble and, as we go on to see, was reversed after the bubble imploded.

The uniquely favourable background of the 1990s faded as the current decade progressed. The implosion of the technology bubble was closely followed by the Twin Towers terrorist attack of 11 September 2001. The combined impact slowed global growth, inevitably affecting the Irish economy which itself had developed an inflationary problem as a consequence of the growth experienced earlier:

Table 14.5 The Irish Economy

	Real GNP Growth	Inflation (HICP)
2000	10.1%	5.3%
2001	3.8%	4.0%
2002	2.7%	4.7%
2003	5.1%	4.0%
2004	4.0%	2.3%
5-Year Period	5.1% p.a.	4.1% p.a.
		(Source: Dept of Finance)

Not surprisingly, the returns generated by Irish assets were significantly lower during the period 2000 to 2004 than those prevailing in the halcyon decade of the 1990s:

Table 14.6 Real Returns on Irish Assets, % p.a.

2000–2004	
Bonds	4.2
Equities	2.6
Cash	(0.6)
Property	8.1
	(Source: © 2005 E. Dimson, P. Marsh, M. Staunton, IPO)

Bonds outperformed equities as disinflation, excess global savings and strategic switching by pension funds from equities into bonds pushed real and nominal yields to levels that have not been seen since the Great Depression. Irish bonds participated fully in the international trend, no longer inhibited by the path of domestic inflation because of our membership of the wider Euro zone.

Table 14.7 Inflation, % p.a.

2000–2004	
Ireland	4.1%
Germany	1.5%
Euro Average	2.2%
UK	1.2%
US	2.5%
HICP for EU countries, CPI for the US	
	(Source: Dept of Finance)

Returns on Irish equities slowed as the pace of economic growth slowed. Nevertheless, Irish equity returns compare very favourably with those generated by Ireland's key trading partners:

Table 14.8 Real Return on Assets, % p.a.

2000–2004		
	Bonds	*Equities*
Ireland	4.2	2.6
US	7.6	(3.8)
Germany	6.7	(9.1)
UK	3.0	(4.9)
	(Source: © 2005 E. Dimson, P. Marsh, M. Staunton)	

The performance of Irish equities in this period was partly attributable to the lower exposure of the Irish market to technology at the peak of the bubble in March 2000. The downside therefore was far more severe for the US and for the UK. German equity returns were undermined by the poor performance of the German economy in the period. It is likely that the Irish market also benefited from two important underlying trends in global equity markets in the period – the outperformance by small capitalisation stocks of large capitalisation and the outperformance of value stocks over growth stocks.

The performance of the Irish equity index in the period was greatly influenced by wild gyrations in the share price of Elan Corporation, an important index constituent. Nevertheless, the superior economic performance of Ireland during the period was clearly a key driver of the better out-turn in Irish equities.

Table 14.9 Economic Growth[1] 2000–2004, % p.a.

Ireland[2]	4.7%
Germany	1.1%
Euro Average	1.7%
UK	2.7%
Euro Average	1.9%
US	2.7%

1 GDP volumes
2 GNP volumes

(Source: Dept of Finance)

Property, of course, was the outstanding performer in this period, supported obviously by the strength of the economy and importantly by low borrowing costs. Property returns had already been strong during the second half of the 1990s. In the five years to end-1999, property generated a remarkable 25.1% per annum return in nominal terms. By the new millennium, therefore, enthusiasm for property investment, both on the part of property investors and lenders, was overwhelming. Property was outstandingly the investment asset of choice in Ireland during 2000 to 2004.

The Irish investment assets in the period, therefore, enjoyed the benefits of relatively high growth, while escaping the adverse consequences of relatively high domestic inflation. Irish inflation, because of our membership of the Euro zone, is no longer a significant influence on official interest-rate policy.

PROSPECTIVE RETURNS

Index-Linked Bonds

The long-term investor seeking maximum certainty of future returns will opt for index-linked bonds for their guarantee of a real return over the rate of inflation. Market enthusiasm for long-dated, index-linked issues was illustrated in September 2005 by the success of the UK Government's issue of a fifty-year index-linked stock at a real return of 1.11%.

At end-September 2005, real returns on long-dated, index-linked issues compared to historical real returns on conventional fixed-interest bonds as follows:

Table 14.10 Real Returns, % p.a.

	Market Yield September 2005	Historic Bond Returns	
		Real Return 1900–2004	Real Return 1950–2004
US	1.51	1.9	2.0
UK	1.41	1.3	1.7
France	1.36	(0.3)	4.9

(Source: Financial Times © 2005 E. Dimson, P. Marsh, M. Saunton)

Real yields currently are in low ground, based on the above comparisons. However, the real yields currently available are not dramatically lower than long-run historical levels. The current perception that they are extraordinarily low is due to the folk memory of high real returns generated by bonds during the 1980s and 1990s. Nevertheless, it cannot be denied that the investor buying long-term, index-linked bonds at today's values is locking into relatively low returns. French yields are used rather than German, because of the availability of French index-linked issues.

Fixed-Interest Bonds

Whilst the investor in fixed-interest government bonds receives returns that are guaranteed in nominal terms, these returns may be eroded by inflation. Again, investor enthusiasm for long-dated, fixed-interest bonds is exemplified by the recently issued UK Treasury $4^{1}/4$% 2055, which at end-September 2005 yielded 4.14% to redemption.

Table 14.11 Nominal Returns on Fixed-Interest Bonds, % p.a.

	Market Yield September 2005	Nominal Return 1900–2004	Nominal Return % 1950–2004
US	4.57	4.9	5.9
UK	4.25	5.3	7.6
France	3.62	7.2	10.1

(Source: Financial Times; © 2005 E. Dimson, P. Marsh, M. Staunton)

The contrast between the yields currently available and historical long-run returns is rather more demanding in the case of conventional government fixed-interest bonds, particularly in comparison with the post-war experience.

Today's buyer of fixed interest is locking into returns that compare unfavourably with the long-term historical returns, and even more unfavourably with the returns generated since the 1950s.

A crude estimation of the bond market's view of future inflation may be calculated by subtracting the current real yield from the current fixed-interest yield – although strictly the nominal fixed-interest yield includes an inflation risk premium that rewards the fixed-interest investor for the risk he takes on inflation.

Table 14.12 Inflation Expectations v. Historical Levels, % p.a.

	'Forecast' Inflation	Inflation 1900–2004	Inflation 1950–2004
US	3.06	3.0	3.9
UK	2.84	4.0	5.9
France	2.26	7.5	5.2

'Forecast' inflation in the US is actually extremely close to the long-term level, but substantially lower than the post-war level of 3.9%. Of course, the post-war average level was bounded by extremes of 7.4% p.a. for the ten years to end-1979, and 2.5% p.a. for the ten years to end-1999. On the face of it, the US fixed-interest investor is currently allowing little margin for error on inflation.

The UK bond investor is more adventurous still. The market expectation of 2.84% is well below the long-term number and less than half the post-war average. In the UK the post-war average was bounded by an extreme of 13.1% per annum for the ten years to end 1971, with the lower boundary being 3.5% p.a. for the ten years to end-1999. Warren Buffet argues that investors, instead of looking forward, look into the rear-view mirror at recent experience, and that is rarely a reliable guide to the long-term future. There appears to be a clear risk that UK investors are overweighting the recent experience. French investors, too, in looking ahead appear to pay little regard to the long-term experience, clearly expecting that a more disciplined fiscal and monetary framework under the EMU will result in a trans-formation of long-term inflation.

The two components of nominal bond yields are the real yield and expected inflation. Clearly, current bond yields at end-September 2005 are built upon low numbers for both. Bond investors see a low-inflation, low-risk world.

There is no escaping the conclusion that bond-market returns going forward will be low.

Equities

The government guarantees the real return of the index-linked bond investor and the nominal return of the fixed-interest bond investor. The equity investor receives no such guarantee. The equity investor takes more risk than the bond investor and therefore is entitled to expect a higher return. This reward for taking higher risk is known as the Equity Risk Premium (ERP). Long-term equity returns, in nominal terms, are made up of the yield on fixed-interest bonds plus the Equity Risk Premium.

An examination of long-term bond and equity returns shows that over the long run the equity investor does indeed receive an Equity Risk Premium. Of course, if he did not then investors would no longer take equity risk and the capitalist system would collapse.

Table 14.13 The Equity Risk Premium: Long Term, % p.a.

	1900–2004	1950–2004
Ireland	3.6	5.6
US	4.7	5.8
UK	4.1	5.9
Germany	4.8	4.9

(Source: © 2005 E. Dimson, P. Marsh, M. Staunton)

The table above indicates a reasonably consistent ERP across the markets over the long run. However, over shorter-run, ten-year periods it has displayed dramatic volatility, including an extended period of negative ERP in Germany in the 1970s.

Table 14.14 The Equity Risk Premium: Shorter Term, % p.a.

	1950s	1960s	1970s	1980s	1990s
Ireland	4.6	13.2	5.7	4.5	3.7
US	17.9	6.6	1.0	3.8	8.5
UK	16.0	8.0	3.0	7.5	1.9
Germany	28.5	0.8	(4.4)	9.6	4.3

(Source: © 2005 E. Dimson, P. Marsh, M. Staunton)

More recently, in the unusual conditions of recent years of strong bond markets but with equities in their post-bubble depression, the ERP has been heavily negative in the major international markets.

Table 14.15 The Equity Risk Premium: 2000–2004, % p.a.

Ireland	(1.6)
US	(11.4)
UK	(7.9)
Germany	(15.8)

(Source: © 2005 E. Dimson, P. Marsh, M. Staunton)

These negative rewards for equity risk taking may be partly explained as a reaction to the very handsome excess returns enjoyed by equity investors in the 1980s and 1990s and portrayed as part of the process of reversion to mean. However, the violence of the reaction has resulted in a significant overshoot on the downside, with the results that:

i) Over the past twenty-five years the ERP is well below the long-term historical average in the four markets examined.

Table 14.16 Equity Risk Premium: 25 Years to End-2004, % p.a.

	1980–2004	1900–2004
Ireland	2.9	3.6
US	2.4	4.7
UK	2.1	4.1
Germany	2.1	4.8

(Source: © 2005 E. Dimson, P. Marsh, M. Staunton)

ii) Over the past fifteen years the ERP has been half of the historic level in Ireland, about one-third of the historic level in the US, and heavily negative in the UK and Germany.

Table 14.17 Equity Risk Premium: 15 Years to End-2004, % p.a.

	1990–2004	1900–2004
Ireland	1.8	3.6
US	1.6	4.7
UK	(1.7)	4.1
Germany	(2.8)	4.8

(Source: © 2005 E. Dimson, P. Marsh, M. Staunton)

That equity investors have been underrewarded, or indeed penalised, for taking risk for such a sustained period underlines the unique conditions created by the severity of the 2000–2003 equity bear market and the prolonged fall in bond yields.

Pessimists might consider these numbers to indicate a permanently lower level of equity risk premium (and therefore equity returns) going forward. The more optimistic, pointing to the violence of the recent undershoot, might expect a higher ERP in the short to medium term as the pendulum swings back.

The usefulness of the ERP in facilitating forecasts of equity returns is thus quite constrained. Reversion to mean points to a premium of perhaps 4% to

$4^{1}/_{2}\%$, say $4^{1}/_{4}\%$. The sobering impact of the more recent periods argues for a lower number, perhaps 3% to $3^{1}/_{2}\%$, say $3^{1}/_{4}\%$. Applying these outcomes to current bond yields points to long-term equity returns as follows:

Table 14.18 Projected Long-Term Equity Returns, % p.a.

	Bond Yield	ERP	Expected Return
Ireland	3.60*	3.25–4.25	6.85–7.85
US	4.57	3.25–4.25	7.82–8.82
UK	4.25	3.25–4.25	7.50–8.50
Germany	3.60	3.25–4.25	6.85–7.85

*3.6% for long-dated (German) bond

By deducting our earlier calculation for 'Forecast' Inflation from these returns we get a picture of how projected long-term equity returns stack up against the long-term history (1900–2004).

Table 14.19 Projected Real Returns from Equities, % p.a.

	Nominal Return	Forecast Inflation	Real Return	Historical Return
Ireland	6.85–7.85	2.26*	4.59–5.59	4.7
US	7.82–8.82	3.06	4.76–5.76	6.6
UK	7.50–8.50	2.84	4.66–5.66	5.4
Germany	6.85–7.85	2.26*	4.59–5.59	2.9

* as calculated from French bond markets

Projected long-term equity returns on this basis, with the exception of the US, compare relatively well with the long-term historical experience. Certainly, a more reassuring picture than that discussed earlier for bonds is presented.

Whatever the constraints around using the ERP for forecasting long-term returns, the volatility exhibited over shorter-run periods makes it quite unsuitable for forecasting short-term outcomes.

An alternative approach to the calculation of equity-market returns is to assume that, in the long run, the equity investor's return is comprised of the opening dividend yield on his investment together with the growth in that dividend over the long term. For a market as a whole, dividend growth may be assumed to be made up of expected inflation and real growth in the economy (i.e., that profits and dividends will grow in line with nominal growth in the economy).

Table 14.20 Projected Equity Returns, % p.a.

	US	UK	Germany	Ireland
Opening Yield	1.9	3.1	2.1	2.2
Forecast Inflation	3.1	2.8	2.3	2.3
Forecast Growth	3.3	2.8	2.0	4.0
Projected Return				
– Nominal	8.3	8.7	6.4	8.5
– Real	5.2	5.9	4.1	6.2

'Forecast Inflation' is the forecast for inflation derived earlier by subtracting real yields on index-linked bonds from nominal fixed-interest yields. 'Forecast growth' is based on assumed long-term growth trends in the different economies. The trend number assumed compares to recent experience as follows:

Table 14.21 Assumed Trend Economic Growth, % p.a.

	Trend Growth	**1995–2004**	**2000–2004**
Ireland	4.0	6.7	4.7
US	3.3	3.3	2.7
UK	2.8	2.8	2.7
Germany	2.0	1.3	1.1

Equity returns projected on this 'dividend plus dividend growth' basis compare with those generated earlier using the Equity Risk Premium, and with long-term historical returns, as follows. The comparison is based on real returns; 'forecast inflation' as calculated earlier is excluded.

Table 14.22 Real Returns on Equities, % p.a.

	Projected ERP Basis	Equity Returns Dividend Basis	Historical Returns 1900–2004	1950–2004
Ireland	4.6–5.6	6.2	4.7	7.4
US	4.8–5.8	5.2	6.6	7.8
UK	4.7–5.7	5.9	5.4	7.6
Germany	4.6–5.6	4.1	2.9	8.9

Many observers agree that prospective equity returns are unlikely to match the exceptional levels generated over the period 1980–2004. These returns are clearly a significant influence on the out-turn for the period 1950–2004. This latter period also included, however, the very difficult decade of the 1970s. Current market levels indicate that prospective returns for equities will be significantly lower than those generated in the post-war period of 1950–2004.

Taking a point roughly between the midpoint of the ERP range, the dividend-based return and the long-term historical return gives the following expectation for prospective long-term equity returns:

Table 14.23 Projected Real Equity Returns, % p.a.

Ireland	5.6
US	5.5
UK	5.5
Germany	4.5

The markets appear to be telling us to expect a reversion to mean, with perhaps the US experience likely to be disappointing when compared to the long-term historical number.

Property

As discussed in Chapter 8, equities and property share common drivers in growth and inflation. Over the long run, therefore, property and equity returns might be expected to be broadly similar. They will diverge over short-run periods, as they are influenced by developments specific to each asset class.

Unfortunately, reliable long-term property returns are not as readily available as those for the other investment assets. Returns are available for Ireland back to 1970, based on the Jones Long Wootton Irish Property Index for 1971, returns from the Irish Pension Fund Property Unit Trust from 1971 to 1982 inclusive and from The Investment Property Databank (IPD) thereafter. IPD have calculated returns on UK property from 1971.

Over the thirty-five-year period to end-2004, real returns on property compare to real returns on equities in Ireland as follows:

Table 14.24 Real Returns: Ireland, % p.a.

	Irish Property	Irish Equities
1970–1979	(2.6)	0.5
1980–1989	1.5	14.0
1990–1999	12.5	11.8
2000–2004	8.1	2.6
35 years to end-2004	4.2	7.7

(Source: Property as above; © 2005 E. Dimson, P. Marsh, M. Staunton)

Over the full thirty-five-year period, Irish equities have significantly outperformed Irish property. Much of this outperformance is attributable to the dramatically better out-turn for equities from 1980–1989, when despite a relatively poor background for economic growth Irish equities performed dramatically well, generating real returns of 14.0% per annum. As discussed earlier, the Irish investment assets benefited from falling inflation and interest rates in the 1980s. An important feature of the Irish equity market in the period was sustained activity in overseas investment and acquisitions by the leading Irish companies. This had the effect not only of reducing exposure to the difficult Irish economy, but of attracting inflows of institutional monies as the domestic institutions, constrained by stringent exchange controls, built their overseas exposure via purchases of Irish equities. Meanwhile, property returns were subdued at 1.5% per annum in real terms, despite the benefits of lower interest rates. Here, a crisis in the public finances caused the Irish government, the largest occupier of office space, to effectively withdraw from new lettings for a period.

The 1990s saw both property and equities perform extremely well and broadly in line with real returns of 12.5% and 11.8% respectively.

The most recent five years, to end-2004, saw property returns running well ahead of equity returns, which suffered from the implosion of the technology bubble.

The outcome over the full thirty-five-year period clearly illustrates the importance of factors that are specific to one asset or the other.

Interestingly, real returns on UK property and equities, while extremely divergent on a decade-by-decade basis, are much more aligned than in Ireland over the thirty-four-year period for which returns are available.

Table 14.25 Real Returns: UK, % p.a.

	UK Property	UK Equities
1971–1980	2.3	(5.0)
1981–1990	5.0	11.7
1990–2000	6.1	12.1
2001–2004	8.6	(4.6)
34 Years to end-2004	4.2	3.9

(Source: UBS)

In forecasting long-term property returns the obvious reference point is the forecast for equity returns. In terms of volatility, property is less volatile and therefore less risky than equities. Property returns might be expected, therefore, to be lower than those available from equities. However, property's lower volatility is at least partly attributable to its valuation basis, whereas equities employ a market-based pricing mechanism. It is arguable that property's illiquidity makes it a riskier asset than equities.

On balance, despite the divergent returns generated in Ireland by property and equities over the thirty-five years for which figures are available, but encouraged by the more even outcome in the UK, prospective long-term property returns in line with those calculated earlier for equities are assumed.

Cash

Cash is normally regarded by the investor as a temporary home for monies awaiting investment. However, there is a phase in each investment cycle when cash becomes an important investment asset in its own right. When the prices of the other assets are falling, cash cushions the fund against the full impact of market weakness and also provides the wherewithal to purchase assets at lower prices after the fall.

Long-term returns from cash are unpredictable. Unlike bonds, it is not possible to lock into fixed, long-term returns. Cash returns fluctuate with economic activity, with inflation and with changing monetary policy.

Long-run cash returns in real terms emerge at 0.7%p.a. for the period 1900 to 2004, and at 1.2% p.a. for the period 1950 to 2004. As Table 14.26 shows, cash returns ranged from a negative 3.1% p.a. in the period 1970–1979 to a positive 5.4% p.a. in the period 1990–1999.

Current levels of interest rates, given our 'Forecast Inflation' numbers calculated earlier, would generate long-term real returns as follows if nominal money-market rates remained constant:

Table 14.26 Real Returns on Cash, % p.a.

	3 Months Money	Forecast Inflation	Real Return
US	4.20	3.06	1.1
UK	4.58	2.84	1.7
Germany	2.19	2.26	(0.1)

Nominal money-market rates will not remain constant, of course; therefore these numbers cannot be regarded as a reliable guide to prospective real returns on cash. In the absence of any reliable guide from the market, we revert to considering long-term, historical real returns:

Table 14.27 Historical Real Returns From Cash, % p.a.

	1990–2004	1950–2004
US	1.0	1.0
UK	1.0	1.3
Germany	(0.4)	1.9
Ireland	0.7	1.2

(Source: © 2005 E. Dimson, P. Marsh, M. Staunton)

A prospective real return on cash of the order of 1% per annum would appear to strike a reasonable balance between the historical, long-term, 1990–2004 outcome and the higher returns of the more recent, broadly post-war period. Admittedly, settling on 1% ignores the very poor German experience. This, of course, was significantly influenced by periods of heavily negative returns, e.g., the period 1910 to 1919, when real returns of –13.6% per annum were generated, and 1920–1929, when negative returns of –6.5% per annum were seen.

PROJECTED RETURNS

Pulling together the projections outlined above produces the following matrix of projected long-term real returns, compared to the long-term, historical, 1900–2004 experience:

Table 14.28 Real Returns from Investment Assets, % p.a.

	Bonds Proj.	Bonds Hist.	Equities Proj.	Equities Hist.	Property Proj.	Cash Proj.	Cash Hist.
United States	1.5	1.9	5.5	6.6	5.5	1.0	1.0
United Kingdom	1.4	1.3	5.5	5.4	5.5	1.0	1.0
Germany	1.3	(1.9)	4.5	2.9	4.5	1.0	(0.4)
Ireland	1.3	1.1	5.6	4.7	5.6	1.0	0.7

The precise projections here are relatively unimportant, given the broad assumptions employed in their calculation. What is important is the general level of long-term returns they indicate going forward. Prospective bond returns will be lower than the long-term norm, and therefore well below the relatively high returns seen in the post-war period and particularly since the 1980s. Equity returns also will be lower than the post-war and post-1980s experience, with US equity returns likely to be well below the long-term historical numbers. Investment returns going forward are likely to be low.

Portfolio Returns

By applying expected representative return numbers to the asset mixes of the various categories of managed funds discussed in Chapter 9, an overview may be formed of the likely returns available to investors in diversified managed funds:

Table 14.29 Projected Real Returns from Managed Funds, % p.a.

	Cautious Mix	Cautious Return	Cautious Portfolio Return	Balanced Mix	Balanced Return	Balanced Portfolio Return	Aggressive Mix	Aggressive Return	Aggressive Portfolio Return
Bonds	30	1.4	0.42	16	1.4	0.22	6	1.4	0.08
Equities	14	5.4	0.76	73	5.4	3.94	88	5.4	4.75
Property	11	5.4	0.59	8	5.4	0.43	3	5.4	0.16
Cash	45	1.0	0.45	3	1.0	0.03	3	1.0	0.03
			2.22			4.62			4.92

Projected real returns range from 2.2% p.a. for the Cautious Managed Fund, through 4.6% p.a. for the Balanced Managed Fund, to 4.9% p.a. for the Aggressive Managed Fund at the high-risk end of the spectrum.

However, as discussed in Chapter 9, there is some controversy attaching to the exposure to real assets, and particularly to equities, in the asset mixes of the balanced and aggressive managed funds. There is a concern that the appetite for risk of the typical retail Irish investor in managed funds is overstated by equity exposures of 73% and 88% for the balanced and aggressive managed funds, respectively.

However, to the extent that equity contents are reined back, expected returns fall accordingly.

Similar concerns surround the equity exposures of Irish pension funds generally. Here, too, the concern is that high equity exposures overstate the appetite of trustees for the downside risk associated with equity investment, as seen so vividly during the period 2000 to 2003.

CONCLUDING COMMENTS – THE PENSIONS TIME BOMB

The analysis set out in this chapter draws us towards the conclusion that investment returns in the coming decade will be much lower than those of the 1980s and 1990s. The consensus of investment opinion does seem to be in agreement, and the persistence of ultra-low bond yields combined with improved mortality is leading to an intense debate, in particular across the pension fund industry. We conclude this chapter by setting out some of the key issues that we believe will continue to exercise the minds of investment practitioners, policymakers and ordinary investors for some time. We identify three core issues, namely:

i)   equities as the dominant asset;
ii)   the search for the riskless asset;
iii)   expanding the investment frontier.

Equities – The Dominant Asset?

The 'cult of the equity' reached its apotheosis towards the end of the 1980–2000 period. As set out earlier, a secular bull market began in the early 1980s and eventually led to ever-rising equity exposures in pension funds in Ireland, the UK and the US in particular. The industry came to feed off the accepted wisdom that equities should be the dominant asset in pension fund portfolios.

- Actuaries and investment consultants developed the concept of competitive peer-group performance and dictated that the role of the investment manager was to generate first quartile returns over the short term, with little reference to total portfolio risk.

- Pension fund trustees became obsessed with short-term performance in an environment where historically high investment returns distracted them from the concept of risk.
- Finance directors saw high returns as an opportunity to reduce company contributions to the pension scheme.
- Investment managers recognised that investment performance was the critical driver of marketing success and they jettisoned core beliefs of diversification and balance.

The implosion of the technology bubble and the severe equity bear market of 2000–2003 led to a realisation that equity exposures at the market peak had been pushed to levels bordering on the imprudent. Some funds have altered their asset mixes dramatically, but many have maintained their high equity contents.

Our analysis is that the lessons from history clearly indicate that equities are the asset category likely to deliver the highest investment returns. The price will remain the inescapable higher-risk nature of equity investment. Although pension trustees will take a much more prudent approach than heretofore, it is hard to avoid the conclusion that equities will continue to play a very large role in the long-term funding of most pension schemes.

The Search for the Riskless Asset

Pension funds and their advisers now approach risk from a perspective that embraces assets and liabilities. For a pension fund the 'riskless' asset is not a government bond or cash instrument, but an asset that perfectly mimics liability behaviour. The behaviour of a pension fund's liabilities will reflect the nature of the pensions promise, which will vary from fund to fund. Unfortunately, in this new world of asset–liability overview there is no ideal asset, so that the search for the riskless asset leads back to the search for the asset mix that best matches the requirements of a particular fund. The search, therefore, is for the **Appropriate Asset Mix**: that mix that best matches the requirements of the particular fund. In their analysis of their fund's requirements the trustees will consider:

- the nature of the pensions promise – whether it is based on final salary or is a defined contribution scheme; whether pensions in payment are fully or partially linked to inflation
- the time horizons arising from the liabilities
- the balance between active and retired members
- the current financial strength of the fund
- the ongoing strength of the corporate sponsor's guarantee
- the capacity of the fund to cope with short-term volatility.

The examination of the fund's requirements may be qualitative or, increasingly, it might be undertaken in a quantitative manner as part of an Asset/Liability Modelling exercise.

Expanding the Investment Frontier

In the UK there is a strong view emerging that the equity content of pension funds will fall sharply over the long term, to the benefit of government and corporate bonds. Many UK funds are maturing at a rapid pace and many defined benefit schemes have been closed to new entrants. In Ireland the age profile of many schemes is much younger, even though the asset mix of Irish pension funds has mirrored that in the UK. In contrast to the 1980–2000 period the liability structure of a fund is becoming the driver of the strategic asset allocation. Consequently the risk/return characteristics of assets are being analysed in greater depth, as trustees and their advisers seek to cope more explicitly with both the return and risk dimensions of portfolio construction. In this context hitherto non-mainstream investment assets are being considered. As well as the traditional asset categories, trustees are increasingly considering private equity, hedge funds, high-yield bonds and structured products as alternatives to equity and bonds. Some US funds now allocate a substantial portion of assets to these so-called alternative investment categories. Irish pension funds have traditionally invested in property and to a lesser extent in venture capital or private equity. They have yet to embrace in a significant way other alternative categories such as hedge funds, managed futures funds and commodities.

SUMMARY

- The high-inflation 1970s proved to be an especially traumatic decade for investors, as inflation surged following two oil shocks and inappropriate government responses, both in Ireland and in our main trading partners.
- Equity performance in the 1980s was particularly noteworthy, as it was achieved against a relatively poor growth background.
- The combination of a favourable international background and a transformed domestic economy permitted the Irish financial assets to generate returns in the 1990s that compared with the very best of those generated by our major trading partners.
- The returns generated by Irish equities were significantly lower during 2000 to 2004 than those prevailing in the halcyon decade of the 1990s.
- Property was outstandingly the investment asset of choice in Ireland during 2000 to 2004.

- The equity investor takes more risk than the bond investor and therefore is entitled to expect a higher return, which is known as the Equity Risk Premium (ERP).
- Many observers agree that prospective equity returns are unlikely to match the exceptional levels generated over the period 1980–2004.

Index